Islamic Law

Also available from Bloomsbury

The Bloomsbury Companion to Islamic Studies, edited by Clinton Bennett
The Bloomsbury Reader on Islam in the West, edited by Edward E. Curtis IV
Religion or Belief, Discrimination and Equality, Paul Weller
Islamic State Practices, International Law and the Threat from Terrorism, Javaid Rehman
Human Rights and Religion – The Islamic Headscarf Debate in Europe,
　Dominic McGoldrick

Islamic Law

Cases, Authorities, and Worldview

Ahmad Atif Ahmad

Bloomsbury Academic
An imprint of Bloomsbury Publishing Plc

BLOOMSBURY
LONDON • OXFORD • NEW YORK • NEW DELHI • SYDNEY

Bloomsbury Academic

An imprint of Bloomsbury Publishing Plc

50 Bedford Square	1385 Broadway
London	New York
WC1B 3DP	NY 10018
UK	USA

www.bloomsbury.com

BLOOMSBURY and the Diana logo are trademarks of Bloomsbury Publishing Plc

First published 2017

© Ahmad Atif Ahmad, 2017

Ahmad Atif Ahmad has asserted his right under the Copyright, Designs and Patents Act, 1988, to be identified as Author of this work.

All rights reserved. No part of this publication may be reproduced or transmitted in any form or by any means, electronic or mechanical, including photocopying, recording, or any information storage or retrieval system, without prior permission in writing from the publishers.

No responsibility for loss caused to any individual or organization acting on or refraining from action as a result of the material in this publication can be accepted by Bloomsbury or the author.

British Library Cataloguing-in-Publication Data
A catalogue record for this book is available from the British Library.

ISBN: HB: 978-1-4742-7448-7
PB: 978-1-4742-7449-4
ePDF: 978-1-4742-7451-7
ePub: 978-1-4742-7452-4

Library of Congress Cataloging-in-Publication Data
A catalog record for this book is available from the Library of Congress.

Cover design by Dani Leigh (danileighdesign.com)
Cover image: Panel with Six Lines of Islamic Prayers in Nasta'liq Script, on diagonal / alamy.com

Typeset by RefineCatch Limited, Bungay, Suffolk
To find out more about our authors and books visit www.bloomsbury.com.
Here you will find extracts, author interviews, details of forthcoming events and the option to sign up for our newsletters.

Contents

List of illustrations	vii
Acknowledgments	viii
Preliminaries	x
Calendars, terms, and conventions	xiv

	Introduction	1
1	**Three Cases**	7
	Saudi Islamic law	9
	Why are US courts interested in pre-national Islamic law?	14
	Borders crossed	19
	Laws and societies	23
	Conclusion: The nature of Islamic law	24
2	**Madhhabs**	27
	Jurists and schools of law	29
	Tools of legal reasoning	38
	The profile of a jurist	46
	Conclusion	47
3	**Theorizing the Shariʿa**	49
	The subject of Islamic law	52
	The sources of Islamic law	53
	Consensus, disagreement, and conflicting arguments	59
	Conclusions	68
4	**The Social Shariʿa**	71
	Authority in the social world	73
	Social standards	77
	Marriage, divorce, and the rest	84
	Conclusion	92
5	**The Personal Shariʿa**	95
	Legal but unlawful	97
	The personal realm	99

Rituals and dietary laws	101
Science and medicine	106
Conclusion	110

6 The National Shari'as — 115

Colonial and post-colonial transformations	118
Islamic law and modern nations	124
Conclusion	137

7 The Transnational Shari'a — 143

Islamic financial jurisprudence	145
Markets, banking, and mortgages	152
Modern Islamic finance: The hybrid	157
Islamic cyber jurisprudence	161
Conclusion	163

8 The Triangle of Society, Law, and Government — 165

The past couple of centuries	165
Older structures of state and society	169
Moving parts	178
Conclusion	182

Final Review — 183

Appendix I: A debate between Shafi'i (d. 204/820) and Ahmad Ibn Hanbal (d. 241/856) (On a Muslim who does not deny the prayers are obligatory but does not perform them.)	189
Appendix II: Map of Muslim populations around the world	191
Appendix III: Preamble to Pakistan's Constitution (4/12/73)	193
Appendix IV: Inheritance tables	195
Appendix V: Islamic mortgage form	197
Further reading	199
Index	201

Illustrations

0.1	Mecca City	2
1.1	Muslim prayer mats, Yemen	16
2.1	Mausoleum of Imam al-Shafi'i on the Southern Cemetery of Cairo	30
2.2	Alhambra de Granada	44
3.1	Mosquée Zitouna de Tunis	55
3.2	Al-Karaouine University (Al-Qarawiyyin) in the city of Fes, Morocco	65
4.1	*Book of Curiosities of the Sciences and Marvels for the Eyes*, copy of manuscript originally written in the first half of the eleventh century	74
5.1	The Sultan Hassan Mosque	96
5.2	Seventh-century CE Quran manuscript held by the University of Birmingham	103
6.1	Frontal view of the Citadel of Aleppo	116
6.2	Supreme Court of Pakistan	133
7.1	Housing Bank & Islamic Jordanian Bank's Branches in central Amman	158
8.1	View of Islamic architecture from inside the Al-Aqsa Mosque in Jerusalem	167
8.2	Cairo Citadel	175
8.3	Ibn Rushd statue, in Córdoba (Spain)	177

Acknowledgments

Without Lalle Pursglove's invitation, I would not have attempted to draft and edit toward the goal of publishing my teaching notes for an upper division course at the University of California in Santa Barbara that goes by the number RS119a and the title *Introduction to Islamic Law*. My gratitude goes also to the students who took the class and put up with my experimenting with this material until I was able to settle on what to and what not to include.

In February 2016, I invited a small group of scholars who teach the subject (or subjects) of Islamic law to the campus of the University of California in Santa Barbara for a two-day event to discuss "best pedagogical practices" in this field from actual teaching projects the guests had implemented. For their contribution to this forum and influence on my thinking I am indebted to Sherman Jackson of the University of Southern California, Clark Lombardi of the University of Washington Law School, Haider Ali Hamoudi of Pittsburgh Law School, and UCSB's Kathleen Moore, Chair of Religious Studies and former Chair of the Law and Society Program. The discussion allowed me to see many things I had probably been "looking at" for years without being able to fully notice and understand. An example would be achieving a good degree of clarity about the implications of both the historical and positivist approaches to the subject, which I make a point of rejecting and diminishing. This event gave me much hope that the best days for teaching and learning the subjects of Islamic law in the anglophone world may just be ahead of us. I hope this textbook will be a positive contribution. I also want to thank those who participated by attending and asking questions. The audience included a group of graduate students, future professors of either this subject or adjacent and similar subjects, and undergraduates who either attended my *Introduction to Islamic Law* or other courses I teach, which touch on many areas that are addressed, if briefly, in this text.

Professor Muhammad Munir of the Islamic University in Islamabad patiently read sections of the text and made corrections and suggestions. Prof. Dato' Mohamed Ismail bin Mohamed Shariff, of the Global University of Islamic Finance in Malaysia, supplied me with Islamic finance cases. A small flat on the twentieth floor on 8 Rue Boucry in Paris's 18th *arrondissement* (quite a contrast with Santa Barbara) is responsible for much of the editing of the text; discussions with my brother Tarek Abouelgamal, a rising scholar of Arabic linguistics and language pedagogy, who had many valuable thoughts about textbooks and teaching, benefited me in that final stage significantly. Someone who could not be sufficiently thanked by well-crafted words is copy-editor Lisa Carden. Her reader-focused edits pushed my text closer to intelligibility and simplicity, even if I could not totally avoid marathon sentences.

Apology is due where my stamina stopped me short of reviewing my material and juxtaposing it with other sources besides the ones I used, elaborating where I could have elaborated further, and smoothening each and every sentence. I hope future editions of this text will allow me to ameliorate the shortcomings of this one.

Preliminaries

What is in this textbook

This textbook introduces the basic doctrines and practices of Islamic law and explains their foundation. The target reader is a college-level, anglophone student. The student may or may not have any Muslim heritage; there is no presumption either way. After a prefatory unit linking the contemporary with the historical picture, the book is divided into eight units.

Unit 1 introduces three modern cases whose starting point is the United States. These cases take us into religious laws Muslims live by in the US as well as laws of national jurisdiction that are taken into account by American courts and government agencies. This will also allow us to get an initial sense of the broad sweep of Islamic legal reasoning in areas as far apart as crime, rituals, property, and the family. Students will note that some aspects of Islamic religious law that do not apply in courtrooms in Muslim countries (such as rituals) can be brought up in a courtroom in non-Muslim countries. US laws that prohibit religious discrimination (most notably The Civil Rights Act of 1964) permit this.

Unit 2 covers the premodern authorities of Islamic law, focusing on the schools of law (*madhhabs*) that acquired social and moral authority over Muslim individuals, given their historical value that is often seen as simply "religious" value. This will draw on biographies of major shari'a figures, give an idea about the geographic distribution of schools of law, say something about the seeds of disagreement among subsequent jurists, and finally, draw a basic picture of the evolution of Islamic law over its long journey.

Building on Unit 2, Unit 3 covers the basic theoretical apparatus of shari'a reasoning, how it classifies human action and the sources of laws, both textual and extra-textual, including the Qur'an, the Prophet Muhammad's *Sunna* (tradition), legal scholars' consensus, and reasoning from both standard analogy and subtle analogy. The unit also addresses how consensus and disagreement among authorities are theorized.

Units 4–7 cover substantive aspects of Islamic law, starting from how it governs social life (Unit 4), personal life (Unit 5), where it appears in national laws (Unit 6), and where it has transnational presence (Unit 7). Unit 4 covers the nature of authority in the social world, the production of legal and moral knowledge via *fatwas* (non judicial case law) as well as adjudication; we will also think about basic social commitments in a Muslim community that show up in legal reasoning, including the laws of alms, the marriage contract and its possible sequels (divorce, child custody, child support), and how legal deduction is founded on a theory of nature as much as it is founded on texts and tradition. Unit 5 covers the shari'a as a personal law, where individuals consult its doctrines when they make *life and death* and other *ethical* decisions where national laws are either silent or accommodative of religious laws. Unit 6 covers the modern authorities that serve as a source of support for the shariʻa, most notably the State itself, which is seen by some of the most accomplished (though historically minded) scholars of the subject in the field as mutually exclusive with the shariʻa—a view not shared by the author of this text. This will allow us to look at examples where, to various degrees, modern Muslim nations employ Islamic legal doctrines in their national laws. Unit 7 covers where the shariʻa functions within global financial institutions and where it appears in cyber debates on religion and ethics.

Unit 8 covers the interaction of government, society, and law. This discussion addresses the *caliphate* (the successional mantle of the Prophet Muhammad) in theory and in history, the jurisprudence of political revolution in Islamic law, the intersections and divergences of laws and morals in the shariʻa, and non-state and regional actors that represent Islamic law's viewpoints.

Two short units of primary source material in translation are placed after Units 5 and 6. The first consists of two texts from a nineteenth-century CE source from a school of law or *madhhab* (Ibadi) of limited following, and the second a text by a twentieth-century CE Hanafi scholar—a follower of the *madhhab* with the widest spread and most numerous accolades in Islamic legal history. The Ibadi texts address the questions of authority in the law, the relationship between the laity and the scholars, and whether God's law is one or multiple. The Hanafi text addresses the conflict of legal and executive authorities within the society, when the reach of these authorities is narrow or broad.

To the instructor

Every text reflects its author's understanding of his or her material. The instructor using this text for pedagogical purposes is, needless to say, not expected to share this understanding. I used this material to teach an introductory course in Islamic law at the upper division level (juniors and seniors) at the University of California in Santa Barbara, where the academic clock is set at quarter intervals of ten to eleven weeks. If you use this text, you may assign additional material in tandem, depending on the issues that interest you and your students. You will likely use this text as a set of conversation starters and a means to emphasize the aspect of the subject you enjoy teaching and researching. I hope you will find using this text helpful for your purposes.

The focus of this text is Islamic legal reasoning, with examples of its interaction with sundry worlds of social, political, economic, and personal lives throughout what is now close to a millennium and a half. There is an increasing number of excellent studies on Islamic law, all narrow in scope, many focusing on social, anthropological, or political elements. There are students who will find these studies a natural next step that would have remained unreachable, were this first step never taken.

As I used the ensuing text in my instruction, I aimed to satisfy the standard of "student comprehension" and left the more complex work of further philosophizing and historicizing Islamic law to the appropriate contexts. I wanted students to learn how Islamic legal reasoning works, as far as I see it from my limited viewpoint. Instead of coining a ritzy neologism to name and describe this approach to legal reasoning, I push to claim for it the well-worn terms "realism" and "realistic." The text's main point of reference is certainly that of an *observer*, rather than a participant, but an observer who would like to make sense of the acts of two kinds of participants: the *participants* in making laws that have an authoritative value and the *participants* who accept this authority and apply the laws in their lives. (In my mind, to remove a potential misunderstanding, there is no association between "observer" and "objective.")

The short "Further Reading" list at the end of the text references some Arabic sources. A few of my students at the University of California were able to check out these sources for focused and limited consultation. Just being able to see a fifteen-volume volume commentary on Hanbali law (*al-Mughni*, #17 on the list) and to look inside one of its volumes was an experience for them. The two primary sources in English translation (#1 & 2) were also a good starting point for them to cement their relationship with the subject and acquire some confidence that they could learn about it on their own in the future. Secondary sources all have their pluses and minuses, and instructors are bound to follow their preferences in how to choose which ones to recommend. Each instructor can suggest his own list of sources in English and in Arabic for further studies.

Tools of study

Cases are one of the basic tools for the study of law, but they are not the only one. The *term* "cases" as I use it here includes both court cases (Arabic: *qada'*) and *fatwa* cases. These are different in important ways. *Qada'* cases:

1 are decided by a judge who ends conflict between opposing parties;
2 do not decide purely religious matters such as rituals; and
3 deliver binding resolutions relating to the point of conflict in question.

Fatwas are non-binding but more comprehensive in scope.

Islamic law is more naturally studied as "principles" and legal scenarios. Principles reflect abstractions the legal mind observes (eg, lesser harms are suffered to avoid greater harms), and legal scenarios allow for an elaboration of legal doctrines, which are legal determinations at a broader level than specific cases (eg, a sale and a rent combined as one contract is an invalid contract). There are layers of legal doctrines and generalizations at different levels right above the case-level and all the way to the maxim or principle level.

Interest in presenting legal materials in case format is not a simple interest in conforming to the habit of law school professors in the US (dating back, one must note, only to Harvard Law's Christopher Langdell (d. 1906), but clearly conducive to studying a legal system that claims the pedigree of the common law tradition). Interest in cases is what distinguishes the foundational form of Hanafi legal theory from its Shafi'i counterpart, according to Ibn Khaldun (d. 808/1406), and it is also an important quality in Maliki legal reasoning. In all Sunni and Shi'i schools of law, a student who knows the principles or maxims of legal reasoning and learns no cases can be regarded only as someone standing at a distance from the full practice of legal reasoning, even if some tolerate this person as a theorist (*usuli*).

The anglophone audience clearly has a preference for the case-law method in treating legal material, which (preference) shapes the way they think of law. For the purposes of this text, the case form is also an aid against perpetuating the historical narrative method which has dominated the teaching of Islamic law for over a century, and which makes it that much harder for students of the subject to understand why Islamic law is relevant in the contemporary world.

To the student

While there are a few inherent difficulties in the subject, what made this subject hard is mostly the way it is presented. The textbook by itself, without the class, achieves much less than you should desire. If the instructor assigns the sections of this text in the order of their appearance, you may still "secretly" take a peek ahead into subsequent sections. Many sections reference other sections, but each section should be intelligible on its own.

In the grand scheme of the course, the different units re-enforce one another. They confirm and complete one another. You will most likely be reading a third or a half of a unit at a time in the order in which the text is presented. Take notes and write the questions you think of. You may find answers to these questions later on. This will link things up for you. If you think there is a contradiction, read again; read more carefully. If the sense that there is a contradiction is still there, ask the instructor about it.

This book is meant as an introduction. One sign that your interest in the subject is increasing is that you will want to move to further studies of it. The core of this textbook is based on primary sources. You will notice that there are quotes from legal scholars who died many years ago. There are also contemporary Muslim authorities who are in the business of trying to develop Islamic law further and further. These are also one possible next step you may want to make if you go farther in the subject(s) of Islamic law.

Calendars, terms, and conventions

Calendar

Taking its point of departure from the Prophet Muhammad's emigration (Arabic: *hijra*) from his hometown of Mecca to Medina, the Islamic calendar begins in the year 622 of the Common Era. Hence the Islamic year 1 (roughly) = 623 CE. The Common Era calendar is a solar calendar, based on the year being (ostensibly) a cycle of 365.25 days. The year 2017 CE corresponds (also roughly) to the year 1438 (they overlap by nine months). If the lunar (Islamic) year were 365.25 days long, it should have been the year 1394 (2017 − 623 = 1394). But the lunar calendar year is only 354 days, which goes *11.25 days faster* than the solar *every* year, and hence three *years faster* than the solar year every century. After fourteen centuries, the gap has become forty-two years. In this textbook, dates are sometimes indicated by two numbers, the first indicates the Islamic calendar and the second the CE year. For example, if you see Ibn Hajar (d. 852/1448), this means he died in the Islamic calendar year of 852 (or after *hijra*, AH), which corresponds to the Common Era year 1448.

When you do approximated date conversion, keep in mind (to round things up), the starting point 620 CE = 0 AH and at the end 2000 CE = 1420 AH. The difference was about 620 years at the start of the timeline and about 580 by the end of the twentieth century. Assuming there is a 600-year difference puts you in the right ballpark, give or take twenty years. You will be closer to the correct guess if you convert dates from the fourteenth century of the Common Era to their Hijri equivalent. For example, when you read about Ibn Taymiyya, if you are given the CE date of his death, it is 1328, and the Hijri equivalent is exactly 728.

	Prophet Muhammad								Iran's Revolution	Arab Spring
Birth	Revelations	Migration	Death							
570	610	622	632	1000	1300	1500	1700	1900	1979	2010 CE

	Prophet Muhammad								Iran's Revolution	Arab Spring
Birth	Revelations	Migration	Death							
−53	−12/3	0/1	10	390	699	905	1111	1318	1399	1432 AH

(CE = Common Era; AH = After Hijra)

Another Islamic calendar is used in Iran, which uses a *solar* calendar that also takes its point of departure to be the Prophet Muhammad's emigration from Mecca to Medina. On this calendar, the year is 365.24 days (using an observation-based, more modern, method than the one used by the Gregorian calendar we use to determine the length of the solar CE or Common Era year). This way the 40+ years gained by the faster pace of the lunar calendar are lost. This means that a solar Islamic calendar year that corresponds to 2017 CE (= 1438 AH, lunar) is the year 1396.

Terms and conventions

Arabic terms are nearly always "transliterated" into English inadequately, but this is the best one could do. Words like shari'a are pronounced with a guttural stop toward the end, which is only represented by the right-faced apostrophe. The "dh" in the word *madhhab*, meaning school of law, indicates a sound similar to "th" in the word "this." This textbook will limit itself to basic and essential Arabic terms, without which a student could not engage in any meaningful discussion about Islamic law.

A convention of Islamic jurisprudence is to think of the shari'a as indicating practical laws, such as praying five times a day, refraining from drinking intoxicants, steering away from usury and from transactions whose commitments include elements of ambiguity or which are too risky, etc. The word shari'a does, in its general sense, include the entire system of Islamic beliefs ('aqa'id), in addition to the practical laws, but this broader usage is all but excluded here.

All translations from Arabic primary sources are my own, whether or not the original is available in translation. For example, Shaybani's (d. 189/805) book *al-Hujja* (from which excerpts are translated in Unit 2), is not available in English translation; Mawardi's (d. 450/1058) *al-Ahkam al-Sultaniyya* (excerpted in Unit 8) is fully available in English under the title: *The Ordinances of Governance*. The student may wish to consult other English translations of the texts I employ here when available.

As I said earlier, the term "cases" here includes both court cases (Arabic: qada') and *fatwa* cases—that is, non-binding rulings of the most comprehensive scope. Qada' cases, which are decided by a judge who ends an adversity, do not decide purely religious matters such as rituals, and deliver binding resolutions of their point of conflict.

Introduction

In a conference on *The Globalization of Law* held in Doha, Qatar, in 2009, a number of judges and lawyers, some practiced in the area of international law and some within national laws, in addition to some academics such as myself, gathered to discuss the degree to which different laws in the world today can be streamlined for further efficiency. There were also debates about global commitments to human rights and shared global values. The shadow of the ongoing economic and financial crisis that had begun the previous year loomed large over the conference, and a candid question arose as to whether markets can be genuinely regulated, given that they govern the (states and hence govern the) laws, rather than be governed by them. On a basic level, everyone seemed to think that reconciling together laws of different provenance, and reconciling these laws with economic imperatives, was something of a dream. But it is a persistent dream.

Because the meeting was in Qatar, and because many of the high-level judges and scholars understood that Islamic law was an underlying element of the laws of many other countries, Islamic law was not absent from the discussion, and it was on this occasion afforded a degree of respect that it is not always guaranteed. At another conference I attended in 2008 at Bad Blankenburg in Germany, for example, Islam would be used as a scapegoat in Europe's struggle to normalize human rights within its borders given the retrograde views some immigrants in Europe hold and live by.

What is this Islamic law, anyway? One side of Islamic law indicates a set of ideas and practices that pervade many national legal systems, as well as moral and religious traditions, that affect the behavior of many people around the world. The debate about the impact of the medieval legal tradition on this law's modern manifestations is still a lively one, which is sometimes held out in the open, but is mostly discussed behind closed doors in legislative hallways in Pakistan, Egypt, Saudi Arabia, Iran, Indonesia, and Malaysia, among other countries.

Historians and political scientists have emphasized that all our modern concepts of "state," "secular," "religious," and the rest of this family of concepts could not be projected on to the premodern world. Some understand this to mean that all attempts at speaking of a continuity between a medieval legal tradition and a modern one, or at speaking of a modern appropriation of the medieval ideas, are doomed to fail. There is a fallacy here. If we say that *modern* distinctions (precisely tailored) between secular and religious could not be found (in their exact form, as tailored) in a *premodern* society, this is both true and useless. It is both true and useless because the conclusion is already in the premise. (All tautological statements are useless; think of "the socialist notion of *justice* does not qualify as *justice* outside of a socialist system.") When this assertion comes from those who are uncurious about the past or bothered by its invocation in the present, it also indicates a lack of courage to address the freedom many contemporary communities have exercised to appropriate their legacy in the manner in which they choose.

A description of a premodern instance of thinking and reasoning, when the full picture is available, will certainly show differences and divergences with modern kinds of reasoning. The insistence that the medieval and the modern are separated by a thick wall, you will note, is most comfortably made by scholars of the modern world with only a marginal interest in the past. If someone is exposed sufficiently to medieval and modern documents, they can begin to compare and see what is different and why. But a modern theorist who is unfamiliar with premodern legal reasoning can only abstain from saying anything about the medieval traditions, what they are or are not like.

Saying that premodern ideas could never possibly be appropriated in the modern world because they would be "anachronistic" does not quite help us when we attempt to observe how old ideas are actually appropriated in new contexts. One must also note that for *both lawmakers who are not opposed to drawing on old traditions and the consumers of religious laws*, not all distinctions that historians find interesting actually are. Religious individuals and lawmakers in the Muslim world alike search in their tradition for elements they find appropriate to incorporate or *account for* in their personal and social life and the lives of their population. And, in the final analysis, these appropriations, which are seen as a problem from outside perspectives, are solutions to problems for those who adopt them.

The medieval Islamic traditions that are the subject of many modern discussions and appropriations have a high pedigree. And, within the medieval Islamic traditions, Islamic law took pride of place. It was an art and a science that was served by all the medieval branches

Figure 0.1 Mecca City. Author: Meshal Obeidallah. Image accessed via Wikimedia.

of knowledge, which correspond to what may be called the fundamentals of the humanities today: Language; history; and philosophy. It commanded the best of minds, and it attracted much effort and analytical work. A fourteenth-century Egyptian scholar known as al-Zarkashi (d. 792/1390) quoted one of his teachers as saying that fields of knowledge are of three types [applying a culinary metaphor here]: fields that are undercooked, such as rhetoric and Qur'anic exegesis; ones that are cooked and have not been burned, such as grammar; and ones that have been cooked and burned, such as law. In this case, burning does not have a negative overtone but rather is meant to indicate both the quantity and the intensity of the contributions to the field.

Islamic law has been part of the lives of Muslims for close to 1,500 years, and seems to continue to be part of it. It has changed a lot over time, and across geographic areas, and it is hard to make a persuasive argument that the borders of modernity (just because we inhabit it) must be more important than any other borders this tradition crossed. This insistence that modernity changed everything stems more or less from our lack of interest in studying, or lack of ability to study, paradigm shifts (to use Kuhn's much-abused term) that occurred in Islamic legal reasoning. For example, significant changes occurred at the time of the Mongol invasions of the Muslim world (which was followed by their conversion to Islam), as Islam spread in maritime southeast Asia, or during the changes attending the rise of military Turkish and Turko-Mongolian leadership in the Muslim world in the thirteenth through sixteenth centuries, with its significant cultural, political, and legal consequences.

In this late stage of modernity, understood to have emanated from Europe's renaissance and enlightenment, the Muslim populations of the world have gone searching for new hybrid identities that accommodate their traditions *and* their commitments to modernity. Imagining yourself a referee of a shari'a *v.* modernity boxing match is not the best way of relating to the subject. More productive than worrying about independent judgments of how the shari'a fared in the modern world is to attend to the real task of realizing the broad spectrum Muslim clerisies and societies occupy in understanding tradition in our time. Let's see how today's eclectic views of Islam's legal traditions in the Muslim world involved the aspiration to define the role of tradition in contemporary Muslim society.

New hopes

Today, one may want to start with the hopes of reestablishing or enhancing the Islamic character of modern Muslims' life, which came to the fore after the events of 2010–2011 and which went by the label of "the Arab Spring." Earlier, Muslim communities in the twentieth and twenty-first centuries had indicated in different ways that they were interested in reconsidering their legacy, which had been affected by their colonial history and their post-colonial governments. This development led to the dissatisfaction of the population. We have now reached a watershed moment in Islamic history. One of our tasks is to understand how Islam plays a role both in the language and activities of many Muslims right now.

Disagreement among Muslim populations within the same nation, whether a Sunni or a Shi'i nation, inhibits us from generalizing. In each country, there are secular, Westernized elites, Islamists with energy and enthusiasm

> Islamic law cannot be reduced to rules made by an Islamic government; yet, government is not irrelevant here.

for an Islamic cause, and many in between. Yet, Islam remains an important element in each and every Muslim nation's politics and everyday life. And these political and everyday activities are the territory of Islamic law.

In Unit 6, we will speak about the rise of what may be called the "national" shariʻas, the modern forms of referencing and employing the Islamic shariʻa in the laws of the nation state. Here, however, we can content ourselves with a broad sense of what is going on today in the Muslim world.

There are, as many know, Sunnis and Shiʻis. In the seventh and eighth centuries, two communities disagreed on legitimate *political authority*. Though not direct ancestors, these two communities are the nuclei, the seeds, of what we call Sunnis and Shiʻis today. It is quite nonsensical to say that Sunnis and Shiʻis have been fighting for fourteen centuries. In fact, what is today the largest Shiʻi country in the world, Iran, was a majority Sunni country well into the sixteenth century, having passed through a remarkable transition, unattended by wars or invasions. Muslims, in fact, have maintained a higher degree of flexibility about what we refer to as Muslim religious "identity" than many, both non-Muslims and Muslims, seem to think.

Unit 2 will tell you more about the details of the rise of Sunni and Shiʻi jurisprudence. For now, we must note that, from the viewpoint of legal and juristic sources, the distinction between the two in terms of hard and fast legal maxims or principles is not easy to draw. This is because of the constant reliance of each side on the other, even as they tried to polemicize against one another. (And note that polemics that address legal and religious norms are more intense *within* Sunni (popular and scholarly) communities and *within* Shiʻi communities themselves.) For early authorities, no distinction is drawn: They cited one another's works and opinions, and thus even an imaginary locus of separation between Sunni and Shiʻi (and those who are neither Sunni nor Shiʻis, as you will see also in Unit 2) could not be pinpointed.

Before we go further in explaining the relevance of public politics and government to "legitimacy" in the Muslim world, we must note, or remind ourselves, that the scope of Islamic law encompasses life outside of the public realm. In this textbook, you will see that a personal version of the shariʻa can be just as complex as the social shariʻa. The aspects I selected of the personal shariʻa in Unit 5 address one's relationship with his or her body in dietary laws, fasting, and prayers, one's relationship with medicine, and one's sense of the value of the human soul and body parts. We will also see later that Muslims residing in non-Muslim countries live by aspects of Islamic law. *It would still be wrong to argue, as many will do passionately, that government is irrelevant to a Muslim life.*

The Arabic Spring, that recent episode which encapsulated (hitherto frustrated) hopes of a new life—which some would understand to be a secular life infused with solid community values, while others would consider simply to be a life that meets a religious ideal as adjusted to the modern—is an invitation for us to think of the shariʻa from a realistic stance. It encourages us to see the complexity of the reality before us and a refusal of simple (to some, comforting) narratives about the death of all preindustrial, pre-Darwinian, and pre-statal systems as simply anachronistic and hence imaginary.

Legitimacy

The durability of Iran's Islamic revolution in 1979 made it a focal point for all discussions of legitimate modern government from an Islamic perspective. Before and after this revolution, modern Shi'i thinking ventured into many new areas, from modern family to modern science, unburdened by a heavy and rich tradition, and this may have slowed down the development of Sunni Islamic jurisprudence. These two elements now come together to play an important role in today's conditions and forms of the shari'a worldwide.

How is there a single Islamic law if there is no single Muslim society? This is the question

(BUT IT IS NOT AN ESSAY QUESTION).

The Arab Spring was not an Islamic revolution. The first democratic elections in Tunisia and Egypt indicated the popularity of the idea of establishing government with Islamic undertones, but subsequent action showed the dissatisfaction of the populations in these countries with Islamists' rhetoric and activities. Libya, Yemen, and Syria did not have a chance to speak up and remained mired in internal and external conflicts that made the character of their revolutions hard to discern. (Foreign intervention did not help, but I hope we can get out of the habit of seeing agency as limited to outside and foreign forces whenever we speak of the Muslim world.)

Yet, it is also true that many Arab, Muslim populations hope for an Islamic revolution, and only an opportunity for these forces to shape the future in these countries will show how persistent and strong this hope is. The relevance of Muslim life to politics in Arab Muslim societies has been confirmed in the context of the events of the Arab Spring, and it is hard to argue that it did not move many of those who contributed to the initial uprising. This mix (of elements that explicitly appeal to the Islamic tradition in their revolutionary act and elements that do not) was also true of the Iranian revolution itself. The rejection of the authority of Iran's *Shah* (king) was not limited to a call for Muslim government. But the subsequent formation of an Islamic republic in Iran allowed its revolution to take a certain shape. It seems to only make sense to hear it being named the "Islamic revolution" of Iran. By contrast, an Arab Islamic republic did not ultimately transpire in the case of Arab Spring countries.

The "shari'a" element is, therefore, neither overwhelmingly present nor irrelevant in debates on Islam's role in law and politics in the Muslim world, and this generalization is not limited to Arab Spring countries and Iran. Algeria, which is not an Arab Spring country, experienced its own internal conflict twenty years prior when an Islamist political party won a majority in its main legislative body, leading to the president's resignation and the ensuing civil war.

Analogies between the Arab Spring and the Iranian revolution of 1979 have been and will continue to be drawn and rejected vehemently, depending on who you are speaking with. The dis-analogies are multiple, but for those who see the similarities, the point of both upheavals is that at least one strong current within modern Muslim societies, Sunni or Shi'i, has become infused with the aspiration to lead Muslim lives with the support of a modern state.

$$(\text{Arab Spring} - 31)^n = \sum_{k=0}^{n} x^k \text{Iranian Revolution}^{n-k}$$

Assume that "**n**" possesses a certain value, then ask what would "**x**" have to be for the Arab Spring to be comparable to the Iranian revolution and at what point, where thirty-one indicates the number of years intervening between 1979 and 2010.

> (The point of this mock equation is to give you an image to remember that there is no way we can easily compare Iran's 1979 revolution and its subsequent Islamic Republic to the events following 2010 in the Sunni world.)

The lag between the two events clearly created important differences. The Sunni population in Egypt, for example, could not ask in 2011 for the same thing that the Iranians requested in 1979, even if the countries were similar. The experience of Iran since 1979's Islamic revolution, which was seen as an example of either the triumph or failure of Muslim politics in the modern world depending on one's viewpoint, played a role in the imagination of the Sunni populations in places like Egypt, when these populations contemplated a Muslim state.

There are still other entanglements here. Arab Spring countries are not, in their modern form, equal or similar. The difficulty in describing the commonality, however, does not negate the commonality itself. The first real challenge in studying Islamic law is that its study does presuppose a structural commonality in Islamic legal reasoning, a common language, or much overlap in the reference materials or in the authorities to which participants in shari'a discourse appeal. None of this bespeaks the presence of a single Muslim society, but none of it negates the impact of diverse social standards on all shari'a answers and even on the questions themselves.

What also makes this discussion challenging is the recentness of the Arab Spring and its unclear outcome, added to its lack of a clear Islamic flavor to parallel almost four decades of Iran's Islamic Republic. The basic point remains simple, however. For those who hope to recover a fuller Muslim life, an Islamic government is desirable. After that, the question becomes: What makes a government Islamic? And if an existing government is not legitimately Islamic, could one revolt against it to bring about an Islamic government?

Though not couched in these terms, these questions of legitimacy and revolution are ultimately over one thousand years old. Medieval Muslim jurists have issued many authoritative rulings on the standards by which a government could be legitimate, and the legitimacy of revolution. Modern jurists re-read these opinions in modern *fatwas*—legal opinions. We will come back to these themes throughout the book and especially in the last unit.

Keep in mind that the presence of shari'a reasoning in today's and tomorrow's world is a work in constant progress. Both in national laws and transnational institutions, there can only be a description of the state of the laws and the institutional development at a certain time. What counts as a very accurate, detailed description in 2017 may not be adequate in the future.

1 Three Cases

If you want to study or practice law in the United States, you go to law school. There is a rigorous, often three-year, program of legal studies, which you need to undergo after you earn a college degree. That is, by the time you are done with your law degree (appropriately called a JD, *juris doctor*, or doctor of jurisprudence), you will have studied for seven full years following high school. It's true that not *every* person to have practiced law in recent American history has had a law degree, of course: In fact, a man by the name of Harry Truman, who ended up being President of the United States, was county judge in the 1920s without ever finishing college. This is not meant as a slight to Truman—we are all fond of him—but he is an exception, and a man of an earlier time. In principle, if you want to practice law, you go to law school, and after that you normally have to take qualifying (American Bar Association) examinations.

How can we study Islamic law in one course of study, rather than clock up extra years at law school? You will, of course, need a law degree to practice law in any one of the 50+ Muslim countries whose laws owe some of their doctrines to Islamic law, and you will, then, have to be acquainted with legal knowledge that goes beyond the borders of Islamic law. What this textbook attempts to accomplish is much less and a little more. It is attempting to offer a panoramic view of both the *historical* system to which modern Islamic law arguments appeal and the *modern* ways of looking at this old law today.

When we talk about the relevance of Islamic law today, we do not have to limit ourselves to 50+ countries. This is because Islamic law has a presence in majority-Muslim countries as well as in countries where Muslim religious beliefs are accommodated, such as the United States. In recent years, the relevance of shari'a to the life of Muslims in the world has been debated intensely. Some scholars hold that the shari'a is incompatible with modern communities and the modern state. Following this argument, the Islamic Republic of Iran (as of 1979) and any Sunni equivalents that some *hoped would arise* or that they *think arose* out of the Arab Spring (as of 2010) are novel and unprecedented forms of "governing" by Islamic law. This new "governing" does employ elements that still go by the name "Islamic law," the imprecise expression we are forced to use in English in order to loosely indicate the Islamic shari'a.

Some authors state that the Islamic shari'a is, plainly and simply, Islamic law; others that it refers only to the stable aspects of Islamic law; by yet others that it refers to the heavenly principles that all Muslims accept. If you go further still, you will read that it includes the basics of the Islamic faiths, that it also encompasses ethics and social practices—and so on, and so on. "Shari'a" is an Arabic word whose full meaning and elastic definitions allows those with an understanding of medieval Arabic to think of examples of how it is used differently by different authors in different contexts. Its English usage only complicates this picture; one could certainly offer a graduate seminar on the uses and abuses of the word in both modern Arabic and foreign languages. This textbook aims to help readers understand what the word refers to in a fairly comprehensive way, without dwelling on definitions, tailoring, and argumentative stances.

The Islamic shariʻa in history covered an area that would have in other contexts and times been covered by Roman and Canon law aggregated together. In some areas, the latter combination encompassed legal doctrines whose equivalents are unknown in the shariʻa (an equivalent to regulating bishops or ecclesiastical hierarchy is nowhere to be found in Islamic law), while in other regards the Islamic shariʻa operates where these two were silent. In the past century, Islamic shariʻa entered into national and transnational laws. In this textbook, we will accept the views Muslim scholars apply in their contribution to how Islam may be practiced, as the expression goes, whether or not we think that there are historical and conceptual arguments against considering whether the traditional shariʻa has disappeared.

Sink or Swim

Islamic law can be seen in action in principles, legal scenarios, and cases. In this and later Units, you will fully understand that principles and maxims are points of departure for legal reasoning and generalizations about the law. We will discuss these in some depth. Legal scenarios are broad practical legal questions with fewer details than cases and are addressed by "legal doctrines." For example, how should a man wanting to sell his house behave toward his neighbor before selling it to a stranger? The answer is that he must offer the house to his neighbor for sale at market price first; if the neighbor declines to buy it, the owner is free to sell it to anyone else. If the owner fails to offer the house to the neighbor, however, the latter has the right to "pre-empt" the sale to a stranger and offer the same price paid by the stranger for the house according to a legal doctrine called the "right of pre-emption." (A modern application for this will come up in Unit 6, section 2.5).

Cases are more specific. Our sense of cases includes the oxymoronic sounding "non-judicial case-laws" or *fatwas* (see below). The familiar judicial type of cases will make frequent appearances. There is neither a universal Islamic court hierarchy nor a universal Islamic Supreme Court that adjusts "lower-level" court decisions to fit or stabilize any type of universal Islamic doctrine. In fact, there has never been that type of hierarchy or that type of court: Muslim societies have lived with divergent doctrines for centuries, and continue to do so today.

This first Unit covers three cases. Get used to this procedure when you encounter a case: Articulate the **facts** of the case; identify the **ruling** (or multiple rulings when there is a disagreement); and determine the **rationale** of the ruling or rulings. *Facts,* then *ruling,* then *rationale.* Facts are absolutely crucial. Unpacking the case may involve studying precedents and unearthing additional information, but only after you have stated the salient facts of the case correctly. If you do not do that, you will be lost trying to find relevant data to understand the case and why the ruling(s) went one way or another.

You are starting your study of the subject based on views for which I am responsible, which I provided in these three cases. While I played a minor role in these cases, I had access to sources that allowed me to see in each one of them an occasion to show the relevance of Islamic legal doctrines to contemporary Muslim life inside and outside the United States. Confidentiality constraints limit my ability to publish the full extent of the information available to me about these cases; the accounts below are redacted and abbreviated versions of them. That said, the material presented should be sufficient for our purposes.

1 Saudi Islamic law

Let's turn now to the facts of the first case. MMK is a Saudi woman, who was born in 1985 and moved to the US on a student visa in 2010 with her husband and son (born 2009). She had been stopped by the religious police in Saudi Arabia in 2006 on suspicion of accompanying a non-relative and was detained for ten hours but later released. Her marriage took place in 2008 in Saudi Arabia, and she was divorced in April 2012 in the Los Angeles Saudi Consulate.

Between July 2012 and July 2013 MMK shared an apartment with a man whom she did not marry. Between July and October 2013 she rented accommodation from an American woman who, after a falling-out with MMK, was later to inform the Saudi Consulate in LA of MMK's living arrangement with a non-relative. (The Saudi Consulate assumes a supervisory role over Saudi citizens on scholarships paid for by the Saudi government, and were asylum never sought, MLK would be going back to Saudi Arabia at some point, in which case her record at the Consulate accompanies her back to her homeland.) The Consulate investigated the matter and contacted MMK repeatedly, suggesting that her son undergo therapy, given his exposure to his mother's unlawful consorting with a stranger. Should she return to Saudi Arabia, MMK may face the following:

1 Capital punishment for adultery, in case of: confession; the availability of four witnesses (testifying to the sexual act); or being pregnant in the absence of a current or recent marriage that could have produced the child. Capital punishment is an unlikely outcome in this case, given the high (confession, four witnesses) or irrelevant (pregnancy) evidentiary requirement. (Note that the rental agreement is only circumstantial and does not establish adultery. We'll cover suspicion later.)

2 Corporeal punishment for unbecoming behavior—that is, sharing a private space with a non-relative for a year. This is a high probability for three reasons: first, the latitude Saudi judges have in applying judicial jurisprudence in the absence of a long and established criminal law tradition based on a penal code (and until 2001, the absence of a code of criminal procedures); second, the record of MMK's ten-hour detention in 2006 at the Riyadh Police Facility; and third, Saudi LA Consulate's investigation of her behavior after the divorce. Legal precedents indicated below will confirm and clarify this point.

3 Physical punishment by the religious police in the case of public presence with men, which would confirm suspicions based on her earlier offenses.

MEN AND WOMEN WHO MAY NOT MARRY

Every Muslim man is prohibited from marrying any one of the following categories of women (with most of whom, apart from numbers 13, 14, and 15, he may share private space): 1) a mother (this category includes grandmothers on both side); 2) a daughter (including granddaughters); 3) a sister (from one or both parents); 4) a paternal aunt (= half- or full-sister of father); 5) a maternal aunt (half- or full-sister of mother); 6 & 7) a niece (whether a brother's daughter or a sister's daughter); 8) a mother via nursing (= a woman by whom the man was breastfed as an infant); 9) a sister via nursing (= a female who shared a breastfeeding arrangement with a male when they were both infants); 10) a mother-in-law (wife's mother); 11) a step-daughter (daughter of wife in a consummated marriage); 12) a son's wife; 13) a wife's sister; 14) a married woman; 15) a father's former wife.

If this is hard to follow, remember this: The heart of the matter here is that MMK has shared a private space with a *non-relative:* sharing a space with her brother or father, for example, would be permitted, as in Islamic law, if a man and a woman are considered close relatives (eg, brother and sister), they may not marry and thus in most cases could share private space together. (See the list of men and women who may not marry and are considered close relatives, although there is disagreement about this issue in some cases.)

The facts of this case are given in the context of an asylum case heard before a US judicial entity. In asylum cases before US courts, Islamic law—as it applies in Saudi society—is salient because its application in a Muslim land may allow an individual in the US to be granted the status of an asylee. The application of Islamic criminal law in Saudi Arabia is argued to be a foundation for granting this woman asylum status in the US, given that this application of Islamic law is considered a case of unwarranted "violence against women" by American legal standards. This situation would arguably constitute grounds for asylum, if all of the following conditions are met:

1 That an asylum seeker face potential persecution.
2 That the asylum seeker belong to a social group (see below).
3 That the *persecution* be related to the belonging to *that group*.

American lawyers have argued that women are considered one such group, as are political opposition groups, religious groups facing discrimination, and those fearing discrimination based on sexual orientation.

In this asylum case, an expert in Islamic law would be expected to provide the American court with information they need about Saudi judicial practice and an assessment of the probability that MMK would face violent punishment should she return home. If the American court is convinced, asylum status may be granted.

In Saudi Islamic law, the subject of the expert report is essentially Islamic law and the context in which it applies in Saudi Arabia. Below are redacted selections from the expert report accompanying the asylum claim, which highlights possible actions against MMK from Saudi judicial entities. The report will repeat some of the information we have just covered.

1.1 Re. The asylum of MMK: Summary

MMK falls into an unfortunate category of females who have, after reaching the age of majority, entered into and consummated (here evidenced by bearing a child) lawful marriage at least once, and are hence considered capable of distinguishing "clean" and "lawful" sexual intercourse from its opposite, and who are subsequently accused of freely entering into an unlawful sexual intercourse. If this is proven, she faces the death penalty. If unlawful sexual intercourse is not proven, MMK faces lesser punishments for "unbecoming behavior" from a woman who is *muhsan* (Arabic for "married," or more specifically, as Hanbali legal doctrines phrases it, someone who has been married at least once. The Hanbali school of law is the dominant school of law in Saudi Arabia).

This report includes first an introduction addressing basic qualities in Saudi criminal and family law. This is followed by sections on adultery and guardianship respectively. It becomes apparent from considering the laws of adultery and guardianship that MMK faces some probable danger, either from the governmental authorities directly or from her family, the latter threat being tolerated by the government on the grounds of acceptable social propriety standards. The next section addresses child custody in Saudi law. MMK's chances of winning joint custody of her son, SFA, are slim, given her alleged repeated disregard for Islamic moral behavior, notably her arrest in 2006 with a male stranger and also her involvement in a kind of domestic partnership with another stranger between July 2012 and July 2013, of which the Saudi Los Angeles Consulate was informed.

Aside from the specific references to cases, the report was based on medieval legal commentaries, including Mansur al-Buhuti, *Kashshaf al-Qina'* (Beirut: Alam al-Kutub, 2003—the collected five-volume edition), p. 3001; Ibn Qudama (d. 620/1223) (eds Turki & Hilw), *al-Mughni*, Vol. 12, pp. 314–17 (Riyadh: Alam al-Kutub, 1997), Vol. 9, p. 345; Vol. 11, p. 414; Vol. 11, p. 409; Vol. 12, pp. 309–10; Vol. 12, p. 528; Saudi Ministry of Justice: Committee on the Documentation and Publication of Court Decisions, *Court Decisions Digest* (2008), Vol. 1, pp. 297–9; Vol. 2, p. 107; Vol. 3, pp. 158–62. Cases are identified by numbers, dates, and court type, rather than names of plaintiffs and defendants.

1.2 Saudi criminal and family law

Saudi criminal law applies judicial reasoning based on medieval juristic works and does not (or at least did not, until recently) employ a penal code. This gives the modern judge much freedom in drawing on medieval jurisprudence; this is arguably an advantage in that it allows a higher degree of attention to the circumstances of each case, but it also carries some disadvantages for MMK in her particular case. Under Saudi law, corporeal punishment is accepted as one category of punishment in the two main classes of offenses: *hudud* and *ta'zir*. Hudud are specified punishments for a limited number of crimes (adultery, slander, theft, highway robbery, apostasy, anti-government rebellion), while *ta'zir* is a broad term for discretionary punishment in cases other than *hudud* crimes.

The severe punishments given for *hudud* crimes is offset by the high evidentiary standards required for incrimination, and judges typically consider the much less severe *ta'zir* penalties should those standards be unmet. Unwarranted presence inside someone's property, in cases where theft is unproven, would be an example of an act that does

> "Discretionary punishment is sometimes founded on evidence of culpability, and sometimes on the defendant being not above doubt of culpability."
>
> Fourth Circuit, Mecca Appellate Court, Saudi Arabia, Case 34338020, hearing of June 10, 2013. Court Digest of Lunar Year 1434, Vol. 14, p. 349.

not ascend to the level of the crime of theft but serves as a foundation for discretionary punishment—here assigned in the context of an unproven crime. Such presence will carry a punishment below the severe (and rarely applied) hand amputation ordered in the case of proven theft.

Family ties are strongly held and protected, and inappropriate behavior by either single or married individuals that may undermine the family structure is punished. As the adultery section (in this report) will show, in cases where these standards are violated, unmarried individuals are treated more leniently than those who are or have been married.

The punishment for witnessing (not engaging in) lewd action can be severe. Decision 169/1392 by the Supreme Court in Riyadh on 8/5/1972 (Islamic calendar: 6/25/1392) provides an example; a witness was imprisoned for nine months with an assignment of thirty-nine lashes per month for witnessing lewd acts without reporting them—for voyeurism, essentially. This is a case where the offense is witnessing, as opposed to participating in, lewd action. For additional recent cases, Volume 14 (of a thirty-volume set) of Saudi court decisions in the *hijri* year 1434 (corresponding to November 15, 2012–November 3, 2013) includes many examples of where *khalwa* (being safely alone) involving a female and one or more males also entailed severe punishments (pp. 301–68), including imprisonment and 200 lashes, administered in multiple doses, and deportation (in a case involving a Filipino man) after imprisonment and lashing.

The courts can certainly be lenient when evidence is lacking and when the consideration of protecting the privacy of presumptively decent people and families are involved (the requirement of *satr*), but when evidence of inappropriate behavior has been presented, the punishments are severe. In one case a Riyadh court employed leniency with a married, former officer cadet: the defendant was ordered to receive 150 lashes in two doses with a ten-day interval as well as a prison term of two months, but the sentences was not implemented in recognition of his status and previous good behavior (pp. 331–3).

1.3 Adultery and suspicion of it

Once a free (non-slave), adult female of sound reasoning has had vaginal intercourse in a valid marriage to a peer (the male has to also be free, adult, of apparently sound reasoning, etc.), her consorting sexually outside of marriage, if it includes sexual (anal or vaginal) intercourse, is punishable by stoning to death. The offense can be established by one of three evidentiary standards: the testimony of four "upright" (that is, trustworthy) males; confession; or pregnancy unaccompanied by a current or recent marriage that may have caused the pregnancy. Disagreement arises as to whether stoning should be preceded by flogging or whether flogging is specific to unmarried offenders. An unmarried individual, male or female, is punished by a hundred lashes only if unlawful coition is evidenced.

As noted above, failure to produce the high evidentiary standard for a *hudud* (specified) crime usually moves the judge to consider discretionary crime, which does not require the same high evidentiary standard. The very act of two unmarried adults sharing a private space is ground for discretionary punishment. In a case of 3/18/2002 (= 1/5/1432), a man was sent to prison for eleven months and 220 lashes, to be administered in five doses, for hosting a woman to whom he was not married.

1.4 Guardianship

Despite acknowledging many of an adult female's rights, including financial independence during the marriage, Hanbali law provides supervision rights for her family as a means of protection. If MMK's divorce in the LA Saudi Consulate is not contested as the result of duress, her guardian would be her oldest full brother. If the divorce is contested, her husband reclaims his guardianship roles as male spouse. The leeway for husbands in applying physical punishment to their wives when the wife is considered disobedient (*nashiz*) is high. In Hanbali law, a reasonable physical punishment leading to accidental death does not lead to compensation (*daman*).

Guardianship by family members (father, brother, etc.) is justified by the principle of protection of women and facilitating their marriage. In the absence of a relative, the government (*Sultan, Qadi*) carries this responsibility. In the case of marriage, the husband is given the responsibility of taking care of his wife/wives. This does not concern private property, as noted, where MMK would be free to run her possessions, but it concerns public behavior.

1.5 Child custody

Her circumstances being as described here, MMK unfortunately falls into a category where she has a next to nil chance of getting joint custody of her son, even if her husband refrains from seeking custody of him, or is deceased. Hanbali legal doctrines unequivocally state that a mother who is unqualified for custody is as good as a non-existent mother. MMK would have had a weak chance of getting joint custody of her son if she was simply considered a non-obedient wife (*nashiz*). In principle, a non-obedient wife loses her nafaqa (maintenance payment) but does not automatically become unfit to have custody of her child. A worse fate awaits MMK, because of the suspicion attached to her character.

IN MODERN SAUDI LAW

- A married Muslim female is free to use her money without consulting her husband, but her social behavior is under his supervision.
- A divorced mother is the presumptive custodian of her young children (7 years for boys), and her husband is the presumptive custodian of older children, especially if the parents live in different cities.

Residence is an important factor in custody battles when parents seek joint custody. When the two parents far apart, the father is the presumptive custodian once the children are considered capable of living without their mother. In one such case, the mother lived in Dammam, the father 237 miles away in the Saudi capital Riyadh, and the son was eleven years old. Here, the mother refrained from remarrying in order to keep custody of her two boys. She subsequently asked the father to take care of the children, as she struggled with their growing older and being less controllable, only to then regret that decision and ask for joint custody. The problem was the distance between the city where she resided and the city where her husband lived. The mother lost her case at three levels of adjudication, all the way to the Saudi Riyadh Supreme Court, the decisive factor being her living alone, where her abstention of marriage did not strengthen her case. (*Digest of Court Decisions*, Vol. 1, pp. 297–9.)

. . .

Before you leave this case and move on to another, take a minute to restate the facts, then the ruling (treat the expert's view as a ruling), then the rationale.

Exercises

1) True or false:

In Saudi society

- A judge decides cases based fully or mostly on medieval legal texts.
- A married woman who consorts sexually with someone other than her husband receives the death penalty.
- A mother of bad character loses custody over her son.
- When divorced parents live apart, the husband is the presumptive custodian for a boy above the age of seven.
- An adult female has more control over her property than over her public behavior.

2) If two of your acquaintances, a roommate or a classmate, are willing to assist, assign them roles and act the case out, and see if this exercise helps you remember the case.

2 Why are US courts interested in pre-national Islamic law?

If the question was simply "why should US courts be interested in Islamic law?," you may have already guessed part of the answer. In cases such as the MMK application above, US courts have had to learn about Saudi courts and how they might handle MMK and women like her should they return to their home country. Islamic law, as part of Saudi law, is relevant here. But why would an American court be interested in an unenforceable, non-binding part of Islamic law?

2.1 Religious practices in the workplace: Title VII case—HALIYE et al. *v.* CELESTICA CORP.

Facts first. A group of Muslim workers in a manufacturing plant in Arden Hills, Minnesota, complained that their need to take breaks from their shifts in order to perform their daily

ROUGH PRAYERS TIME (CHANGES BY GEOGRAPHIC REGION & BY SEASON, FALL/WINTER/SPRING/SUMMER):

- Dawn/Fajr: An hour before sunrise;
- Noon/Dhuhr: Midday (around 12 noon);
- Late Afternoon/'Asr: Midway between noon and sunset;
- Sunset/Maghrib: At sunset;
- Night/'Isha: An hour after sunset.

prayers was not accommodated by existing shift breaks. US State (Minnesota) law requires companies to provide adequate break-time during shifts, where the length of the breaks is proportionate to the length of these shifts, and the company has complied with this requirement.

What is still in question is whether a special accommodation should be made to this group of workers on the grounds that the employer should not leave them vulnerable to having to make one of two bad decisions: Losing their jobs or disobeying their religious conscience. After multiple rounds of negotiations between the workers and their superiors (from shift leaders to senior managers), the workers decided that they were not being accommodated sufficiently. They then decided to sue their company, which if found in breach of these workers' rights, would be required to offer a compensation. But why was it hard for the company to accommodate the workers, assuming they made a good faith effort?

By virtue of the First Amendment to the US Constitution, the US government is not allowed to either support or thwart any religious belief or expression. By virtue of other US federal laws, like the Civil Rights Act of 1964, non-governmental entities, such as private businesses, could not discriminate based on religion (Title VII) and are accordingly required to accommodate Muslim religious beliefs in order to avoid religious discrimination lawsuits.

In this case, the workers' sincerely held beliefs are based on religious laws that, at least traditionally, would have no judicial jurisdiction in many Muslim courtrooms but may be discussed and explained before an American judge. Again, expert testimony will need to be sought, but it will tell us about an aspect of Islamic law that is not enforced in principle in Muslim countries. It is a voluntary aspect of Islamic law, which believing Muslims choose to obey out of their own volition. So, what are these legally non-binding, yet religiously binding, laws?

DAILY PRAYERS

Time windows for the daily prayers in Islam shift depending on the season. If you look up how prayer times changed in Minneapolis in September 2015, you will note that the time for the:

1. **Dawn** prayer was at 5:11 am at the beginning of the month and 5:51 am at the end of the month, and sunrise times ranged from 6:34 am to 7:09 am over the same period;
2. **Noon** prayer (much more stable): 1:14–1:04 pm;
3. **Late afternoon** prayer: 4:56–4:19 pm;

4 **Sunset** prayer: 7:51–6:56 pm;

5 **Night** prayer: 9:16–8:17 pm.

On short days during the winter, the times change, and the window of the daytime prayers gets shorter.

This fact makes a permanent, year-round plan for break-time during work shifts that matches prayer time-windows hard to come by. As you can see in the list above, prayer windows are set in relation to (natural) day and night time-marks such as dawn, noon, late- or mid-afternoon, sunset, rather than specified hours, such as 8 am or 6 pm. The changing times of the daily prayers force Muslim workers to either not perform their prayers or lose their jobs.

The question of how to reconcile work and rituals was answered by jurists from the Muslim world at the beginning of the twentieth century as the rise of industrial jobs caused this issue to come to scholarly attention. One answer (recorded by *Abd al-Rahman al-Jaziri* in the 1940s and increasingly adopted by many modern Muslim jurists) was to apply a traditional religious license to combine the second with the third prayers and the fourth with the fifth. Note also that Muslims also have a religious obligation to support their families. (This is often assumed to be the duty of adult males.) Reconciling these two religious duties is what is at work in the religious law in this case.

2.1.1 SUPPORTING ONE'S FAMILY

Muslim workers are required to support their families, which means that they cannot simply refuse to work to fulfill their religious duty of the daily prayers at the expense of other religious

Figure 1.1 Muslim prayer mats, Yemen. Author: Rod Waddington. Image accessed via Wikimedia.

commitments. While disagreeing on some details, Muslim jurists stipulate broadly that a husband must make basic items available to his wife and children, and a son may also be required to support a needy parent (and, if appropriate, a grandparent). In cases where either one's father (or grandfather) or offspring is in need of financial support, one must also shoulder the duty of offering this financial support.

2.1.2 LICENSE IN RELIGIOUS LAW

One solution to the problem is for the Minnesota workers to take advantage of the license to combine prayers, which stems from medieval Islamic law. This is allowed only in the case of prayers #2, 3, 4, and 5, however: the first prayer of the day (the Dawn Prayer) must be performed uncombined. (Acceptable combination is also limited to performing 2 with 3 and 4 with 5.) But the license to combine prayers is not accepted by all Muslim legal scholars: some believe that it should be allowed only in limited conditions, such as the cases of sickness, traveling, or adverse weather that might prevent trips back and forth to the mosque or collective prayer room, while others hold that it is allowed when there is a reasonable need (which would include the factory workers' scenario). Indeed a wide range of views exists, some strict and others relaxed.

The view that this religious license is not available to the workers in this instance was taken by one of the case's expert witnesses. He argued that the workers could not benefit from this "combination" license because the workers (being Somalis) follow the Shafi'i school, which does not allow it. The District Court decision can easily be located and need not be reproduced here with all its subtleties.

[Case No. 06-CV-4769 (PJS/JJG). (D. Minn. Jun. 10, 2009). One thing to be aware of is that the fact of the disagreement among the workers as to what they believed their religious duties were led to a denial that they represented a "class" in the legal sense. Muslims don't all believe the same thing about whether they can take advantage of this license of even whether they could delay performing the prayer until the end of its window. The Court states that: "The four prerequisites for class certification under Rule 23(a) are numerosity, commonality, typicality, and adequacy. After careful consideration, the Court concludes that plaintiffs have failed to meet the prerequisite of commonality."]

Which of these two views do you sympathize with? And why?

. . .

Before we leave this case, think of the context—the capitalist US world. Companies have an unusually strong advantage in negotiating in circumstances such as these. The writer of the expert report who suggested that the workers *could* combine their prayers agreed that companies often ignore the religious and personal needs of workers until these workers are able to take their employers to court. The other side also acknowledged that the license to combine the prayers existed in Islamic law but argued that Shafi'i law, to which the workers subscribe, does not allow combining. Debates like these may go on in many workplaces, and as such the sincerely held religious beliefs of other faiths may also not be consistently accommodated.

LEGAL SCHOLARS VIEWS ON COMBINING PRAYERS

HANAFI SCHOLARS: Prayers may be combined only during pilgrimage.
MAJORITY OF MALIKI AND SHAFI'I SCHOLARS: Prayers may be combined for traveling, sickness, bad weather, guests' visits, and similar reasons.
HANBALI AND SHI'I SCHOLARS: Prayers may be combined if there is a reasonable need. (Some of these scholars stipulate that this must not become a habit, however.)

The argument for using the religious license is that Muslims do follow the view of their *muftis*. A *mufti* is a religious counsel who provides an authoritative, albeit non-binding, opinion. Laypeople are not expected to engage in religio-legal discussions before they decide how to practice their religion. Most people often take the answers of religious authorities on faith and accept their limited explanations without argument. If the workers received the answer that they may combine their prayers to fulfill the two religious obligations of "supporting their families" and "complying with the requirement of the daily prayers," they would likely follow that religious instruction or *fatwa* (place this as number #1 on the shortlist of important Arabic terms) without hesitation. The presence of external pressure from American society and its perception of Muslim workers' un-pragmatic, or even unreasonable, stances makes this hard to do.

This particular argument would never have been resolved through religious reasoning. Both sides probably went home thinking they won the argument. The US court decision was ultimately to reject the claim that the company had an obligation to accommodate this one religious belief, for all the reasons mentioned, especially the complexity of religious beliefs and the disagreement among workers about their sense of what is required in a faith context.

Cases such as these can be concluded before or during the trial via an agreement or a "settlement" between the parties. All acknowledge the difficulties involved in reconciling the various considerations of religious laws and US laws against religious discrimination. New American legal doctrines continue to be devised in order to attend to the different considerations involved here.

One more set of exercises

- How would you have wanted this case to be decided?
- What information would you need to form an opinion?
- Check online for similar Title VII civil rights cases involving discrimination claims (that apply to the religion category).
- Check commentaries in different schools of Islamic law and see how they discuss this matter. Consult the first two items on the "Further Reading" list (after the Appendixes).
- Check the arguments for and against Oklahoma laws that attempt to restrict the reference to Islamic law (among other religious laws) in American courts in civil rights act cases and similar cases.

3 Borders crossed

In the United States, the Internal Revenue Services (or IRS), overseen by the Federal Treasury Department, has a mandate to apply the Revenue Code (1986), which allows the government to collect taxes and seek to identify cases of mistaken filing and fraud. What follows is a case that appeared before the IRS and required a law firm to seek knowledge of aspects of Islamic law. It is a tax case in which American lawyers represented a US citizen, who grew up and had property in Iraq but whose ownership of this property remained in question even after he lived in the United States for years and acquired his citizenship, having filed multiple tax returns in the meantime. Among other things, the question involved property and inheritance laws in Islam, as they appear in Iraqi personal status laws.

In this case, it became apparent that a property/business in question would not be considered the property of a US citizen (identified for our purposes as A.J.), since he is named only an interest holder, as opposed to a title holder. A.J.'s father holds the title to the property. Inheritance laws assign the son in this case a small share in his father's inheritance and restrict the father's ability to offer the property to his son in his will. This condition was at the root of this complicated arrangement. The father's wish was that his son take over the business after his death, but he did not transfer the property's title to his son. In other words, what appears to be an unwarranted confusion in the ownership status of the business in question is explicable in terms of fairly simple legal principles and practices in Iraq, which are based on national customs and traditions. Below are edited excerpts from the expert report in this particular case. The report starts with a quote from a lawyer explaining the question at hand and proceeds to considering relevant laws, with a special reference to Iraqi personal status laws and their amendments.

3.1 Property and inheritance in a foreign land

I write this report to offer an answer to the question of how Islamic inheritance law, as applied in Iraq, dictates the distribution of the inheritance of A.J.'s father (Client's father), after he is deceased. The question, as stated by C.D. of G, P, and H [LAW FIRM], is as follows:

> The hypothetical decedent's family is comprised of the following people:
>
> 1. Hypothetical Decedent ("HD")—born in 1943;
> 2. HD's wife—born in 1948;
> 3. HD's 1st son—born in 1969, died in 1991, was never married and had no children;
> 4. HD's 1st daughter—born in 1972, died in 2012, had two sons and one daughter (all presently living);
> 5. HD's 2nd son—born in 1974;
> 6. HD's 3rd son—born in 1985 (the Client);
> 7. HD's 2nd daughter—born in 1988;
> 8. HD's 4th son—born in 1992;
> 9. HD's 3 brothers (born of same parents as HD);
> 10. HD's 3 sisters (born of same parents as HD).

Organizational documents describe the Client as the interest holder of several companies (the "Companies"). However, the Client states that the Companies are actually his father's companies and list the Client as the interest holder only because the Client's father wants the Client to run the Companies upon the Client's father's death . . . . how [would] the Client's father's estate be distributed under Islamic law in the following hypothetical situations:

- **(Hypothetical 1)**: Assume that the organizational documents describe the Client's father as the interest holder of the Companies. Thus, assume that the Client's father is the only person who holds any interest in the Companies. Also assume that the Companies comprise 90 percent of the Client's father's estate. Next assume that the Client **had a will** (if such document exists under Islamic law) and wished to devise all of his interests in the Companies to the Client. Under Islamic law, is such a distribution possible? If not, how is the estate distributed? We were told (by the Client) that a person can only devise a certain portion (around one-third) of their estate and that the rest of the estate is distributed under Islamic descent and distribution rules. Is this correct?

- **(Hypothetical 2)**: Assume that the organizational documents describe the Client's father as the interest holder of the Companies. Thus, assume that the Client's father is the only person that holds any interest in the Companies. Also assume that the Companies comprise 90 percent of the Client's father's estate. Next assume that the Client's father **did not have a will** and therefore, the Client's father's estate was distributed under Islamic descent and distribution rules. How is the estate distributed?

3.2 Property and personal status laws

This case involves the laws governing "ownership," "compulsory wills," and "inheritance" in the Islamic legal tradition and modern Iraqi laws. Iraqi inheritance laws, as laid out in the personal status laws of 1959 and their amendments, are based on Hanafi law but as of the late 1970s began to show modifications that derive from Ja'fari laws. (Iraqi scholars themselves disagree about how to interpret these amendments' reflections of Ja'fari doctrines. See, for example, Qahtan Hadi Ubayd, *Mirath al-Bin fi al-Fiqh al-Islami wa al-Qanun al-Iraqi* (= *The Daughter's Inheritance in Islamic and Iraqi Law*), Takrit Journal of Legal and Political Sciences, Year 2, Vol. 7, pp. 270–309.) The future of Iraqi law promises a larger impact for the Ja'fari (Shi'i) school of law, depending on how things turn out there, but as things stand, Sunni law is embedded in current national laws.

There are several differences between the two systems. The two (Hanafi (Sunni) and Ja'fari (Shi'i)) schools would disagree, for example, on how to distribute the inheritance in situations where a daughter and a father are sole inheritors, the case of a husband or wife with a father and a mother, and the case where maternal (that is, enate) brothers inherit with full (cognate) brothers, among other situations and scenarios. The Ja'fari (Shi'i) school of law also does not allow the resizing of shares (*awl*), if an aggregation of the shares exceed the perfect arithmetical value of one (which corresponds to the full inheritance; this resizing procedure is needed in this inheritance case). In Ja'fari law, the remainder of an inheritance is not distributed among male agnates after the share-carriers are given their shares (al-Allama al-Hilli (d. 726/1325) (ed. I. Qadiri), *Tahrir al-Ahkam* (Qumm, Iran: Sadiq Org. 2001), Vol. 5, p. 8).

Sunni and Shi'i laws, however, do not disagree as to the inheritance case where the sole inheritors are the wife, sons, and daughters of the deceased, as we see in this case. In most cases, they arrive at similar conclusions in addressing inheritance questions. Islamic inheritance law is certainly complex, but one may venture at least one simplification that tends to be true in most cases: Children, spouses, and parents are favored over siblings, and siblings are prioritized over other relatives. My answer follows Sunni law as it is stated in national Iraqi personal status laws.

In the first hypothetical, the Client's father would have a "will" that may benefit the Client. In Islamic law, such a "will" would be void without the permission of the rest of the inheritors. This is because the deceased is restricted to benefiting non-inheritors when he assigns parts of his inheritance to others upon his death. If such a will assigns shares (below or up to the third) to a charity (or any entity other than the inheritors), it is implemented unless it exceeds a ceiling of one-third of the inheritance. The two hypotheticals, therefore, will be treated as one. The rest of the report will then address the general principles that govern the case as presented.

3.3 Owner, possessor, and business representative

In Sunni Islamic law, **ownership** (*milk*) is a condition allowing the possession and dispensation of both a physical entity and its utility. For example, a tenant of an apartment is not an owner because s/he has access only to the utility of the apartment. Mere **possession** (*yad*), on the other hand, is only a factual rebuttable indicator of ownership. That is, absent evidence of ownership by another, person **A** is a presumed owner of an object/asset if s/he has physical possession of it (or lives in it, in the case of a house), but this presumption may be refuted with a deed of sale and title where person **B** is named as owner, for example. Another distinction in Islamic law is between a **business representative** (*wakil*) and an owner (*malik*). Islamic law does allow "delegation," founded on the permission of the owner, which gives full access to a property, including sale and dispensation without price (as in a gift), but the owner has an owner's claim to the value of the property, if it is transferred to another for a price. The delegate in medieval Islamic law is usually (but not always) an individual and not a company or fund. Modern Iraqi civil law, given its partial derivation from the 1949 Egyptian civil code, which in turn derives from French legal institutions, allows for additional types of delegation/representation vis-à-vis property, which evolved from the further development of the concept of *personnalité juridique* (unknown, in the modern form, in medieval Islamic law). An interest holder is a translation of a term that indicates this function (business representative), and A.J. (the Client) is hence not an actual owner of the property, which leads to dividing the property upon his father's death as I will explain below.

3.4 Wills voluntary and compulsory

Upon an individual's death, three obligations apply to her/his owned possessions, in the following order, according to both medieval Islamic law and Article 87 of Law 188/1959 (Iraqi Personal Status Law): **funeral costs; debts of the deceased;** and **as provided for in a personal will**. As noted above, the deceased gets to assign up to one-third of his money to any person or charity **excluding his inheritors** (lest this be a way to redistribute the inheritance, or as some Muslim jurists would have it, continue to own one's property after death).

In medieval Islamic law, writing a will before death, although recommended as an act of charity to needy non-inheritors, is not an obligation. (It is in fact one of very few matters where consensus is fairly strong among all Sunni jurists.) In modern Islamic law, based on a view that originated within the Maliki school of law, the grandchildren of the deceased whose parents died within the lifetime of their grandfathers, collect, within the limits of one-third of the inheritance, a share that is characterized as a compulsory will (Article 74, Law 188/1959 (personal status law) as amended by Law 72/1979). This "compulsion" is posthumously placed on the shoulder of the deceased grandfather (in our case, A.J.'s father). That is, jurists assumed he had a duty to provide a will for his grandchildren whose parents (who are in turn the deceased's offspring) died within his lifetime.

3.5 Standard inheritance law and its application in this case

Under Islamic law, inheritors fall into one of several "ranks."

1 A group of relatives comprising twelve classes (four of whom are male—father, grandfather, husband, maternal brother—and eight of whom are female—mother, grandmother, maternal, paternal, or full sister, wife, daughter and son's daughters). In any inheritance case, there can only be eleven categories, because there is either a husband or a wife/wives, and under each category one may have a single or multiple individuals (eg, multiple sisters from both parents). Each one of these categories is assigned a specific share that is a fraction of the number 1 (ONE, representing the inheritance itself) (fractions being one-eighth, one-sixth, one-third, one-half, and so on), and each one/inheritor's share is affected by the number and presence or absence of others.

2 The second rank is that of male agnates who collect the remainder of the inheritance.

Absent this category, other relatives (via the mother, such as a maternal grandfather) inherit. In some cases, the treasury (or the State) comes in. Our case does not require enumerating other inheritors.

To apply these rules to the case, the inheritance will be divided as follows (after funeral cost, debt, and any valid will):

- The wife collects one-eighth. It will turn out that this one-eighth is applied to the remainder of the inheritance *after* the grandchildren receive their compulsory will share, which is calculated below.

- The remaining seven-eighths are shared by the three sons, the living daughter, and the children of deceased daughter. Each (one of the three) males here receives two shares per each share for their sisters—the deceased's daughters. The deceased daughter's share transfers to her living children; note, in addition, that they will collect their share before anyone else, because it is considered part of the deceased's will—a will he should have assigned before his death. The total shares within the seven-eighths are hence 8 ((2 times 3) + 1 + 1). Each son then gets a quarter of the seven-eighths, and each daughter one eighth of the remaining seven-eighths of the inheritance. Thus each son (A.J. [the Client] being the case at hand) collects one-quarter of seven-eighths (= 7/32). The living daughter collects half of that (7/64). The two sons and one daughter of the deceased daughter collect their mother's share (7/64) as if she were alive.

We can now go back and recalculate each share, other than that of the grandchildren, in relation to the remainder of the inheritance, after the grandchildren's share. (They end up with smaller amounts, but not significantly so.) The chart below shows the inheritors' shares. Note that each of A.J.'s brothers is indicated collectively as Son B (equal share).

. . . .

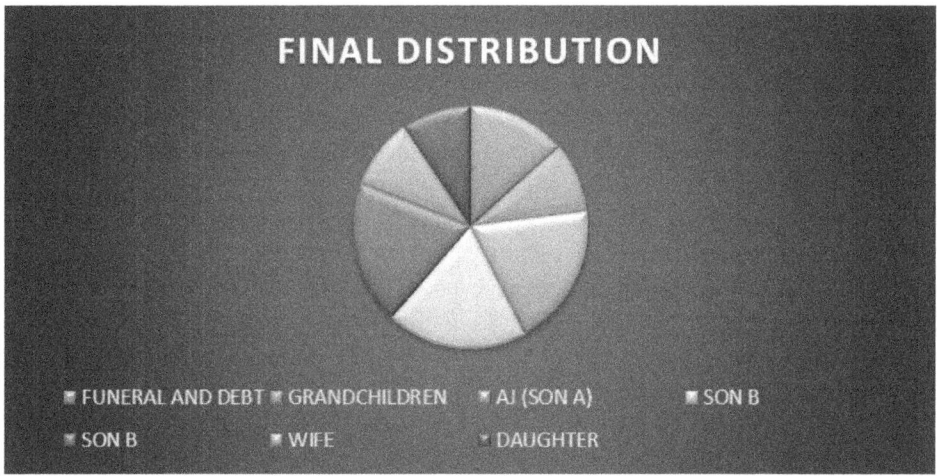

Suppose the deceased left $74,000.00, his funeral cost $2,000.00, having also left a debt of $8,000.00. He assigned no legacies to a charity or an outsider. The inheritance here equals $64,000.00. In this case, the children of the deceased's daughter divide $7,000.00, which does not exceed one-third of the inheritance (the grandchildren's shares are their mother's share of 7/64th of the inheritance after the wife's share (one-eighth) is collected, as I explained, but they collect their share before anyone else). A.J.'s mother (the deceased's wife) ends up with $7,125.00 (one-eighth of $64,000.00 (minus) $7,000.00), A.J. with $14,250.00 (a male's share of the one-quarter of seven-eighths, that is, taken from the $57,000.00 that remained after the grandchildren received their compulsory amounts); the same amount goes to each one of his living brothers (the deceased's sons), while the living daughter collects a share equivalent to half of A.J.'s share.

(For more on inheritance law, see section 3.4 in Unit 4.)

4 Laws and Societies

When words such as *ifta* and *fatwa* are introduced, questions arise. For example: What is the relationship between the seekers of *fatwa* and those who offer it?

We agreed to think of the expert reports we read so far as *fatwas*, or religious legal advice. Just as much junk science has flooded the courts, especially in tort cases (where harm compensation was in question), pseudo-Shari'a expert reports could also be found in many court docks. In the *Haliye* case, one advice was that the workers could perform their prayers only within the normal prescribed time-windows, while the expert stated that combining certain prayers *would* be an option for them. In a Muslim environment no one is surprised that *muftis* or *fatwa* providers disagree.

In premodern times, the *mufti*'s authority was conceded because of his or her knowledge of the religious law. She or he is a religious authority and is also a judge-like authority, but a judge without the backing of the police. The *mufti* is not a lawyer in the sense of someone who will take your side and make up supporting arguments for it. The *mufti* is often not compensated, but payment can be made if the scholar has an official position. The compensation is certainly not paid for by the questioner, and not organized per an hourly rate.

The *mufti* is supposed to be dispassionate and must not solve the problems at the expense of arriving at a truly reasonable and sensible answer that is consistent with solid legal reasoning. Yet in times gone by, it was appropriate for these figures (most of whom were male), to act in a rather paternalistic fashion and become invested in solving the questioner's problems. In modern times, much of the sense of responsibility for the questioner is maintained in the minds of *muftis*, yet they must constantly stive to provide a degree of neutrality that is unavailable to one's natural father or paid lawyer. In the modern context, to complicate things farther, the questioner, the person seeking religious advice, sometimes turns the *mufti* into something of an older brother, father, or psychiatrist figure in a process called *transference* and *countertransference* by psychiatrists. This is when the questioner projects onto the *mufti* the image of a father or other confidante, while the *mufti* allows that to happen. In such cases, the *mufti*'s goal becomes allowing the questioner to find a solution to their personal problem—whether it is a question of divorce, investment, or something else—rather than provide an answer that can be used in the case and similar cases.

There are premodern precedents for the use of so-called stratagems or *hiyal*, where a scholar exploits his mastery of the law to find ways out of legal obligations for the questioners. Experienced *muftis* are not supposed to do that. This aspect of Islamic law continues to puzzle scholars of the subject. Check out websites of Islamic centers that have *fatwa* sections: The larger the website, and the greater the number of questions and answers, the more representative it will be, and the easier it will be for you to get a sense of how lenient or stringent these centers are, what school of law or *madhhab* (put this as #2 on the short-list of important terms, if *fatwa* is #1) they tend to cite, and how diverse their Muslim population is.

5 Conclusion: The nature of Islamic law

The questions we have looked at so far (extramarital affairs, criminal punishment for lewd and unbecoming behavior, prayer–work schedule adjustments, inheritance) show the extent to which Islamic law operates and the diversity of its tools. It is not in question that Islamic law regulates all life affairs, from social life and public manners to rituals. It is also obvious that the law has an enforceable side to it and a voluntary side, which causes some of those who study it to think that some aspects of it are not law at all. It is also, finally, true that Muslims, whether living in a majority-Muslim community or living as a minority, have interesting questions about how to live their lives based on Islamic law.

This takes us to the second real challenge (remember the first one from the Introduction) in studying the subject of Islamic law and raises a central question we have to answer at least provisionally, before we move on to additional material. What is the nature of this beast? What is the nature of Islamic law?

COULD THIS BE AN ESSAY QUESTION?
Which one is the more important foundation for the law in Islam: power or morality?

Islamic law seems to indicate "law" as we understand it in the modern sense of the word, a system of *rules backed by the force, normally of a modern state* or equivalent power. Islamic law also includes *morality-like, non-binding, opinions* (some may say), or religious *edicts* (other would call them), or simply *viewpoints*, which these *fatwas* convey, backed, however, only by the vague authority of the *mufti*, or the *fatwa*-issuer. Islamic law incorporates both of these elements, and some of the heated debates among scholars of the subject revolve around the extent to which each scholar sees one of these two elements as the more important and which is secondary.

Once again, Islamic law is an imprecise, if necessary, expression of an amalgamation of orders and opinions. Islamic law is the basis for the Saudi laws that punish an individual, in this case MMK and her "boyfriend" if he were to reside in Saudi Arabia with her. It is obvious that the *prohibition of fornication and adultery* is moral in its nature, but the government gives this moral instruction a legal value, in the modern sense, by enforcing it.

Islamic law is also the reason why the workers in Arden Hills, Minnesota, wanted to break from work to perform their daily prayers. There are Muslim countries, such as in Tunisia and Egypt, where no court of law claims a jurisdiction in this matter. But a US court, bound by respect for religious beliefs if not Islamic law's authority, will hear the case and may grant relief to the plaintiffs here—that is, guarantee that their employer relax shift-time rules to accommodate the religious beliefs of its employees.

As we look at these cases where the shari'a is brought up in different contexts, a realist's attempt to show the relevance of the shari'a in today's world also shows the limits of this relevance. At this stage, the potential sweep of this system is what we need to have a sense of.

For those who still find this broad sweep strange, let me try to think of a (partial) parallel. In a 1816 decision,* American Supreme Court justice Joseph Story (1779–1845) proclaimed: "It is the case, not the court, that gives jurisdiction." With this the Supreme Court asserted its jurisdiction over matters decided by state Supreme Courts (eg, the Virginia Supreme Court) and negated being limited to reviewing decisions of only federal entities. This means that the US Supreme Court could decide any matter where the constitution of the United States is in question (with other limits that you may want to pursue in constitutional references). There is constitutional law *in potentia* (law that may arise when requested or sought) now and in the future. But it is the subject, then, that makes this court operate. Keep this in mind when you advance in this text and learn about the theoretically global preview

---

* *Martin v. Hunter's Lessee*, 14 U.S. 304 (1816).

of Islamic law. Seek an understanding of its limits in understanding where it limits itself to Muslim subjects and land ruled by Muslims, which you will understand gradually.

Where does all this come from? Who made up all these rules and gave the foundation for these opinions? If you think it is all or mostly all in the Qur'an or the Prophet Muhammad's sayings and actions, think again. Or, just move to Unit 2.

Review and think ahead I

- Islamic law includes non-binding instructions (*fatwas*). These regulate important aspects of a Muslim's life, including rituals (prayers, fasting), diet (prohibition of pork and wine), as well as matters of public nature, such as whether one is expected to revolt against unjust rule.
- Islamic law also includes court decisions that are enforced by the police and political power. A contract including an element of "usury" may not be valid. If a man goes to a court and says that another man is forcing him to pay usurious interest, he may receive the protection of the court and his party may be asked to demand only the debt's principal.
- In Saudi law, a woman accused of unbecoming behavior may receive physical punishment, imprisonment, or lashing.
- Islamic law regulates both personal and social affairs, including family, trade, and crime.

Tips

- When you define *fatwa*, make sure to indicate the role of the questioner in shaping the conditions for the scholarly or juristic answer to it.
- Court decisions don't normally cover rituals but are binding; *fatwas* have a broader scope but no force beside the authority of the scholar who provides them and the faith of the questioner.

Material for reflection

- There are two views (in *Haliye vs Celstica*) on whether workers can combine their five prayers into three instances of prayer. There seems to be only one view on whether MMK has acted inappropriately by sharing an apartment with someone other than a husband, while her minor son is with her. Can you argue against this view from a non-liberal viewpoint?
- Zayd is Laila's half-brother (their mother's two marriages gave them two different fathers) and Laila is Maryam's half-sister (same father, different mothers). Can Zayd marry Maryam? Why? (Tip: One is prohibited from marrying one's full or half-brother or sister. Does this include the sister of one's sister?)

2 Madhhabs

Islamic law derives its "ultimate" authority from the Qur'an, God's revelation, and the Prophet Muhammad's sayings and actions (*Sunna*). In its long history, Islamic law has experienced calls for a return to the textual umbrella (the Qur'an and the Prophet's *Sunna*) whose air of authority gave it both its outer limits and its distinctive flavor. The modern era, in particular, brought about tendencies that are most emphatic on seeing the Qur'an and the *Sunna* as the only law's true sources. But it is a common mistake to think of Islamic law as either Qur'anic or Muhammadan law. The European notion, preserved out of habit in casual conversations today, that Islamic law is either Qur'anic law or Muhammadan law distorts the subject more than it clarifies it.

In this book, each time we refer to God's law, God's truth, or employ a similar expression, we indicate a search scholars undergo to "discern" God's ways from His revelations (Qur'an) and his messenger's path (*Sunna*). God rarely speaks explicitly; hence the need for interpretation. God's language, rich and full of indirect hints, then requires jurists to figure out its meaning and make it into laws.

One of the early Sunni authorities, Malik ibn Anas (93/711–179/795), who was known to have built his law on the tradition and practices of the residents of Medina, the Prophet's city and burial place that preserved its residents' lived traditions and practices, is reported to have been asked what someone should do who missed a corner of his body (or a body part, such as his elbow) as he washed out for the prayers. (The ablution, a prerequisite for the prayers, includes (at a minimum) washing one's face and feet and wiping one's hair (or the balding head for the hairless), in addition to the lower part of the arm, including the elbow.) Malik said that if missing that corner of the arm was unintentional, then the person ought to only wash the missed body part and then redo the prayer; if it was intentional, the whole "ablution" must be redone before the prayer can be redone; if the person *was in the middle of* the washing process, he must start again from the beginning (Ibn 'Abd al-Barr (d. 463/1071), *Ikhtilaf Aqwal Malik wa Ashabih* (eds H. Lahmar and M. Muranyi) (Dar al-Gharb, 2003), p. 49.) These answers, while not surprising, have no textual basis. This, in a question of rituals, raises doubt about generalizations that assert, as many European scholars have imagined over the centuries, that law in Islam is truly based on texts and traditions that appeal to revelation in the narrow sense.

Islamic law has some fairly identifiable human authorities. The early authorities of Sunni and Shi'i law were companions and debating partners. Many of them were even relatives and family members. True, all appeal to the first teacher, the Prophet himself, but *the details of the law*, as they elaborated it, were extensions of practices after the

وقال مالك فيمن نسي في غسله لمعة من بدنه حتى صلى أنه إن كان عامداً لذلك ابتدأ غسله من أوله وأعاد صلاته وإن كان ناسياً غسل الموضع وحده وأعاد صلاته وإن لم يغسلها الناسي حين ذكر كان عليه أن يعيد الغسل من أوله.

اختلاف أقوال مالك وأصحابه لابن عبد البر (تحقيق حميد محمد لحمر وميكلوش موراني) نشر دار الغرب الإسلامي – بيروت – ٢٠٠٣ – ص ٤٩.

Prophet's death. There is really no way to tell the stories of the founders of Sunni and Shi'i law as separate tales: They certainly developed interesting intellectual disagreements, which tells us something about the power of human reflection on the same events and arriving at different conclusions, but they inhabited very much the same world of ideals and social parameters.

Sunni and Shi'i doctrines diverge in many areas, but they also are interdependent. The revival and robust development of Shi'i jurisprudence since the thirteenth to fourteenth centuries (if you really, really can't wait, see the section on al-'Allama al-Hilli later in this unit) was achieved with an extensive conversation with the (then) much more developed Sunni jurisprudence. In the past half-century, the process seems to have gone in a reversed direction. Shi'i legal philosophy and doctrines have become more developed than their Sunni counterparts in many areas. This may lead to important changes in Sunni law in the current and subsequent centuries.

According to the Shi'i view of the matter, the Prophet Muhammad bequeathed his knowledge, which he received from God, to the closest members of his family, most notably a young cousin named Ali, who was later to be known as the *Imam*, or leader of the community. The word *Shi'ah* or *Shi'a* means "partisans," and Shi'i is the common adjective for those who ascribe their practices to the family of the Prophet Muhammad, whose knowledge was inherited by Ali and subsequently his descendants.

According to the Sunni view, the most important contributors to the making and development of Islamic law were the *madhhabs*, or schools of law. It is also true that Muslim governments have played an important role in developing the law as a system and carved a space for its "public" application. A degree of separation between government and *madhhab* (paralleling only in a limited way the separation of state and church in the United States) has always obtained, but competition and collaboration could also be identified.

There is a good case for an argument that Islamic law, both in its Sunni and Shi'i variations, was mostly made in Kufa, a city in Iraq that was founded about seven years after the Prophet Muhammad's death (in the reign of the Prophet's companion 'Umar ibn al-Khattab (d. 23/644), a great and independent lawmaker in his own right) and which hosted many immigrants from the south (Arabia) and the north (Mesopotamia and Iran). Though this argument will likely be made in a tongue-in-cheek, rather than a serious, manner, there is a lot that supports it, as we will see. In less exciting and also less reductive versions, Islamic law was made in Kufa and Medina (the latter being the Prophet's burial city and his home during the last ten years of his life, where both early Shi'i and Maliki law started out); it was also made and developed a generation later in Fustat, Egypt (currently a suburb of Cairo); and it was disseminated to centers of learning proximal and distal in the Islamic West (ie,

North Africa and Spain), which left us with memorable monuments of learning such as the Zaytuna in Tunisia and Qarawiyyin in Morocco, two of the most significant centers of Islamic learning all the way to the modern era.

The early history of the *madhhabs* can be a matter of angry academic quibbling in Western scholarship. This is caused by an overemphasis on the early history of Islam in this scholarship, which itself is caused by multiple factors. One of these is orientalists' interest in identifying the Jewish and Christian (and other) roots of ideas in Islam, a search ultimately triggered by trends in European scholarship that emphasized the origins of a phenomenon as a foundation for understanding it. Islamic studies in Europe and the United States grew in the midst of "orientalist" scholarship, which was fascinated by the origins of Europe itself, and where inquiries into those origins became a quest in themselves. In some cases, orientalists' speculations about the genesis of ideas that found their way to Islamic legal reasoning, and about the interaction of foreign ideas with the views of Muslim jurists, are plausible. In other cases, however, they are wild and purely conjectural. While this Western scholarship has had an impact on many Muslims, what matters most, to many Muslims and Muslim scholars, in inquiring about Islamic law is what they believe inherited and current religious authority requires them to do. This unit will briefly attempt to sketch the premodern history to the extent that it explains the present.

1 Jurists and schools of law

The *madhhab* is a school of law, but not in the sense of a physical, bricks-and-mortar building such as the UCLA or New York University Law Schools; rather, it is a way of thinking, a battery of method tools, and a set of doctrines or answers to legal questions. There are four *Sunni* schools of law, which spread all the way from western China to Morocco and from Russia and Eastern Europe to the belly of Africa. We will limit ourselves to two major *Shi'i* schools of law, which flourished in Yemen, Lebanon, Iraq, and, much later, in Iran. There are also schools that are neither Sunni nor Shi'i, such as the Ibadi school in Oman and small areas in North Africa, as well as *extinct* schools, ways of thinking, and doctrines that did not survive the test of time or may have very few followers today, such as the Zahiri School and those schools founded by Sufyan al-Thawri and Ibn Jarir al-Tabari.

Madhhab broadly means "way" or "direction"—which applies to ways of thinking, whether about theology or even politics and trade—but its definition has narrowed down over time for a good reason, namely its frequent usage in the specific sense of "ways of thinking," which applies most usually to legal and theological matters. Let's look at it like this: If used in a general matter, there could be a literary *madhhab*, a theological *madhhab*, and a political *madhhab*. Without qualifications or context, it would indicate *a way of thinking about practical legal matters*.

1.1 The story of the *madhhabs*

The founders of the main schools of Islamic law lived within 150 years of each other (roughly between 700–850 in the Common Era), but their systems took centuries to fully develop. In addition to their sense that their work fulfilled a religious duty, it was mostly the companionship and intellectual pleasure that drove the founders to develop their

Figure 2.1 Mausoleum of Imam al-Shafi'i on the Southern Cemetery of Cairo. Author: PaFra. Image accessed via Wikimedia.

answers to practical questions, such as how one should conduct one's prayers and what is lawful and unlawful gain. They lent their names to their schools. For example, a man who was known by the epithet Abu Hanifa was considered the founder of Hanafi law. (Hanifa -> Hanafi). A man named Ja'far gave his name to the Ja'fari school of law. Zayd, Ja'far, Abu Hanifa, Malik, Shafi'i, and Ahmad ibn Hanbal are hence the eponymous jurists of the *madhhabs*.

Within that same 150 years, government in the new Muslim societies matured beyond its early beginnings. The first ruler of the Muslim community, Abu Bakr (d. 13/634), ruled from his home at first and refused to take a salary for his services as Caliph (lexically, *successor*, here "leader" of the community as a successor of the Prophet in administering the community's affairs) until close to the end of his reign. He later accepted a wage, but returned it when he was dying, saying he did not really need it. By the middle of the eighth century (750), a hierarchical government apparatus had been established in Damascus for close to 100 years, and a major revolution (the Abbasid revolution (130–132/748–750)) was brewing. The new system established by this revolution was multi-ethnic, mostly non-Muslim in its population, with complex systems of personal and property taxes and a far-reaching (though chiefly province-based) military structure.

Zayd ibn 'Ali (d. 122/740), Jaf'ar al-Sadiq (d. 148/765) and Abu Hanifa (d. 150/767) all lived during what came to be known as Umayyad times (after the name of a family, based in Damascus, which ruled between 40/656 and 132/750). This is the same dynasty that crumbled after the revolution of 132/750, which in turn founded the longest reign in Islam, that of the Abbasid house. Abbasid reign was to last until the invasion of Baghdad by the Mongols in 656/1258.

The "high noon" of the Sunni legal traditions occurred in the first half of the eleventh century. Hanafi legal commentaries have matured and accounted for the lapses of the works of Muhammad ibn al-Hasan al-Shaybani (d. 189/805). Maliki narrators of local customs had accumulated sufficient material from the Islamic West, in small coastal towns in Libya and Tunisia, as well as the larger cities of Morocco and Spain, and ceased to converse with their Hanafi counterparts. Shafi'is in Iraq and Iran produced more law than all early Egyptian Shaf'is, which made the northeastern side of the Arabian peninsula a center for this and not only Hanafi law. There were also Hanbalis in Iran and Iraq, but this school needed more time to develop in its later stages.

By the thirteenth century, an incremental reform was taking place. There was a return to an examination of the early doctrines of the school founders, led by Shafi'i jurists such as Abu al-Qasim al-Rafi'i (d 632/1226) and Muhyi al-Din al-Nawawi (d. 676/1277), and by Hanbali jurists, such as Ibn Taymiyya (d. 728/1328). This movement took the schools in new directions. The concern of jurists before these three scholars was to complete the law by providing answers to the new questions on behalf of the school's founder. This certainly continued, but new paths were trodden. These included correcting mistakes in attributing the views to the founders, and more importantly, judging the school doctrines against the standard of correct reasoning, based on evidence from the sources of the law, namely the Qur'an and the *Sunna*.

Legal scholarly discussions of the *madhhabs* were contemporaneous with important political developments. Some legal scholars were friendly to certain political regimes and some were strongly opposed, yet when the government needed legal scholars, they had no choice but to rely on, and in some cases promote, these private jurists or scholars. In the beginning, many scholars shied away from government service and many remained uninterested in government until later centuries. For a number of them, by contrast, at least serving in judicial capacity was expected and in fact desired.

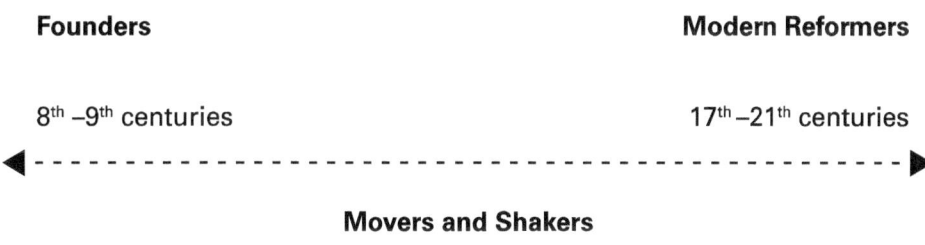

1.2 The founders and their authority

Compared to the major Sunni schools of law, Shi'i and other non-Sunni schools of law rightly claim to have an earlier historical foundation, dating to the last decades of the first century of Islam and the first decades of the second century (roughly the years 700–750 CE). The documentation of non-Sunni schools of law, however, comes later than early Sunni works of jurisprudence. In any case, the foundation of both Sunni and non-Sunni law goes back to similar sources, and they all have influenced one another. The sheer quantity, wide circulation, and power of Sunni law makes it the focus of most studies of Islamic law, although the student is advised not to take this as an indication that non-Sunni law is either less authoritative in its environment or historically posterior.

1.2.1 SUNNI SCHOOLS

The first two Sunni schools of law originated in Iraq and western Arabia almost simultaneously. The first was the Hanafi school of law, led by Abu Hanifa (d. 150/767) and his two students, Aby Yusuf (d. 182/798) and Muhammad ibn al-Hasan al-Shaybani (d. 189/805). While guided by traditions of practice that claim to have come from the Prophet himself, their main method of generating answers to practical legal questions was *reason-based*. Early Hanafi scholars were also focused on structure and consistency, but also on regulating "exceptions" to the rules. The other school of law was the Maliki school of law, led by Malik Ibn Anas (d. 179/795), which was based on *the actual practice of the Muslim population* of the City of the Prophet (Medina or Madinah). By Malik's time, the Prophet's companions and their children and grandchildren had populated the city with five generations of practicing Muslims all of whom possessed the highest degree of knowledge of the Prophet's tradition.

Muhammad ibn al-Hasan al-Shaybani (d. 189/805) studied with both Abu Hanifa and Malik for about two to three years in each case. He was only eighteen when Abu Hanifa died, but he continued to study with a student of his and decided to dedicate himself to defending the Hanafi doctrine, writing the standard texts of the Hanafi school, and ended up writing a legal polemic against Maliki doctrines (which is quoted in this unit on the question of secret marriage). Muhammad's uncle, al-Qa'nabi (d. 221/836), was a major reporter of Maliki doctrines and remained loyal to his school.

The entanglement of Hanafi and Maliki law at its departure point has other elements. Shaybani (d. 189/805) is one of the reporters of Malik's main text of Prophetic traditions— that is, reports from the authority of the Prophet Muhammad. This book was classified in an accessible manner and was known with this title *Muwatta* or the *Accessible Sourcebook*. The other source of Maliki doctrines, which was destined to spread in the western parts of the Muslim world (North Africa), started with questions prepared by a scholar named Asad ibn al-Furat (d. 213/828), who was also a follower of Abu Hanifa and a companion of Shaybani, based on the questions Shaybani answered in his legal commentaries, and which Asad later gave to Ibn al-Qasim (d. 191/806) to answer. Ibn al-Qasim's answers became the building blocks of Maliki jurisprudence as it later developed in the Muslim West, and remained at the heart of subsequent commentaries.

Out of these two schools, a third school was conceived, by the genius of Shafi'i, a man from 'Asqalan (north of Gaza, Palestine) who traveled all over the region and spent his last few years in Egypt, where he died in 204/820 and where he is currently buried. Shafi'i attempted a synthesis of Hanafi and Maliki legal methods, as he studied with both Shaybani and Malik, but he leaned toward Malik's side. The Kufa connection keeps coming back. Not only was Shafi'i an immediate and personal student of Shaybani; Ibn Surayj (an Iraqi second founder and elaborator of Shafi'i law) was said (according to the seventh/thirteenth-century Shafi'i authority Nawawi) to have relied on Shaybani's work to add details and legal scenarios to his *madhhab*.

A student of Shafi'i who was mostly known to collect "reports" of the sayings and actions of the Prophet Muhammad founded the fourth school. This was Ahmad Ibn Hanbal

> In writings about Islam, you will encounter the word *hadith* repeatedly. Remember that it literally means "something new," but in its technical legal sense, it *indicates* a report of something the Prophet Muhammad said or did or tacitly approved of. While "*hadith*" in the technical usage of reporters also includes reports that supply descriptions of the Prophet (his bodily characteristics), these are irrelevant for jurists. Think of *Sunna* and *hadith* as signifying the same object.

(d. 241/855), after whom the Hanbali school is named. This school or *madhhab* remained a minor school in the Muslim world (with an estimated following of only 3 million people in the nineteenth century, when the Muslim population was estimated at 250+ million, according to M. al-Hajawi al-Tha'alibi (d. 1376/1965), but has experienced a tremendous revival in the past century.

Abu Hanifa, the founder of the earliest school, was said to have spoken Persian in addition to Arabic. He wrote no books, but his two students documented the discussions of their often three-person colloquia and gave us the earliest comprehensive texts of Islamic jurisprudence. These included basic, simple, and often beautiful explanations of doctrines.

In one of Shaybani's books, the author debates Maliki jurists in many practical legal matters, where Shaybani argues that Malik's adherence to the reports of the Prophet's sayings and actions binds him to adopt the Hanafi legal viewpoint. Most of these cases are complex, and the difference between the schools centers on subtle distinctions. But Shaybani forcefully defends his view. For example, in Hanafi law, an adult female has the final say in her marriage were her father to object to a prospective groom, while Malikis think that a father's view, which represents the family's, trumps that of his adult daughter, if *this was her first marriage*. Shaybani cites textual arguments, saying that the Prophet has repudiated a marriage that was concluded on a father's consent against the wishes of his daughter, the bride (*al-Hujja*, Vol. 3, pp. 134–8).

Malikis are not without arguments against Shaybani's views, and juristic argument could go on forever, but the point is that Shaybani wanted to make the case that he was conversant with the art of *law as traditions of practice, not only arguments from reason*. From other Hanafi legal texts, one learns also about the internal disagreement within the same school of law in this and other legal matters. Another example of Shaybani's writing in the same book is his debate of Malik's view on secret marriage. (See textbox.)

Shafi'i (d. 204/820) developed a reputation of being rooted both in reason and in tradition. A follower of his, Abu Ali al-Za'farani (d. 260/874), said that collectors of the Prophet's reports were "asleep" and Shafi'i woke them up. (Nawawi (ed. M. N. al-Muti'i), *Majmu*, (Jiddah, Saudi Arabia: Maktabat al-Irshad, 1980), Vol. 1, p. 27; *kana ashabu-l-hadithi ruqudan fa-ayqazahum al-Shafi'i*). This is meant to indicate that, among those who were concerned with reporting the Prophet's acts, he was the one to stimulate them to employ reason in analyzing these reports, as opposed to satisfying themselves with reporting. Shafi'i's followers see him as the focal point of the early development of the schools, and some orientalists seemed to have been enchanted by his work. He was, no doubt, a great debater, who delivered scathing arguments against those who championed reason and discarded *hadith* (or reports of the Prophet's sayings and actions). Some of his opponents

MARRIAGE KEPT A SECRET BUT ATTESTED BY UPRIGHT WITNESSES

Muhammad (Shaybani): Abu Hanifa held that a marriage kept as a secret is permissible, if attested by upright witnesses, even if these are asked not to propagate the news of the marriage.

Medina scholars: Secret marriages are unlawful; even if upright witnesses can be summoned to testify that they had witnessed it but were asked to keep it a secret.

Muhammad (Shaybani) exclaims: How could this be invalid, if attested by upright witnesses? Take a man who married off his mature daughter after her consent, to a husband who is both fit for her (a proper peer) and a man of good character, but for some reason (which reason they wanted to keep unknown) all agreed to make this a private matter: Would this make it an invalid marriage? What if a man marries his daughter off while in hiding from an unfair prince or even from a debt he is said to owe and then asked those who knew (of the marriage) to hide the matter, would this make the marriage itself invalid?

They (Medina scholars, Malikis) argued that the Prophet's tradition has decided the matter, and we could not go against that decision. I (Shaybani) would say to them that in fact a report [from the authority of 'Umar Ibn al-Khattab] narrated by your own scholar, Malik Ibn Anas, shows that what I argue is correct. [Shaybani then proceeds to cite the report, showing that once good witnesses testify to witnessing the marriage, it would not be considered unlawful, because the marriage itself was not meant to be kept a secret.]

SHAYBANI'S HUJJA, VOL. 3, PP. 222–5

limited the sources of the law to the Qur'an, more highly authoritative as the word of God. Shafi'i argued, in effect, that both the Qur'an and the Prophet's statements were the word of God in an important and neglected sense.

His opponents were also formidable, and their arguments correctly pointed to deficiencies in reporting and recording these *hadiths* or *Sunna* reports gathered over the 150 years since the Prophet Muhammad's death, as well as ambiguities in their context and purport. In his own accounts of the debates, he easily triumphed against them by displaying a stronger knowledge of the history of these reports (showing that they complement and clarify one another). Shafi'i also made an irrefutable argument from a simple question: How could the ambiguities of the Qur'an itself be resolved, if these reports were tossed aside?

Shafi'i further debated those rejecting *hadiths* based on their transmission by a single reporter or a handful of reporters. He showed that the companions of the Prophet, his Muslim contemporaries, had accepted reports of trustworthy single individuals. His opponents also showed that 'Umar (the Prophet's companion and the second chief of the Muslim community after the Prophet's death) hesitated in accepting the reports of some individuals, some of whom he trusted more than others. This shows that skepticism about reports that are not abundantly attested is reasonable. Shafi'i argued that 'Umar's was only a research diligence measure, but 'Umar bowed to the content of the reports once the reports were confirmed. 'Umar, for example, accepted levying the poll tax from Zoroastrians (while some Muslims assumed only Jews and Christians were asked to pay it) based on trustworthy, albeit *single-chained* reports—reports that lack multiple reporting or recurrence of reporting in each generation; reports where one reporter (some definitions include a handful or a small number of reporters) carries the story in each generation. Similarly, 'Umar went against his own early assumption about how to compensate for assaults on the body after learning of the Prophet's ruling in the matter, when reports showed the Prophet's practice to be in opposition to his own.

The early debates show that "*reason*" always played a large role in developing legal doctrines, but the arguments of Shaybani and Malik's students also show that *tradition*—that is, what the Prophet and his followers were believed to have said or done—was important. Over time, tradition became more established. But within each school of law, there were also "traditions" of *thinking and practice*. The authority of the schools' founders became in themselves the foundation for the views of later authorities. Against this backdrop, calls for returning to the sayings and actions of the Prophet himself came from time to time.

There was then, a confluence, and at times, a clash, of traditions, in Sunni Islamic law. On the one hand, there was *a tradition of reports*, which themselves also became multiple and complex, and multiple *traditions of reasoning*, or ways to solve practical legal matters. Similar conditions existed in Shi'i law, but the latter would follow a different pattern of development.

Before we leave the early masters of Sunni law and the long shadow they cast on subsequent legal reasoning, be aware that "polemics" showing that one of them was much smarter than the other are sometimes subtle. One story goes something like this: Shaybani (the student of both Abu Hanifa and Malik) started his relationship with Malik with a little showing-off. Unknown to Malik, he attended one of his classes and asked the master one question: What would a man who wants to do his ablution (wash his face, arms, and feet and wipe off his head before the prayer) do if water is available only inside the mosque, but the man is in a particular state of impurity that prohibits him from entering the mosque. Malik said "No one in this state could enter the mosque under any circumstance." Shaybani then insisted that the master give a way out. Malik could not be saying that this man would remain absolved of his prayers until water is available outside of the mosque. Malik kept insisting that the man could not enter the mosque. Then Malik, taken by the stranger's insistence, asked him if he thought there was a solution to the problem he presented. Shaybani

How does legal tradition contradict reporting *hadith* traditions?

The Hanafi software that sifted through "reported" Prophetic tradition to winnow out the spam—to use a modern metaphor—was aggressive. It rejected many of these *hadiths*/traditions. It established, against some *hadiths* for example, that capital punishment applies in murder cases, regardless of the religion of the criminal and the victim. Other schools, accepting the reported *hadiths*/traditions, thought that the family of a Christian murder victim deserved a financial compensation, thus sparing his killer the death penalty, if the killer is Muslim. Centuries down the road, the principle of equality as applied to criminal law became a tradition within Hanafi legal thinking. This is (legal) tradition against (*hadith*) tradition.

said "he could do dry ablution [tapping the surface of the earth, the symbolic substitute for regular ablution if water is absolutely unavailable], then enter into the mosque and get a regular ablution." Malik supposedly thought this was a good answer. He then inquired as to where this stranger came from, and Shaybani supposedly mumbled something about being from a certain direction nearby. Malik objected that he knew his neighbors and could not imagine Shaybani being a local, and Shaybani said there were many Malik did not know. Malik's students later explained to him that Shaybani did not mean what Malik thought he meant, and Malik was left wondering which failure on his part was worse (not knowing the solution or being unable to notice what Shaybani meant when he indicated where he was from).

1.2.2 SHI'I SCHOOLS

As noted above, the early founders of Shi'i jurisprudence were older or exact contemporaries of the founders of the four Sunni schools. The major Shi'i schools we will discuss are the Zaydi and Ja'fari (named after founders who died in 122/741 and 148/765 respectively). But Shi'i law took much longer to develop true "classics" or legal digests. Shi'i law was also different from Sunni law in another important regard: The reports of the family of the Prophet (who were scholars of the law) were its source, which made the two kinds of tradition (reports and reasoning) go together from the beginning.

Zayd ibn Ali (d. 122/741), from whom the Zaydi school descends, was the son of 'Ali, who in turn was the son of Husayn, the grandson of the Prophet Muhammad. Of all the eponyms of the schools that survive to date, he was the most senior and closest to the Prophet Muhammad's time and family. His school of law, however, has the smallest number of followers of all the major six schools, the four Sunni schools and the two main Shi'i schools. This school engaged Sunni schools of law earlier than the Ja'fari School, but it lost followers in Iran and Arabia and today is mostly concentrated in Yemen.

Zayd's nephew Ja'far, who was close in age to his uncle, gave his name to the Ja'fari school. Ja'far was almost an exact contemporary of Abu Hanifa (they were born either the same year or around the same date, and Ja'far died only two years before Abu Hanifa in 148/765) and lived in Medina, like Malik. Ja'far was held in high esteem by both Abu Hanifa and Malik.

On his father's side, Ja'far descended from 'Ali, the Prophet's cousin and fourth successor, and his mother was the daughter of a grandson and a granddaughter of Abu Bakr, Muhammad's immediate successor and long-term companion. (Yes, these two parents of Ja'far's mother were first cousins.) Ja'far was a polymath and a great debater. No Sunni or Shi'i disputes his intelligence and knowledge.

The school of law that bears Ja'far's name considers the human intellect or reason ('aql) to be a source of law in two important ways. First, there are many matters where *reason is able to decide independently of revelation*, which Muslims and non-Muslims agree on. In some situations, human reason is capable of discerning the good and bad qualities in human actions. An example would be the good embedded in truth-telling and the bad in lying. In these cases, reason is a good foundation for deciding good and bad (without much attention to context). This, in itself, is not a deviation from revelation, because the revelation asks us to do what is good and avoid what is bad. In some cases, *the revelation shows that the context of an action makes it good or bad*. Attacking the enemies of one's community is good (if provoked, or when ongoing hostilities justify it), while attacking one's community is bad.

The second manner in which reason works in tandem with revelation is when *reason dictates that a matter undecided by the revelation but which is similar to another that has been decided by it, should be similarly adjudicated*. This is a broader sense of analogy than the typical Sunni version thereof. Ja'faris, like the rest of Shi'is, reject "reasoning based on analogy" as a source of laws. The point may be reductively made that revelation and reason are two tools that help us arrive at sensible laws.

Until the fifth/eleventh century, Ja'fari legal texts continued to be less developed than their Sunni counterparts. In this century, one of the most extensive legal encyclopedias of Shi'i law (titled *al-Mabsut*, meaning *The Detailed*) was written by a scholar who started his career as a Shafi'i and then shifted to the Ja'fari *madhhab*. He was referred to as the master of the sect (*Shaykh al-Ta'ifa*), which is usually followed by his epithet Abu Ja'far al-Tusi (d. 460/1067).

Thereafter Shi'i law experienced two stages of revival and development, one in the seventh AH/thirteenth century CE at the hand of scholars predominantly from Iraq and Lebanon, who were later instrumental in the spread of Shi'ism in Iran, and another in the fourteenth/twentieth century after the Iranian revolution.

1.2.3 OTHER LIVING SCHOOLS

Other schools of law that do not fall under either the Sunni or Shi'i rubrics include the Ibadi school of law. Ibadi legal reasoning is even less developed than the Shi'i version and relies mostly on Sunni sources of law. However, Ibadis have disagreed with both Sunnis and Shi'is in some important matters. Two Ibadi texts are available after Unit 5.

1.2.4 EXTINCT SCHOOLS

Historical schools of law with no real followers include the schools of Tabari (d. 311/923) who studied to be a scholar of Shafi'i law but ended up with views of his own. There are extinct schools of law that are older than all four Sunni schools of law, such as the school of Ibn Abi Layla and Sufyan al-Thawri. The reason we even know about these schools is that their views continued to be reported in Sunni sources, despite their lack of following, mostly because of the debt the extant Sunni schools owed to them.

The Zahiri school of law, which is counted among non-popular Sunni *madhhabs*, is one of these extinct schools of law. It was formed by a student of the students of Shafi'i named Dawud al-Zahiri (d. 270/884). Dawud rejected reasoning based on analogy, which judges new cases by identifying similarities between the new and old or already decided cases. For example, when a new drink is made that is not identified as a type of wine but which has the same effect as wine, regular Sunni reasoning would think it is prohibited, because it shares *the basis of the prohibition* of wine. Dawud would say that he needed "textual" evidence (a statement from the Prophet) to say that the new drink is prohibited. In many cases, this disagreement was not a real disagreement, because Dawud would interpret the Prophet's language broadly enough to perform analogical reasoning without acknowledging that he did that. So, he would say the word *khamr*/wine did mean every intoxicant, which would encompass newly designed drinks that intoxicate. But in some cases, language alone would not do it, and Dawud found himself in disagreement with the mainstream of Sunni legal reasoning.

2 Tools of legal reasoning

The basic story of the origins of Islamic law tells us that Islamic law grew in the eighth and ninth centuries CE due to the efforts of some private jurists. These jurists' authority built what I will refer to with some hesitation as "systems of thought" which later generations of scholars developed further. Let us describe the big picture, including how *madhhabs* or schools of law developed their doctrines (their laws) and with what tools and how the movers and shakers in later centuries reshaped these schools, or systems, or *madhhabs*, as they added important contributions to those of the school founders.

2.1 Sunnis, Shi'is, and Zaharis on reasoning from analogy

Both the Qur'an and the Prophet's *Sunna* are often silent about situations that demand rulings. This led Hanafi jurists to devise multiple tools for providing answers to questions untreated (and even un-hinted at) in the revelation and the Prophet's record. They accepted reasoning based on general, rational principles, but were fixated on consistency in their own rulings more than on following the apparent language of a text from the Qur'an or the *Sunna*. They focused on considering important differences between cases that led to different rulings. This kind of jurist, then, thought in terms of *analogies and disanalogies*, similarities and dissimilarities between or among cases decided and undecided by the revelation.

The Arabic term *qiyas* will keep coming up over and over; so, add it to your short-list of key Arabic terms along with *madhhab* and *fatwa*. The word *qiyas* itself means "measuring" or "gauging." (Think of a small tool like a thermometer that measures the body's temperature when you think *qiyas*' narrowest sense—the sense that a jurist *compares* two acts, one whose law is known and another whose law is not, and decided to judge them similarly, because of what they share.) The next unit will give you more on this, but here we go on to explain how the different schools of law looked at this tool.

Hanafi law, in fact, developed a fascination with both simple analogies and what they call counter-analogies or subtle analogies. The Arabic term for subtle analogies is *istihsan*. This term comes up very frequently in Hanafi literature, and it is particularly common in long commentaries by the masters of the school. The lesson of *istihsan* is simple in the abstract: Two human acts may be similar and hence judged similarly, but when one looks closely, dissimilarities might prevent us from giving these two acts the same ruling. The application of subtle analogy to specific cases is a challenge, not only to newcomers to the subject, but even to those steeped in it.

If in its basic lexical meaning, the Arabic word '*qiyas*' means measuring, it was also the chosen translation of both the word "syllogism" (which logicians use to study Aristotelian reasoning), aside from indicating this juristic "analogy" (which would apply in language and law). This did not help. Many literalist successors of the Zahiris were suspicious of foreign influences on their thinking, feeling that philosophers and theologians made excessive use of imported ideas, which forced them to change their language usage and thinking habits.

If this was not sufficiently complicated, the word '*qiyas*' even more commonly in Hanafi law indicates for many jurists a simple principle that must be followed. This is because the essence of analogy is similarity among cases. A principle stating, for example, that close relatives should not be allowed to get married is a statement that applies to all people (mother–son, sister–brother) who fall into this category. This sense of *qiyas* would be responsible for many debates about the so-called "subtle analogy" or "counter analogy," which is an argument against a general principle based on a reasonable distinction of a case that must be excluded from that overall principle.

Pro analogical reasoning of multiple kinds

HANAFIS — apply direct, standard, and subtle analogy

SHAFI'IS — reject subtle analogy but employ direct analogy

ZAHIRIS — reject reasoning from analogy categorically

JA'FARIS AND ZAYDIS — search for qualities that cause favorable and unfavorable judgment

against all talk of analogy

This spectrum overlaps with an early disagreement that engulfed the early contributors to the art of law in Islam about whether the law derives from reports (*hadith*) or reason (*ra'y*). In its early manifestations, the dispute was inchoate. Some early scholars were not sure that a legal system was even needed to live virtuous, Muslim lives. These were the reports' community. Those who were called, sometimes derogatorily, by the epithet of the people of "opinion" or *ra'y*, came to establish what became, in due time, Islamic law. Subsequent calls to return to the law's textual roots notwithstanding, Islamic law—both Sunni and Shi'i—established firmer roots and longer branches based on equations of reason, which remained a matter of dispute among the different schools.

In a broader sense, *qiyas* (what is normally considered standard analogy) came to indicate obvious lines of reasoning while *istihsan* (here, reasoning from a counter analogy) came to indicate any subtle reflection against the obvious reasoning. Ibn Qutlubugha, a Hanafi jurist from the fifteenth century, reflected on the case of an individual in the middle of her/his daily prayers, who lost herself/himself in private thoughts that were foreign to the prayer (*Rasa'il*, Damascus, 2013, p. 147). The person in question was in the proper position, facing the right direction for the prayer (Mecca), and performing the prayer. She or he may have been kneeling or prostrating and reciting words that are proper to the prayers. Given that lapses in concentration are inevitable, and given that private thoughts may indeed be relatable to this worshiper's affinity with the Deity, obvious reasoning (*qiyas*) might lead us to think that the prayer was valid and needs no correction. Based on further reflection (*istihsan*), however, a corrective prostration (*sujud sahw*) was required to compensate for absent-mindedness. There is no escaping the fact that traveling in thought is foreign to prayer, and any prolonging in the *position* that coincides with thought-traveling (whether it be *sitting*, *kneeling*, *standing*, or *prostrating*) is a deviation in need of correction, if it is long enough to be equal to the time spent in an act of kneeling or standing, etc. (Ibn Qutlubugha was saying essentially that an instance of thought-travel of a half-minute, for example, is too long to tolerate.) *Istihsan* then necessitates a corrective, compensatory prostration at the end of the prayer.

Another example of divergence in the conclusion based on arguing from obvious versus less obvious or controversial lines of reasoning concerns malpractice claims against expert blacksmiths and tailors. If a Hanafi jurist reasoned from analogy or the general presumption of justice principles, expert blacksmiths and tailors should not be liable for their mistakes if negligence was not attested. However, by reflecting further, Hanafi jurists held that these expert workers should have been liable even for inadvertent mistakes. The prevalent consideration in this further reflection was fairness to customers, who would not have wanted to argue with expert workers and make the case that they made this or that mistake for lack of attention, training, or something of this nature. Even if the mistake was an "honest" one, the customer must be protected from having to endure a cost to which a benefit he expected does not correspond.

2.1.1 A IS FOR AMBIGUITY

Hanafis then apply what (as noted above) they called "counter analogy" or "subtle" analogy (*istihsan*), which would allow them to rule based on considerations that run in the face of analogical reasoning or simple logical consistency. If we follow simple analogy, we prohibit contracts that have a degree of ambiguity similar to prohibited contracts (that is, ones that were prohibited by the Prophet) that have an element of ambiguity. The objective of these prohibitions is pre-empting conflict—since ambiguity breeds conflict.

One way to restate the essence of an analogy is to state it as a principle: Ambiguity breeds conflict. Contracts that include an element of ambiguity are prohibited because they are similar in this sense. The Arabic word they use, *qiyas*, then sometimes simply references the overarching principle.

Sunni jurists will agree that, in principle, an exchange in the market ought to be between two knowable quantities or items, as ambiguity threatens the validity of a contract. In a sale, for example, I may agree to give you my watch for $50. In the sale, the qualities of the watch should be clearly identifiable, and the $50 is also a standard that is easy to identify. The point is to pre-empt conflict. If the watch is not well-described, disagreement about what I sold you may arise. So we can agree that a *non-existent watch* should not be sold for $50. Selling a watch *with qualities different from the one described* in the contract is also invalid. But who will tell us what to do if there is ambiguity?

By subtle analogical reasoning, Hanafi jurists allowed commonly accepted contracts and deals that included an element of ambiguity in the commitments of the parties, if no quarrel was reported about these ambiguities. The point of prohibiting dealings with ambiguity, they argued, was to prevent quarrel and make life smoother. And it would make life much less smooth if we were to insist on eliminating ambiguities that are tolerated by those to whom the deal matters. In some cases, very common contracts (such as rental agreements), once contemplated, seem to have a fatal flaw on the principle of ambiguity breeds conflict.

Based on this principle, the "rent" contract poses a difficulty. The exchanged goods here are a "utility"—the use of the apartment—and the rent (say $1,000 per month). This utility is a future value that does not exist at the time of the contract, while the rental amount is paid upfront. The utility of a safe, clean, and quiet residence is presumed to be collectible over time. Yet this may or may not happen. The broad principle that ambiguity threatens the validity of a contract thus goes against the idea of a rental agreement.

Obviously no society can afford to outlaw rent altogether, so the question hinges *on what basis is it allowed*? Kasani (d. 585/1189) states that rental payment is exchanged for a utility that could not be equally compensated with a payment, whether at the beginning or at the end of the rent period, if we followed a strict sense of the principle that ambiguity breeds conflict.

Rent, in other words, is not analogous to the good watch sale, which is positioned to survive future disagreement on the basics of the sale. Yet, *istihsan* saves the day and allows us to provide (basic) explanations of why principles such as these could not be adhered to strictly.

> Those who reason from counter-analogies or "subtle" analogies make up their own law.
>
> *Shafi'i (d. 204/820)*

Maliki jurists also used *istihsan* extensively. They say that it is nine-tenths of juristic knowledge. Ibn Rushd (d. 596/1198) says that *istihsan* for Malik is reconciling contradictory sources (*Bidayat al-Mujtahid*, Vol. 2, p. 278, Beirut, 1982). Many Malikis seem to take it to mean considering social standards. Based on this sense of *istihsan,* they are known to have allowed social standards and customs to dominate in both matters of the market and the family. Here, how people conduct their daily lives is taken into account and prioritized over strict and rigid rules of similarities between human acts in the abstract.

The analogy between two contracts with an element of ambiguity that might lead to conflict is easy to see. Reasoning on "regular" analogy which tends to appeal to similarity in basic qualities between two cases, would lead to prohibiting many dealings. Reasoning on "subtle" analogy, by contrast, appeals to "distinctions" between two cases that share basic qualities. This is why, in one definition of arguing from subtle analogy, the Hanafi jurist al-Karkhi says that it is an argument from distinguishing ostensibly similar cases—that is, by distinguishing cases that would have judged similarly because they appear to be similar, a jurist decides that the similarity is inoperative (in other words, they are only ostensibly, and not truly, similar).

Shafi'i expressed something of an emotional rejection to the idea of distinguishing similar cases. He thought it was a potential slippery slope, one that might lead jurists to making up their own law based on whims. In one version of his reaction, he says "those who reason from subtle analogies make up their own laws"; in another, it is rendered as "those who argue from subtle analogies judge based on desire."

Shafi'is were more systematic but more stringent. Hanafi law gradually won the day and became the dominant system in the Muslim East, but Shafi'is insisted their system was closer to the revelation and accused Hanafis of "making laws up." As hard as it may be to believe, Shafi'is were not the strictest: The Zahiris went farther and even rejected reasoning by analogy as a matter of principle. How could one impede the engine that allows the system to operate? They argued they did not need it. The broad language of the Qur'anic and Prophetic instructions allowed them to derive laws for all the cases they encountered. The animosity against Zahiri thinking and attempts to belittle their stature went as far as to make Shafi'is stipulate that Zahiris were not even jurists, because *reasoning by analogy is the essence of legal thinking* or *fiqh*. Some Shafi'i scholars (as Isnawi (d. 772/1370) records in his writing) stated that a school dedicated to the study of *fiqh* or law could not offer scholarship funds to a Zahiri, because his work would not have met the requisite standard of legal reasoning.

To be fair to Zahiris, their chastisement in Sunni law texts was not limited to their disagreement about the authoritativeness of reasoning based on reason or analogy. They were also made into the butt of jokes for their rejection of "consensus" after the first generation of Muslims and for their unique interpretations of the texts. Today, among Sunni Muslims, Zahiris are present more as objects of criticism than a living tradition, not unlike Mu'tazilis and similar groups. Historically, they shared their skepticism of reasoning from the analogy among cases with many formidable jurists of the old times.

We must note that reasoning based on analogy and counter analogy is different from the idea of respect for precedent. This is because at the level of precedent (a specific case with all their circumstances tailored to adversaries before a judge), no two cases are truly alike. When we speak of analogy, we mean by cases of generic situations. Analogy looks into a quality in a human act that prompts us to consider whether that act is prohibited, obligatory, or something in between. This is also why one can argue from the so-called subtle analogy or counter analogy perspective by looking into what look like similar cases but which end up being different in important ways.

2.1.2 U IS FOR USURY

Let's review the positions we have stated so far. When the revelatory sources (the Qur'an and the *Sunna*) are silent and consensus is lacking, a Sunni jurist thinks that the human act under consideration must be like or unlike another human act in a case that is decided by the revelatory sources. Shi'i (Zaydi, Ja'fari) jurists start from what they see as a starting point that is more fundamental. They say the "actions" under consideration have qualities that allow them to be judged as "good" or "bad." This is what makes the revelatory sources judge them as desirable or undesirable. The revelation, however, is crucial and provides significant guidance, compared to the human intellect that is unaided by revelation, which is at a clear disadvantage.

Zahiris extended their loyalty to the text to a full-blown rejection of reasoning from analogy. They say that if the revelatory sources are silent, they have an open field of choices. Wherever reasoning works and produces sensible results, Zahiris are never impressed. They think it is simply a *law of reason*, rather than a *law of God*. In their defense, Zahiris' apparent austere attitude is justified on a correct description of the jurists' activities. Drawing an analogy is an activity of the human mind. Each analogy assumes a degree of omniscience about the cases that may and the cases that may not fall under the umbrella of any analogy.

Now, another example. The Prophet is reported to have prohibited usury, which literally means "surplus" in an exchange that delivers some injustice to one of the parties. The simple example would be if I agree to loan you $100 on the condition that you pay back $110 after a certain period of time. The Prophet prohibited usury by requiring that the exchanges of goods be immediate in delivery and equal in quantity. He essentially prohibited the exchange of a commodity for the same commodity, unless both are equal in quantity, and simultaneous in delivery. In the Prophet's reports, six examples of commodities are usually mentioned, gold and silver (which were prices) and four other goods, which different reports identify in various ways.

> GOLD EXCHANGED FOR GOLD, SILVER FOR SILVER, WHEAT FOR WHEAT, BARLEY FOR BARLEY, DATES FOR DATES, SALT FOR SALT—EQUAL IN QUANTITY AND QUALITY, IMMEDIATE IN DELIVERY.
>
> THE HADITH COLLECTION OF MUSLIM OF NISHAPUR, #1587

All Sunni jurists recognize that usury applies in the six categories of merchandise and "prices" available at the time of the Prophet (gold and silver as prices; dates, wheat, barley, salt as commonly sought goods). While they disagreed on the basis of the commonality among the four categories that are not prices, all jurists agreed that the list of six categories is not a complete list. Usury also applies if one barters one ounce of green beans for two. Dawud, the founder of the Zahiri school, begged to differ. He said usury applies only in these six categories, because they were mentioned in the texts explicitly. Any other exchange that includes an element of disparity between the two exchanged merchandises or prices cannot be prohibited from an argument based on analogy.

A nineteenth-century Ibadi scholar from Oman, named Jamil b. Khamis al-Sa'di (who flourished around 1256/1840), was of the opinion that the disagreement among jurists in this matter bespeaks the fact that the Prophet simply meant some basic elements of human social life to be based on sharing and charity, not commerce (*Qamus al-Sharia al-Hawi li-Turuqiha al-Wasi'a*, Vol. 1, p. 328.) This, apparently socialist interpretation of the tradition is based on the idea that four elements of life (currency, basic food, basic fruit, and what he calls seeds/seasoning (*buzur*)) should be handled cautiously and not be left to the control of the market.

Other modern interpretations of usury look at its bottom line as being the unfair exchange between one party (the lender) who is guaranteed a return on his loan/investment and another (the borrower) who shoulders all the risk in the operation, even if he or she ends up investing the loaned amount and potentially makes more than the percentage of interest stipulated on the loan. We will look at modern interpretations of usury in Unit 7 when we consider Islamic financial jurisprudence.

2.2 Jurists other than the founders (the movers and the shakers)

The accumulation of juristic works, reasoning, and authorities continued to proliferate over the centuries. At a certain point, what we may call (with license) the Islamic legal system became saturated with opinions. In fact, it was saturated with whole schools of law or *madhhabs*, although these were not equally developed. The Hanafi system had significant success in the Sunni Muslim East, the Maliki in the Sunni West (Libya is the eastern end of the Muslim West, which covers Tunisia, Algeria, Morocco, and Spain for eight centuries), the Zaydi in Iraq then Yemen, and Ja'fari law, especially in later centuries, started to command a strong presence in Lebanon, Iraq, and Iran.

The four Sunni schools that seemed inevitable from the viewpoint of later centuries did not always look that way at the beginning. Ibn Rushd, the twelfth-century Spanish jurist and philosopher, did not regard the fourth school, the Hanbali *madhhab*, as equal to the initial three. In his comparative law work (*Bidayat al-Mujtahid*), he accorded more respect to some of the under-developed Sunni views of *Thawri*, *Ibn Shubruma*, and the like.

A charge of inflexibility and sterility is waged against "eastern" Islamic law by the westerners, or the *maghriba*, who also saw in their Maliki system's accommodation of local social customs a tool unavailable to the Hanafis and Shafi'is who dominated the East. (You may want to pursue these questions further.)

An interesting element of Sunni–Shi'i polemics here is the "closure of the gate of Ijtihad" controversy. Shi'is charged that their juristic system was more of a living system, because this idea of the closure of a gate to new views is nowhere to be found in their jurisprudence. Indeed, Sunni literature does toss around the term "*insidad bab al-ijtihad*," which carries the metaphor of gate closure, as if to describe the situation of someone who arrived after hours and found a gate to a shop to be closed. When this happened, if it ever happened, is another question. The term means in essence the end of an opportunity to found new schools of law, instituting a cap above the number four. As we have shown, there arose more than four Sunni schools of law. The debate, then, was whether these "extras" were to be seen differently from the initial four and whether constant founding of schools in later centuries made sense.

Al-Maqrizi (d. 1442), in his book *al-Khitat*, thinks of the Egyptian government's appointment of four judges, each from one of the four schools, in the year (664–5/1266), as the decisive moment in limiting Sunni systems to these four. The same moment is seen by some historians as a triumph of legal pluralism in Islamic law overall. This is because the individual and the family inherited or decided first which *madhhab* to follow and were then assigned a judge of their own school. This also assumes that one does not normally keep changing his *madhhab* affiliation.

Central to this discussion is the question of how the law changes, as ostensibly it stays the same. In the Sunni world, the change had to be achieved, clearly, within the dominant schools of law. In the Shi'i world, the schools also dominated the discourse, but important transitions in their school, all the way to the thirteenth century and even beyond, allowed their system to appear more modern and in fact be more modern.

Sunni Islamic law did accumulate a heavy tradition and moved slowly, as all heavy bodies do. But when glossators took up an old text of law to comment on it, they did not simply reiterate what was in it. They often assembled an array of views, which they had to explain and dissect, allowing their readers to understand how legal reasoning works and think of novel solutions to new problems. In fact, the idea that legal commentaries were an indication of the stagnation of the law could be believed by those who had a limited interest in these commentaries.

Past the glossators and their contribution to legal reasoning, we must attend to the presence in the thirteenth–fifteenth centuries of acts of innovation that added even one more element of complexity to existing *madhhabs* as they were inherited. This leads us to address the contribution of Hilli to Ja'fari law and Ibn Hajar al-'Asqalani to Sunni law.

Figure 2.2 Alhambra de Granada. Author: Andrew Dunn. Image accessed via Wikimedia.

2.2.1 AL-'ALLAMA AL-HILLI (D. 726/1325)

A student of the polymath philosopher and astronomer Nasir al-Din al-Tusi (d. 1274)—whom you will meet in Unit 8—al-'Allama al-Hilli or Ibn al-Mutahhar al-Hilli was a towering figure, at least in Shi'i Islamic jurisprudence. His town, al-Hilla in Iraq, produced many scholars who went by the epithet al-Hilli, including al-Muhaqqiq al-Hilli (d. 676/1277), but this particular Hilli is the most famous of all. His fame rested first and foremost on the quantity and the quality of his work, as well as on his comprehension of Sunni *madhhabs* and the views of its scholars, and finally and most importantly on his attempt to clarify the difference between his Ja'fari law and its Sunni counterparts.

At the time Sunni (especially Hanbali and Shafi'i) law was taking a turn toward "tradition," Hilli was busy reading Sunni legal commentaries and supplementing Shi'i doctrines to show that Ja'fari law was as comprehensive in its scope as its Sunni equivalent. The principles of Ja'fari legal reasoning would enable a jurist of his stature to answer the questions that his Sunni predecessors have answered. All he needed was to be acquainted with legal questions and the views of other jurists, which are recorded in encyclopedias such as Ibn Qudama's (d. 620/1223) *Mughni* and Nawawi's (d. 676/1277) *Majmu'*.

This Hilli, in the final analysis, stimulated Shi'i scholars of the subsequent centuries to look into how the principles of their school of law could be developed into answers to practical questions. His immediate successors (a list of major scholars in Lebanon and Iraq) were instrumental into providing the jurisprudence necessary for Iran's future turn toward Shi'ism in the 1500s.

In the Sunni world, a return to the question of the textual sources of the law, the Qur'an and the *Sunna*, accompanied new legal and religious scholarship, particularly so in the fifteenth century.

2.2.2 IBN HAJAR AL-'ASQALANI (D. 852/1448)

Ibn Hajar is another landmark figure, not only in Shafi'i law, to which he subscribed, but in Sunni law overall. This is because he singlehandedly showed that some 4,000 reports of the Prophet's *Sunna*, which al-Bukhari (d. 256/870) included in his collection of reports (*al-Jami' al-Sahih*) could serve as reference points for all of Sunni legal or *fiqh* questions. Ibn Hajar wrote an extensive commentary on Bukhari's collection, covering therein all legal questions from rituals and diet to trade and matters of the family, crime, and state. The name of the commentary is *Fath al-Bari* (literally *Divine Opening*, in the sense of divine support).

He was also an exceptional and an intriguing figure. In honor of Ibn Hajar's life, his student, Sakhawi (d. 902/1497) wrote one of the longer biographies emanating from the Middle Ages: it extends to some 1,500 pages in a modern edition. From it, one learns about Ibn Hajar's love of chess, about his family life, his willingness—distinct from most of his contemporaries, and in fact many scholars in all ages—to actually lend his books to scholars and students. But one also learns about what distinguished his scholarly comprehension and method. This method may be summed up as one that is based on faith in human knowledge of history. This student-biographer himself turned to history and spent more time on it than he spent on legal reasoning.

There are those who strongly disagree with his view that the law is essentially the fruit of religious "tradition" (*hadith*, or sayings and actions of the Prophet Muhammad). To be sure, Ibn Hajar did not invent a path and travel it alone. Before him, the interest of jurists, especially

Shafi'i jurists, in his environment in building a strong connection between "law" and "tradition" (in the sense of the Prophet's *Sunna*) was clear in their scholarship. Nawawi's (d. 676/1277) introduction to a long legal commentary he himself did not live to finish emphasized even his fascination with the language of reports. He took time to explain the linguistic peculiarities in these reports as much as he was interested in spelling out juristic disagreement about whether actions are prohibited, permissible, or obligatory. The relationship between law and tradition, in short, was becoming stronger than the relationship between law and logic.

Ibn Hajar opened up a door for modern reform that added one element of hybridity to modern Islamic legal reasoning that did not exist in the high medieval tradition. He allowed scholars a path to *reconsidering* "texts" or "reports" of Muhammad's life to produce new forms of understanding of these, which were latent in legal reasoning and could only be seen implicitly in *madhhab* reasoning. In Ibn Hajar's time, *madhhab* material, reasoning, and disagreement, were still the only ways to understand texts. Even now they play an important role and cannot be ignored or eliminated. His procedure, however, opened up doors for new reasoning from texts directly. This will be one layer in modern Islamic law that is further complicated by the rise of modern legal elites in the Muslim world who received education in European legal academies.

2.2.3 LAW FROM REPORTS: A MUSLIM WOMAN MARRIED TO A NON-MUSLIM MAN

This is an example of Ibn Hajar's procedure in his commentary (*Fath al-Bari*, Vol. 9, pp. 420–3) in the matter of the marriage of Zaynab, the daughter of the Prophet Muhammad, to a man named Abu al-'As. Zaynab embraced Islam, her father's message, six years before her husband, but the Prophet Muhammad did not repudiate her marriage to her husband. Muslim jurists, as Ibn Hajar and many of his readers know, agree that a Muslim woman cannot initiate a marriage with a non-Muslim man, and that, should a female Muslim convert to Islam while her husband remains a non-believer, the marriage dissolves (see more in Unit 4, section 3.2).

Ibn Hajar's commentary takes the sayings and actions of the Prophet as the foundation of laws, which indicate in this case that the jurists' agreement may not be in line with the Prophet's practice, unless, as they say, this action by the Prophet was *abrogated* (canceled and made ineffective) by a subsequent law. For jurists who follow the standard tradition of legal reasoning, this abrogation is a matter of consensus.

The Prophet's practice in Zaynab's case may have been a necessity in the beginning of the community's life, in other words, and was later abrogated by the Prophet himself when he denied any new marriages between a Muslim female and a non-Muslim male. Ibn Hajar does not always provide his own final answer to the questions he brings up and is, in fact, content to provide a full account of the disagreement in relation to the Prophet's tradition. Modern reformers will employ new kinds of reasoning from Muhammad's tradition that reaches different conclusions about what the law should be in modern times and in places where Muslims live among a non-Muslim majority.

3 The profile of a jurist

The jurist in some cases is a specialist in law, within a specific school of law or *madhhab*, and may have little interest in other branches of knowledge aside from the requisite knowledge of language, logic, and rhetoric, and knowledge of the texts and techniques of legal reasoning. But the jurist was also sometimes someone with broad interests, in medicine or astronomy, in agriculture or trade. These forms of knowledge affected how jurists considered the law and made a mark on their contribution to it.

The activities of the jurist over the centuries ranged from teaching, research, and writing to other tasks such as serving on the judiciary or in consulting positions. The extent to which some jurists spent more time documenting their school of law and others spent time taking questions from people and solving their problems also affect their craft.

There are also interests that affect both the thinking and style of jurists, such as philosophical and mystical interests. It is notable, however, that some jurists are known by their legal production to be traditional and disciplined, and their biographies point up an unusual philosophical orientation that was kept at bay from the legal production. Jurists who experienced violent bouts of doubt, or those who held "heretical" views such as monism or the unity of being (among others), are examples of how juristic writing followed standards that allowed the jurists not to engage their readers in the full extent of their intellectual interests.

4 Conclusion

How can people live Muslim lives? They must derive the norms or rules that guide their lives from an *exemplar*. This would be the Prophet Muhammad, who delivered the revelation of God, which is a concise book containing some practical instructions but one that has also many other themes that do not lead to making a comprehensive law. The Prophet's behavior and example was also a lot of help. But these two sources, the Qur'an and the Prophet's *Sunna*, will not suffice. Here the early authorities disagreed on what to do, and this is what created the schools of law or the *madhhabs* that we learned about in this unit.

The founders of the schools of law thought their job was to answer practical questions and provide general principles for their followers. Each generation after the founders were faced with new questions, but as the schools became established, each new generations of jurists focused on augmenting, or rather *completing*, the old systems. This made the schools even more magnificent and awe-inspiring as time went on.

There were important moments of reflection and reconsideration in the history of most of these systems of law or schools. In the tenth and eleventh centuries, both the Sunni and Shi'i schools, to different degrees, underwent some basic changes. The number of cases or practical legal questions ballooned, some of the schools spread into geographically disparate areas, and the *internal conversations* among the schools added some spice to the meal. Some major events, such as the apparent weakness of the Abbasid government lead to new ideas in Shi'i and Sunni law—not only about government, authority, and war, but also about basic daily practice. In the thirteenth century, a return to the essential sources of the law, especially the oral tradition of the Prophet, which was documented gradually in the eighth–ninth centuries, can be identified. After the fifteenth century, this return to tradition will lead to a virtual split inside the schools about *what the law is* and where its authority comes from. Just at about the same time the major schools of law were being firmly established, there were ways to interpret them afresh.

In the next unit, we will take a break from history and focus on how Muslim jurists even claimed to be able to answer questions about which human actions are desirable and which ones are not. How did these jurists think they could rule on matters of rituals, market, family, and public manners from a limited number of principles of logic and ideas about social standards and customs?

Review II

- In their early stages, the *madhhabs* were established by the efforts of individuals such as Zayd, Ja'far, Shaybani (Abu Hanifa's prize student), and Shafi'i.
- A few centuries after their foundation, the *madhhabs* became "systems" of law or something close to that, and authoritative digests of each system were produced (eg, Marghinani's in Hanafi law). In their middle period, some *madhhabs*/schools were cleaned up of wrong reporting (Nawawi in Shafi'i law) or augmented and brought in line with other systems (al-Hilli in Ja'fari law). In their late premodern periods, many *madhhabs* showed a tendency to a return to the roots (the Prophet's authoritative life) and a reconsideration of some of their doctrines.

Analyze this

- If the essence of the law is not tradition ("it is this way, *because* it has been this way"), then what is it? Is it the human reason? Which human reason, one that works from *qiyas* or standard analogy or one that notes exceptions and competing considerations? What would a law you make be like? Are laws based on the votes of elected representatives more defensible? Do these laws also come from reason or something else?
- Some modern historians of Islamic law think that eclecticism in the law (forum-shopping, picking one view from one school and the next from the next school of law) means the shari'a lost its integrity. Does this integrity go back to the Prophet's time, the time of the school's founders? Is it illusory? If you say it is illusory, what is integrity in the law to you? What does a law do to change but keep its integrity?

3 Theorizing the Shari'a

As stated in Unit 1, Islamic law includes aspects that are *externally enforced* (such as when a judge assigns a land to a certain owner, based on the evidence) and aspects that are *enforced by the person on herself or himself*, as is the case when this person is convinced that their practice is backed up by a strong authority. The part of Islamic law that exists outside of courtrooms and other government entities is represented by *fatwas*, non-binding statements by religious jurists.

Fatwas are detailed answers to specific questions, about prayers or sales or marriages, and are seen by some historians of Islamic law as the way Islamic law got started. That is, these historians think that Islamic law began as answers to detailed questions about everyday life situations, and theorizations and generalizations came about later. The law evolved over time from these detailed answers and similar legal scenarios to general rules or "laws" (in Arabic the term is *furu'*), which appear in law books. To remember this theory, take this image of a man with two faces, like the Roman God Janus, who is a God of transitions.

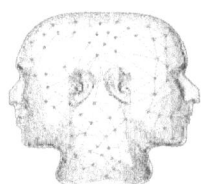

Single cases & legal scenarios
General rules

Janus, the Roman God of beginnings and transitions, is depicted with two faces. Islamic law is said to have transited, on one theory, from answers in detailed cases, into developed general rules or laws.

Real-life questions, according to this view, forced (or allowed) the early lawmakers, who were in fact private legal scholars, to think of a comprehensive system that would one day answer all real-life questions. This could only be achieved if some "hypothetical" (ie, *imagined*) but *realistic* questions were also raised and answered. Hypotheticals are sometimes raised to allow us to clarify a basic point, or to allow some of us to be clear about their bottom line. If you are an opponent of democracy, based on mistrust of people's common sense, I may ask you to hypothesize a society of wise people and then ask you whether you would still reject democracy. If you still oppose it, you must find another reason other than mistrust of common sense. The point of these hypotheticals is to allow people to be clear about the causes and implications of what they think.

> **IBN HAZM (D. 456/1063), AL-MUHALLA**
>
> Sha'bi (an authority from the seventh–eighth century, d. 103/721) says: "Those who enjoy hypotheticals made the mosque less desirable for me than my house garbage."
>
> قال الشعبي: ترك هؤلاء الأرايتيون المسجد أبغض الي من كناسة اهلي

Some scholars, especially *hadith* scholars, found these questions to be pretentious and counterproductive. One of them, Sha'bi (d. 103/721), said that these questions made him not like being in the mosque, where he would meet these *ara'aytiyyun* (literally: *the what-if crowd*) or the fans of hypotheticals. Yet those who employ hypotheticals in their reasoning and pedagogy see them (in the context of a legal system) as useful in that they allow us to ask about the principles that govern all cases, both those that have occurred and those that are still just potentials.

A global position system (GPS) supposedly covers every point on the surface of the earth. Ergo, it is not supposed to miss any spot that falls within this purview. No "possible" human action should escape the purview of the law, just as no "actual" position on the surface of the planet should remain undetected as if it did not exist. While on the GPS analogy, let's take an Islamic law question about prayers and geography. A Muslim worshiper faces one target direction, which is the Ka'ba, the small house in Mecca in the middle of the Holy Mosque (which pilgrims circumambulate during their pilgrimage), each day when she or he prays. All Muslim jurists agree that the direction the worshiper must aim at during the daily prayers is the Ka'ba, but they disagree about the degree to which this direction must be assessed or approximated. Aiming at the Ka'ba is easy enough if one can see the Ka'ba or knows its direction in a rough sense, being in a nearby city. But what happens when one is very far away, and resides in a terrain that is topographically above the valley level of the Ka'ba? Only approximate measures can be made, since a direct line would fall from a higher point toward the Ka'ba. Evidence suggests that the Muslims of Morocco initially got the direction of their early mosques wrong; later, when the mistake was detected, an approximately correct direction was accepted, or a redirection of the line inside the mosques was made. When the deviation was considerable, the mosques were rebuilt.

One of the early hypotheticals drawn by the what-if crowd Sha'bi did not like asks: What if someone was hanging in the earth's atmosphere, not touching the ground? How would this person pray? This is only one step farther from a real-life question, which is praying from the top of the *Abu Qubays* mountain, east of the Holy Mosque and above it by about 1,377 feet. There is no evidence that those who raised this question contemplated airplanes, let alone spaceships, but this hypothetical can be used today for precisely these situations. The answer depends on whether the jurist believes that the small building of the Ka'ba can be imagined to rise up in the earth's atmosphere, whereby the direction would be a direct line to a point above where it is situated in reality. If the jurist thinks an imaginary line must land on the building, the answer would be different. In many of these questions, the answer would be given using the same methods used to answer real-life questions.

Hypotheticals in matters of marriage and divorce, in market dealings, and in criminal matters also helped jurists and judges solve many practical questions. There are legal scenarios in medieval legal literature that make even those sympathetic with the exercise of answering hypotheticals remember Sha'bi's scorn with a wink of agreement.

Hypotheticals are only one theoretical apparatus that is needed to build up a system of legal queries and tools to answer them. A larger theoretical apparatus that accommodates hypotheticals reaches its most abstract form when it determines a set of classes for all human actions, some reducing these to seven, some to three, while the majority of jurists reduce the classes to five. Actions, theorists of the shari'a taught, are the subject of *fiqh*, the field of understanding the detailed law. Just as medicine's subject is the human body, inasmuch as it aims to correct its failed functions, Islamic law's subject is *human actions*, which are either desirable, neutral, or undesirable, with degrees of desirability and undesirability being debated.

Let's now fast-forward from Sha'bi's early 700s to 1876, when a modern attempt at codifying the civil sides of Hanafi law was made in what came to be known as *Majallat al-Ahkam al-'Adliyya*; Articles 2–100 consisted of ninety-nine general maxims or *qawa'id*. In the premodern Hanafi legal doctrines, both *applications* and *exceptions* applied to these legal generalizations. The exercise of devising legal maxims or *qawa'id* as they are called in Arabic, comes from the middle (rather than recent) centuries, but its modern format attempts to look more like European Union statutes.

Article 26, for example, included a principle or maxim stating that "harm delivered to the few is endured to prevent harm suffered by the multitude." In Hanafi doctrines, many laws (comparable to statutes) followed. These include, for example, zoning laws for shops. Blacksmiths and restaurants/cooking businesses are not permitted to open in areas where shops trading in silk had proliferated. A balcony that may harm passersby is removed, even if it is old (which gives it a presumption of continuity [why remove it?] as well as a presumption of architectural value.) In criminal policy, highway robbers may be executed without seeking the permission of the families of the victims (an otherwise standard procedure in criminal cases.) (See Units 6, section 2.5, and 8, section 3.1, for modern applications in Pakistan.) Setting prices for markets in cases of extreme need and monopoly or price gouging; this despite a competing principle that stipulates that gouging should not, as a rule, be assessed by experts and should be left to customers' judgment. Another public policy matter is that the government may remove buildings and houses next to a large fire to stop the fire spreading. The government may also allow (in a manner similar to public domain laws in the US) its agents to pass in people's property to fix a public utility. This does not go as far as confiscation in principle, however (Ahmad al-Zarqa, *Sharh al-Qawaid al-Fiqhiyya* (Damascus: Dar al-Qalam, 1993), pp. 197–8.)

To recap: Theorizing the shari'a is both an old and a new quality in Islamic legal reasoning. In its early phases, it was concerned with covering as many cases as may occur. In subsequent phases, the same need continues but is coupled with another need: Thinking of categories for cases, in which categories allow exceptions. At the root of the whole exercise of *fiqh* or legal research and reasoning, however, are three foundational theories:

1 categorizing human actions;
2 stating the sources of the law;
3 theorizing consensus and disagreement, with a special attention to the conflict of arguments of equal power.

Let's look at each in turn.

1 The subject of Islamic law

1.1 Five or seven categories of action

All Muslim jurists agreed that the subject of *fiqh*, the tool by which laws are generated, is human action. They then mostly agreed that these actions fall under a limited number of categories, five for the majority. An act is either desirable, undesirable, or neither (of a neutral value). If the desirability of an act is emphasized such that its abandonment is punishable, punishment is obligatory; otherwise it is merely recommended. If an undesirable act is equally singled out for blame and deemed punishable, it is prohibited; otherwise, it is reprehensible. An act of a neutral value is called permissible. On a scale from one to five, one being least and five most desirable, human actions are as follows.

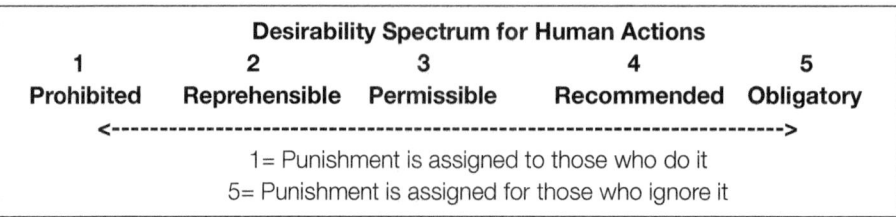

Punishment is economically applicable only at the end of the spectrum. Examples will make this clearer: Drinking wine is prohibited, eating while walking reprehensible, voluntary fasting recommended, and Ramadan's fasting obligatory. Permissible acts are not countable or exemplifiable. They account for the majority of human actions.

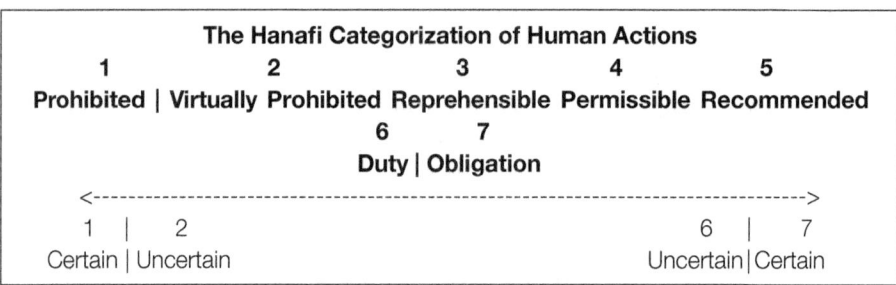

Hanafi jurists distinguished two kinds for each end of the spectrum, very broadly two degrees of prohibition and two of obligation, depending on whether the source of the prohibition or obligation is certain or simply probable. On a scale from one to seven, one being least and seven most desirable, human actions are as follows.

Other legal categories

Hanafi jurists call a "duty" (as opposed to an obligation) a three-unit prayer, the *watr*, that the Prophet rarely missed after the regular (fifth) late-night prayer. Modern Hanafis consider smoking "reprehensible nearing prohibition" because it lacks a definite source of prohibition comparable to the source of the prohibition of wine.

Medieval jurists also offered another classification of specific human activities. Contracts, for example, may be valid or invalid (or a third category, essentially susceptible to correction or invalidation). Rituals may fall under the category of "regular performance," "delayed performance," or "compensatory performance." Other activities may qualify as "causes," "conditions," or "exclusionary elements." While reference is made to some of these categories, we will not pursue the full extent of these classes in this book.

The subject of law in the modern world is rights and responsibilities, rather than human action. A. Sanhuri (d. 1971), the father of Arab civil law, attempted to build the foundation for comparative law in the modern Muslim world by starting to juxtapose the notion of rights with its equivalents in medieval legal literature. The obvious candidate is the notion of *dhimma*. *Dhimma* indicates "commitment" in its lexical usage, and in legal terminology it means a depository of rights and responsibilities corresponding to the human being.* Think of it in mathematical terms, where a positive (+) value is assigned to rights and a negative (–) value is assigned to responsibilities. The simplest type of these are debts owed to and by a person. If I owe you $100, my *dhimma* is occupied with a negative value of $100, and when you later destroy a property of mine worth $200 and hence owe me this value, my *dhimma* is now at a positive $100.

It is not only money that occupies the *dhimma*. A man's *dhimma* is occupied with a duty to raise and teach his children; a woman's *dhimma* is also occupied with the duty to breastfeed her children, if she is supported by her husband. These rights and responsibilities clearly have a potential to clash. (Did you learn something like this in Unit 1 in the *Haliye* case?) In the old Islamic law, the notions of *dhimma* and the regulation of human actions went hand in hand, but actions remained the law's core domain. It is, as you will notice gradually, what makes the scope of Islamic law larger than any modern state law.

2 The sources of Islamic law

2.1 The textual sources: the Qur'an and the *Sunna*

Of its more than six thousand verses, the Qur'an's legal content is limited to a few hundred verses. Even this is a generous estimate, if we speak strictly of verses that directly affect the majority of legal and juristic writing in matters such as rituals, marriage, inheritance, sales, contracts and promises, and crime. Muslim jurists still see the whole Qur'anic text as shari'a-relevant, given the general and deep texture of its language, whose hints are always taken into account as the jurist goes about their day to day work of matching principles to cases. (As we said earlier, this means nothing close to the thought that the Qur'an is the *Torah*, *lex* or *law* of Muslims.) In modern Islamic law, while the medieval tradition's impact on how the Qur'an and the Prophet's tradition remain an essential medium for much legal interpretation, some jurists try to go directly to the texts to squeeze them (as one may squeeze an orange) in order to access new moral and legal instructions to come out.

---

* You will also encounter (in Unit 4) another legal sense of *dhimma* that is specific to the position of non-Muslims who entered into a contract (of mutual commitments) with a Muslim state. This is what makes them called *dhimmi*s.

The rhetoric of the Qur'an being the main source of the law, to be clear, is not a matter of the perception of misguided outsiders. This is a late medieval Ja'fari view of the sources:

> The sources of laws, for us, are four: God's Book, the *Sunna*, consensus, and reason. The authority of God's Book is established by the fact that it contains God's words, to which neither misrepresenting reality (*kadhib*) nor anything deserving of being bad (*qubh*) applies . . . *Sunna* is either the Prophet's [*Sunna*].or an imam's [*Sunna*] . . . this includes statements . . . action.and it may be preliminary (*ibtida'i*), requiring knowledge of its context to make an acceptable argument, and it may also be a tacit approval, in which case, if it is the Prophet's approval, then it is categorically authoritative, because the Prophet is not prone to *taqiyya* (hiding what he believes) or if it is an imam's [tacit approval], then it may not be authoritative, because of this possibility [i.e., that it was affected by *taqiyya*).
>
> Miqdad Ibn 'Abdilla al-Suyuri (d. 826/1423), *Naddual-Qawaidi al-Fiqhiyya*, p.12

After the Qur'an, the Prophet's sayings, actions, and tacit approvals are taken by both Sunnis and Shi'is to be either a source subsequent in power or, as Shafi'i argues, equal in power to the Qur'an, given that the Qur'an is in need of the *Sunna* more than the *Sunna* is in need of the Quran (in the sense that the *Sunna* provides details without which the Qur'an would not convey its full meaning). Juristic consensus, or the Muslim community's consensus, comes next. We will cover consensus and disagreement at the end of this unit. For Shi'i jurists, the *Sunna* reports of the Prophet must come from acceptable sources and interpreted in light of the traditions of the *imams* or legitimate leaders of the Muslim community (from 'Ali, the Prophet's cousin to his sons Hasan and Husayn, etc.) Consensus is also the consensus of the true community, in whose midst the *imam* (or legitimate leader) is counted. After these sources, for Shi'is, comes *reason*, plain and simple.

This is where the analogy debate comes up. I know we talked about this in Unit 2, but we need to revisit this once again. There are a few subjects that you simply cannot afford to ignore. *Qiyas* is one of them; contract theory is another; abode theory is a third. Each one of these will be revisited more than once in this and subsequent units.

Reasoning by analogy, or reasoning by *qiyas*, officially the fourth source of the law, becomes, once you think about it enough, the essence of the whole endeavor of *fiqh* or juristic reasoning. This is at least what Shafi'i argued, as you learned in Unit 2. Another direction of contemplating the extent to which *qiyas* serves the law is when you consider the extent to which it works, even for those who believe in it, which complicates the picture.

2.2 Reason, *qiyas*

Islamic law's subject, as noted, is human *actions* (and *rights* only to a much lesser degree). An Islamic law ruling characterizes an act as obligatory, prohibited, or something in between. *Qiyas* reasoning is understood pedagogically to indicate a matching between two acts (eg, drinking wine and drinking beer) and judging them similarly, because they share a *decisive quality* that is seen as *the rationale or basis* for *the ruling* in one case. In other words, a new case (drinking beer) is judged similarly to an earlier one, because the two acts share a quality that makes them "the same" or comparable in measure. The Arabic word *qiyas*, after all, literally means measuring.

In Unit 2, you learned how defining and employing reason distinguished Sunnis from Shi'is and how the rejection of *qiyas* (or reasoning from analogy, obvious or subtle) was a contested matter among Sunnis (Zahiris' response to *qiyas*? No thanks). Shi'is correctly saw that the *qiyas* mechanism can fail frequently. "To what extent must one extend the rationale that two acts share" is not an easy question to answer. Hanafi jurists, for example, would consider drinking sake—the Japanese intoxicant made of rice—to be a different act from drinking wine. Hanafi jurists, in fact, as you also learned in Unit 2, already designed a mechanism for exceptions and called it *istihsan* (literally, going for the correct way).

Many argue that the whole craft of lawmaking in Islam is nothing but recognizing whether cases are similar or dissimilar. The true jurist points to important differences that affect the judgment and explain away differences among cases that look different but will still be judged similarly.

Al-Allama al-Hilli, a major Ja'fari authority we encountered in Unit 2, assumes that knowledge of *qiyas*—reasoning by analogy—is a requirement in a judge (*Tahrir al-Ahkam*, Vol. 5, p. 111). As we said, Hilli's work was clearly influenced by Sunni sources from the century and a half preceding him. When his school doctrine differs from Sunni schools, he points out the difference and argues the Shi'i position. His view in this matter indicates that in his mind, even a judge of the Shi'i school must be at least knowledgeable about *qiyas*, regardless of how he employs this knowledge in his adjudication.

In practical terms, even a Shi'i who does not think that the label "*qiyas*" is appropriate for a true jurist who is schooled in a good juristic manner, still resorts to some of the same techniques in solving legal problems and characterizing a human action to be good or bad. Let us then review and supplement what we have learned about this legal technique.

Figure 3.1 Mosquée Zitouna de Tunis. Author: Kassus. Image accessed via Wikimedia.

2.3 What is *qiyas*?

Qiyas is a legal technique by which a vacuum in the law is filled by extending the legal logic in cases where the law *is* known to areas where it is not. Remember the usury discussion? If the law prohibits an exchange of two unequal *essential* commodities (eg, food) with a delayed delivery of one of them, a jurist might decide to prohibit similar exchanges, even if the exchanged commodities are *not essential*. Another example would be prohibiting a substance (a non-grape-based drink) that shares the quality of "impeding the mind" with a *grape-based* "wine" whose prohibition is established in the law. In both cases, a *describable* quality is shared (between wine and other intoxicants, between essential and non-essential commodities) that *pertains* to the ruling (prohibition of consumption, commercial exchange). This is called *qiyas al-'illa*, the word *'illa* indicating the shared *quality* that is deemed *efficient* in bringing about a ruling (this quality is also known as a *cause*, since it is, in a non-metaphysical sense, an efficient cause for the ruling. It is sometimes also called a *rationale* or, when you get fancy and want to use Latin, *ratio legis*.

Note that the jurist may have to labor to improve the describability of the shared quality leading *qiyas* reasoning or the *ratio legis*. For example, hardship during travel is a reasonable cause for shortening prayers, but it is not easily describable. A distance of fifty-five miles (a modern equivalent of a distance calculated from journeys where the prayer was shortened by the Prophet and his community) serves as a cause for prayer shortening (and breaking one's fast) during a trip, because it satisfies this condition.

Some legal theorists added other conditions to describability and pertinence. This is how one legal theorist (Juwayni, *Burhan*, pp. 716–18) stated the conditions for a quality that brings an unknown case under the same category as a case whose law is known. The quality must

- be describable;
- be pertinent to the ruling;
- be **consistent with other standards of reasoning** (*usul*); and
- **escape reasonable objections**.

What these last two conditions do is force the jurist to consider all his rulings based on *qiyas* in light of his other rulings.

Qiyas also operates in other ways. Take the analogy between a normal divorce and a strange practice inherited from pre-Islamic Arabia known as *zihar*. *Zihar*, in laymen's terms, is an oath to abstain from sexual activities. A husband's sworn abstention from sexual intercourse (*zihar*) makes the husband responsible for what jurists call "expiation"—in this case either freeing a slave, fasting two continuous months, or feeding sixty destitute individuals. *Zihar* is not a divorce, and divorce is not a *zihar*. They don't share a *quality* that is *efficient* for a law to be based on it, such as the one shared by usurious transactions or intoxicants.

But, for some jurists, they may be analogous in certain situations. In their debates of when a statement of divorce is invalid, Shafi'i jurists consider questions about the mental state of the husband when he divorces his wife. They consider degrees of stress and intoxication. Getting into these debates would make this example go for too long. It is enough to note that they applied the same standards they accept in considering a divorce valid or invalid to *zihar* cases.

This more controversial *qiyas*, the technical term for which is *qiyas al-shabah*, operates without an intermediary quality shared by the two cases which "pertains" to the shared ruling (Ibn Qasim al-'Abbadi (d. 992/1584), *Commentary on Tuhfat Al-Muhtaj*, Ch. *Talaq*, Sub-chapter: *Zihar*). While a degree of analogy between *zihar* and divorce has, depending on where one stands, a weak or no connection with the basis of this law, the ruling here is ultimately based on the objective of making the contractual commitments of marriage immune to impetuous or uncontemplated invalidation.

Now consider an even less stringent extension of the logic of the law. It is prohibited in an Islamic legal and ethical code to interrupt an active bid to buy a commodity by offering an alternative bid. This prohibition is explained by a desire to "pre-empt" animosities among individuals. When this prohibition is extended to a marriage proposal before a bride makes up her mind about an earlier proposal, one cannot find a shared quality (*'illa*) in the two contracts quite readily. What is shared, rather, is a more general goal, or a *maqsid*, of the lawgiver. This reasoning is excluded from *qiyas* (Ibn Ashur, *Maqasid a-Shari'a*, Ch. 3) because the disanalogies between marriages and sales are such that the two cases could only be judged similarly in this context via the abstract goal of pre-empting animosities.

2.4 Vacuum—So what?

The logic of *qiyas*, even in the strong cases of analogy that are based on an indisputably suitable, shared quality between two human acts, has been hotly debated. An entire school of law, as we learned, the Zahiri, distinguished itself by rejecting *qiyas*. But it would be a mistake to understand this position as an acceptance that the law is silent, or concede that there exists vacuum in the law, or that Zahiri law would be significantly expansive, if the *qiyas* procedure is not rejected. That is because conclusions very similar to the ones reached through analogical reasoning can also be attained through other means, for example by appealing to generalities in the language of the revelation, the Qur'an. When *khamr* is mentioned as a prohibited substance, a Zahiri does not understand it narrowly as "wine," but rather all intoxicants. All Muslim jurists abhor vacuum in the law.

But what is wrong with declaring the law silent? The argument has been made repeatedly that the language of revelation is limited while life's affairs and cases are unlimited, which necessitates resorting to *qiyas*. This aversion to acknowledging that a vacuum may exist in legal norms is also emphasized by the principle that "no case is fully devoid of a legal norm" (*la takhlu al-waqi'a 'an hukm li-l-shar'*). In other words, constant engagement with *qiyas*, while acknowledging its many cracks and holes, alleviates a fear that there may simply be no law governing certain human activities.

2.5 *Qiyas'* dialectics

A hidden (or less obvious) *qiyas* may defeat an obvious *qiyas*, according to Abu Hanifa and his student Muhammad Ibn al-Hasan al-Shaybani and their followers. This is what is called subtle analogy or counter analogy, which made Shafi'i worry that jurists may simply be making up the law—in which case this would be not God's law, even in a metaphorical sense.

Here is one more example of how subtle analogy may be employed in a modern argument. We understand that marriage (*nikah*) initiates a marital bond, divorce (*talaq*) ends it, and resuming the marriage (*raj'a*) establishes it again. The requirement of two witnesses to establish any of these three legal activities may be seen as a normal expectation, given the analogy among them all. This is what Ja'fari jurists think, and this is why they don't have a problem here. Sunnis don't think divorce requires witnesses when it is issued by a man, because men, who stand to lose the most from divorce in financial terms, should not take divorce lightly and should always guard their language, not using the word "divorce" lightly. If they do throw the word around, they ought to take responsibility for it. Requiring testimony for divorce gives men much undesirable leeway. This is also why Sunni jurists hesitate to accept the "stress" defense and the intoxication defense from a husband who divorced his wife—although in some cases, it *is* accepted.

Now let us restate this in terms of obvious and subtle analogies among marriage, divorce, and remarriage. All three are similar to one another as events that create or break up a family. The dissimilarity between divorce (on the one hand) and the other two necessitates a distinction. Divorce results in heavy financial responsibilities *for the husband* and hence may be seen as his own burden, which leads to making a simple pronouncement of divorce by the husband sufficient to establish it. Both marriage and remarriage, by contrast, establish negotiable rights by *both* parties (husband and wife), which require witnesses. A modern Sunni jurist arguing that marriage, divorce, and remarriage must require witnesses and even paper documentation would be doing so based on a countering of old analogical reasoning.

2.6 *Madhhabs* and the law

Schools of law in Islam understood themselves to be distinct entities, and in fact, inter-school polemic abounds. That said, there were moments where both doctrines and authorities were shared (example in Unit 4, section 2.4), building on their early symbiotic relationship in the eighth and early ninth centuries. The same is true across the Sunni–Shi'i divide, even when the fog of tetchy disputes seems to dominate the juristic picture. There is, as I said, a case to be made that the original body of Islamic law was made in Kufa, where the masters of Hanafi law developed their legal research and devised its methods. Visits to and from Medina, where scholars of practice- and *hadith*-based law were busy at work, allowed cross-fertilization among these early jurists of Islam. The subsequent centuries also separated, if this is not too much to take, scholars even from the same school. Geography played a role too: Hanafis, for example, were Iraqis or Transoxanian (central Asian), while Malikis identified as scholars of the Egyptian south or the North African west (= the *maghrib*; North Africa).

As the schools of law matured, a new scholar would receive legal education with the scholars of one of these schools (*madhhabs*). This did not prevent *madhhab*-shopping, which biographies of scholars attest to a large degree. It is not uncommon to read about scholars who started studying the law according to the Shafi'i school of law and then turned to the Hanafi school, or vice versa. The direction was not in any way from one specific school (which lost followers) to another (which gained followers); this school-shopping existed in all directions, and it can be found across all centuries and all locations. Of the early Maliki authorities, Asad ibn al-Furat started as a Hanafi, and of the late Hanafi authorities, Ibn 'Abidin started out as a Shafi'i.

Doctrine-borrowing also existed. The Egyptian Shafi'i scholar Suyuti (d. 911/1505) mentioned in his *al-Hawi* that it was not uncommon for Shafi'i jurists to borrow from Maliki and Hanafi doctrines when a clear (Shafi'i) school doctrine was lacking. The justification for this limited borrowing, made by Subki and other Shafi'i authorities, was that Shafi'i (d. 204/820) was a student of Malik (d. 179/795) himself, which means that he received his early training at the hand of this master. A connection of this kind clearly does not guarantee agreement between mentor and mentee, as all jurists learn of disagreements among them in many matters large and small, but in the cases where disagreement is not reported, one may thus justify this necessary "borrowing."

It is rather more surprising to learn that Hanafi authorities themselves borrowed from Maliki doctrines to supplement their own. In one legal scenario, a discussion addressed triple-divorced couples and whether they could resume their marriage and under what conditions. Divorce is capped at three times. If a couple is divorced once, they may revoke the divorce and resume the marriage; the same is true a second time, but a third "strike" means the couple may not remarry each other (except in the unlikely scenario when the wife marries another spouse and gets divorced again.) There was a consensus among all jurists that this new marriage (to another spouse) must occur, where the divorced wife marries another individual, then be terminated before the couple remarry. The question arose as to whether the husband in the intervening marriage may be a young adult (say a thirteen-year-old, since adulthood is taken to begin with natural puberty) or whether he must be a fully fledged adult. Some Hanafis seemed to have taken the lenient position. Ibn 'Abidin demurred that stipulating a fully fledged adult was the best way forward, since Malik in this matter stated that, for the new marriage to be a real as opposed to a *stratagem*-marriage, it must include an element of full sexual pleasure. Ibn Abidin justified his borrowing from Malik by saying that Malik, being a young contemporary of Abu Hanifa, could have been said to be a student of his. (Ibn 'Abidin, *Hashiya* (Beirut: Dar al-Fikr, 1987; Cairo original), Vol. 2, p. 538.) More on law and *madhhab* as they relate to consensus and disagreement below (section 3.3).

3 Consensus, disagreement, and conflicting arguments

Without a consensus among scholars (or professionals in any area of expertise), very little can be achieved. It is especially true in legal systems that scholars must find a few points that are not open to dispute. If every matter in a legal system awaits new thinking and novel interpretation, even on the assumption that all participants in the legal system are accomplished men and women of good moral character, the legal system cannot proceed.

It is true that Islamic law, and the same goes for each one of its *madhhabs*, did not always look or function like a legal system with a community of scholars bound by agreements that could be established, tested, and employed to create a foundation for consistency. And, while we have a good number of cases where even major Muslim *muftis* and judges were "corrected" by contemporaries and subsequent generations of scholars for ruling against a juristic consensus, there were no judicial institutions that could test whether consensuses were respected, rather than ignored. There was, after all, no Supreme Court for Muslim communities or even for each *madhhab* to function as arbiter. So what *is* consensus like in Islamic law, then?

3.1 Consensus

Let's follow a thirteenth-century commentary in theoretical jurisprudence (Qarafi's (d. 684/1285) *Nafa'is*, text glossed: Razi's (d. 606/1209) *Mahsul*, Vol. 6, p. 2561, Riyadh edition (Nizar Mustafa al-Baz, 1316/1995) to get a sense of how this issue is discussed in theoretical jurisprudence. This is a Sunni source, and one must be aware that consensus is a much more important discussion in Sunni law that it is in the Shi'i traditions.

From this source, you will learn at least two points. The first is that Sunni consensus, in principle, is a tool to define the borders of the Muslim community (if you are out of the consensus, you are out of the community) but may also be extended to "conventions" among the scholarly legal community on obscure points unknown to all practicing Muslims. The second is that consensus is not affected, also in principle, by Shi'i disagreement, but practice showed that Shi'i disagreements shook Sunni jurists' confidence in the existence of a consensus.

One also reads that definite cases of consensus were bound to occur within a small window of time in the history of Islam. The window begins with the Prophet's death, because an agreement on "interpretations" of his teaching in his lifetime is not a source of law separate from his (the Prophet's) authority. The window is then closed while ascertaining the agreement of scholars in the vast swathes of Muslim territories became something of an impossible task. Even today good jurists, sharing an intellectual orientation, context, and method of reasoning or school of law, still find reasons to disagree. Even one and the same person may hold two different views at different times in their lifetime. Furthermore, and we are still following the voices in the same commentary, many of us simply assume that Muslims agreed on basic matters, only to learn later that they were at odds over what was included even in the Qur'an itself.

But if consensus is reserved for one generation, why is that so? Why did the companions of the Prophet ever agree on anything? Did they simply share a natural disposition to hold certain views? Our source continues: Consensus could occur after disagreement, and it would be an acceptable consensus. All historical consensuses, then, could have gone the other way. Agreements simply happened after debates in the first generations. In some cases, those in the minority would make an argument that wins the majority and later becomes a matter of consensus. Abu Bakr argued that a group of apostates must be fought, and he was in the minority, and his argument led to a consensus to fight the apostates, but it could have been otherwise.

ومن يشاقق الرسول من بعد ما تبين له الهدى ويتبع غير سبيل المؤمنين نوله ما تولى ونصله جهنم وساءت مصيرا

Whoever conflicts with the messenger, after guidance has been made available, and follow a path other than that taken by the believers, we reward him accordingly, and place him in Hellfire, the worst of all possible destinies . . .

Qur'an, Sura 4, Verse 115

What made consensus authoritative in the eyes of legal theorists, as I hinted, was the language of the Qur'an and the Prophet's instructions that *drew the line between Muslim and non-Muslim at a point of disagreeing with the views shared by the Muslim community*.

An important caveat is given by Juwayni (d. 478/1085) regarding the subjects where the consensus should be taken seriously: These must be matters of reported *religious* doctrines and practices (*sam'iyya*) as opposed to pure rational or empirical matters. Even the Prophet's instruction or ways of doing things are not all to be taken at face value and followed as aspects of the religious law, since he acted as a man, husband, judge (with limited evidence available to him), and not always a prophet communicating with the heavens. If the Prophet is not infallible, how could the body of the Muslim community be infallible? Muslim societies will entertain prejudices and assumptions that may or may not be correct. Hence, giving credence to views common among Muslims or even Muslim scholars has no basis. Consensus, in other words, seems to operate to distinguish Muslim from non-Muslims, in matters where reasonable disagreement plays no part. (Yes, we did say disagreement may have occurred at an earlier time, but reviving this contretemps at a later time would be unreasonable from this standpoint.)

Some technical and obscure points you may want to read or skip. Abu Bakr ibn Furak, a fourth–fifth/tenth–eleventh-century authority, further argued that consensus could occur only when a whole generation of qualified jurists who are to have agreed have all passed away, with their agreement intact. Razi (d. 1209) begged to differ. He posited that the scholars of each generation may educate (rising) scholars from a new generation, who then become authorities in the life of their mentors. Were the above stipulation to be taken seriously, one would have to wait until the field were devoid of legal authorities with the same dominant and undisputed view. This would never happen. Razi instead thinks that this requirement is not needed at all and opts for a standard to establish *more*, rather than *fewer*, instances of consensus, by saying that a consensus occurring for even a moment, albeit after a disagreement, is a binding standard and a source of law.

So those qualified to be members of the community of the consensus may agree after disagreeing and hence create a consensus. If they were to be divided, and held two opinions, then the whole group that held one of the two views would have to disappear (in a natural disaster, say) or abandon the religion before the other group was able to *enjoy the consensus* of the community and the consensus would be binding. While these are controversial matters, this understanding of consensus is the most consistent. But what would be the point of this consensus?

3.2 Sunni and Shi'i

Once again, consensus is supposed to be a useful, rather than restrictive, quality in a legal system. It provides a few anchors for legal reasoning, and allows new scholars to learn how to clarify the points of consensus in order to also learn where one finds areas open to *ijtihad* and research and reflection. But without these reported consensuses, the new students have no guidance for juristic discussion.

The system, at least on its Sunni side, has built mechanisms to get out of a consensus when it is truly a burden for the scholarly community. This mechanism is closer to distinguishing new cases—showing that what looks like the old question where the consensus operates is actually a new question. Or, in some cases, the consensus may have been agreed over a view that would still function in the new conditions but would still be abandoned if it lacks a common purpose. Taking our favorite case of the consensus to fight collective apostasy by war under Abu Bakr again, a new consideration of this question and a fresh look at a similar condition, negates the need to enter into collective wars with apostates, even when a broad view of the conditions shows resemblance to the conditions of Abu Bakr's wars, as it looks into the purpose of the initial apostasy disputes.

The Shi'i view of this matter raises interesting questions. For them, the value of consensus is derived from the group that held a doctrine without disagreement. Zaydi and Ja'fari jurists believe that the *imam*, the only real authority in matters of law, is part of the consensus of the righteous community, and this is what lends this consensus value.

Shi'i law functioned within smaller populations. When one refers to Shi'i authorities, one must note that those intended are not a uniform set; some were seen as authoritative only among Zaydi, Ja'fari, or Isma'ili factions. It did not suffer so much from a surplus of legal views as a deficit and thus had a different task in its pursuit of the standardization of authority. In addressing the potential of mixing authoritative and un-authoritative views, the Shi'i traditions prescribed the ingenious solution of building law around the living imitable authority—an individual, rather than a group of scholars. Those abreast of the law, the learned circles, had to figure out among themselves how to negotiate their own disagreement.

Then there was the phenomenon of "border-crossing" between Sunni and Shi'i legal doctrines and views. Erudite Sunni scholars unhappy with the results of Sunni consensuses found the views of Shi'i jurists (or to be more accurate, scholars whose views were reported in Shi'i sources unknown or unstudied by the bulk of Sunni scholars) to come in handy as spoilers of consensus. One can find at least one reported view by a scholar against the consensus, even if another view attributed to the same scholar that comports with the consensus is found. Ja'far, the Ja'far of Ja'fari law, for example, is reported to have allowed wills to be given to inheritors who are assigned standard shares of the inheritance, while the consensus is that only outsiders, such as charities, can be given from the will, within the limit of 33.3 percent of the inheritance.

The Syrian Hanbali jurist Ibn Taymiyya (d. 728/1328), who attacked Ja'fari and other Shi'i theologians quite a bit, ended up considering their views and defending them. He relied on their "aberrative" views in divorce law and contested the existence of a consensus, despite their disagreement. The subsequent centuries produced followers for him.

Sunni reliance on Shi'i disagreement to argue against consensus is an interesting feature of the debates on consensus, despite an overall sense that even eccentric Sunni views did not spoil an otherwise widely reported consensus. This feature, in any case, clearly indicates that Shi'i disagreements did matter for some Sunni jurists, and was not simply seen as irrelevant.

All this applies to the later centuries of Islamic law, because in its early years, debates in Kufa and Medina were the norm and claimed consensuses were rare. Medina was the birthplace of both Ja'fari and Maliki reflections on practical matters, but no one should imagine councils of scholars debating lists of legal doctrines in the second/eighth century, sifting through which laws had been agreed upon and which ones were a matter of disagreement.

It remained true that consensus in Shi'i law was of secondary importance compared to its Sunni standing. The early Shi'i authorities were limited in number. Once again, and to conclude this section, the crisis in Shi'i law was one of deficit of law, rather than a surplus. If consensus in Shi'i law were to be seen as the agreement of scholars, as opposed to a community within which the *imam* lives, there had to be ways to get around the authority of agreements that did not stand the test of time.

3.3 Law within one *madhhab*

A traditionalist Egyptian scholar, 'Abd al-Ghani 'Abd al-Khaliq (1908–1983), argued that consensus was the only foundation on which one can base any legal doctrine without doubt. The language of the Qur'an and the Prophet's *Sunna* are matters of disagreement, at least if one is undeterred by the rules of traditional interpretation. Of course, within each *madhhab* or school of law, the options are limited by the school's standards of legal reasoning. Once these restrictions are removed, no doctrine is immune to revision.

Some modern Muslims celebrate this development; many decry it. In any case, the Sunni traditions of theoretical jurisprudence provides limited solace. If recognizable authorities in the law agree, as long as they distinguish their questions from those that have been matters of consensus earlier, this may serve as a foundation for new, stable laws.

In the old Islamic legal and philosophical traditions, there were two views of God's cosmic plan and God's obligations for human beings. The Mu'tazili view is that the human mind must be able to assume a consistency in God's cosmic plan and must be able to discern qualities in human acts that allow the jurist to judge these acts as good or bad in the divine eyes. The Ash'aris have relinquished this task and acknowledged that things sometimes do not add up to the limited human intellect, and this is part of why the divine ways are above human comprehension. While this disagreement has some consequences, it is not always consequential. In most juristic debates, the scholars will argue practical solutions, eliminating arguments and supporting others.

Legal knowledge is distinct from natural knowledge by its standing on manufactured authority. If I am the lawmaker, I can say this is the law, and it does not have to be consistent with the way knowledge of nature is imagined or presumed to be. The only meaningful crisis of equally conflicting legal imperatives is transferred to the inside of the jurist's mind (if one jurist is building a system) or to the clique of legal elites inside a legal system (as in modern national laws, for example).

When one and the same person finds conflicting indicators or considerations leading him in different directions, he may not be able to answer the question at all. But he may also answer it twice. This is what we colloquially refer to as being "of two minds" about something. One of the medieval jurists whose ability to apparently produce two different legal systems in the same lifetime was the founder of the school that our Isnawi followed—the Shafi'i school of law.

As we know, the *imam* plays a major role. In the absence of the *imam*, the legitimate leader of the community, Ja'fari jurists wondered how duties such as the Friday prayer may be fulfilled. A consensus is reported that the prayer was obligatory, based on an apparent instruction in the Qur'an (62/9), requiring good reasons for a claim to an exception to be made. (Zayn al-Din b. Ali al-'Amili (al-Shahid al-Thani = the Second Martyr) (d. 966/1558), *Rasail al-Shahid al-Thani* (#8) (Qumm: Markaz al-Abhath wa al-Dirasat al-Islamiyya, 1379/1421/1999), Vol. 1, p. 175.) An opposed consensus stipulates, among other things, the permission of an upright *imam* is required, and draws partial support from the simple fact that people tend to gather for bad reasons more frequently than they gather for good.

The reason we end up with ostensibly equal and conflicting arguments, then, is that there is no question that the presence of the *imam* or his deputy (jurist) is a condition in the prayer and there is also no question that the prayer is obligatory. The continual absence of the *imam* and his deputy does hence create something of a paradoxical situation. But, of course, there are solutions to paradoxes, which will appear to be only illusory after the solution.

Arguing the first position, that the prayer remains an obligation, the Second Martyr, Zayn al-Din al-'Amili (d. 966/1558) first acknowledged the powerful disagreement on the matter. Yet, he was adamant that he had the tools to resolve it. The side that argues that a "call to the prayer" (*adhan*) is valid only when performed by the rightful authorities does have a point. He comes back, however, with a rebuttal:

> Once a command establishes an obligation, my conclusion is established. This is based on the consensus of all Muslims, our fellow scholars [Shi'is] and laypeople [Sunnis] included. The obligation is not, in itself, contingent on the *adhan* or proper call to prayer. It is simply made to appear conditional in order that the call be taken seriously—such that some scholars stated that the *adhan* itself is a separate obligation. The same is true regarding a requirement of 'moving toward a place to perform the prayer, since it is a requirement because it leads to a requirement. But is moving to a place to perform the prayer is a requirement, the prayer itself is actually the ultimate requirement, since the act of moving itself cannot be seen as good (*hasan*) without requiring it . . .

Not unlike their Sunni counterparts, Ja'fari scholars could adjudicate disagreement—eliminate it, in effect—and show that either the equality or the conflict of the arguments is illusory. Many of their ground rules chime with, when they are not a mirror image of, those given by Sunni legal theorists. In an introduction to his commentary on al-'Allama al-Hilli's Summary of the Law (*Mukhtasar al-Shara'i'*), Jamal al-Din Miqdad al-Suyuri (d. 826/1423) provides a statement of method on evaluating conflicting legal dicta. (Jamal al-Din Miqdad Ibn Abdullah al-Suyuri (d. 826/1423) (ed. A. al-Kuhkamri), *al-Tanqih al-Ra'i' li Mukhtasar al-Shar'i'* (a commentary on al-Allama al-Hilli's Mukhtasar), Vol. 1, pp. 8–9.)

He first states that sectarian, often desire-bound, opinions have diverged, the correct path of the People of the House (the scholars of authority in Ja'fari law) being the one chosen by the author. While already reducing the number of choices for a jurist, this fundamental turn toward specific authorities does not eliminate all disagreement. Suyuri moves on to enumerate the authorities of the school (*madhhab*), from Muhammad al-Baqir to his son, the school's eponym, Jafar al-Sadiq (d. 148/765) to al-Kazim (Musa), the fifth, sixth, and seventh of the twelve leaders of the community. He warns that reporting from these authorities is not of the same quality. In some cases, the reporting produces knowledge that is close to certain, having acquired the status of "abundantly reported" (*mutawatir*). In other cases, all you have to go by is a single reporter or a handful of them. The latter, in turn, can be of different (totaling six) types. The author essentially offers two scales, one describing the quality of the reporters, descending from the highest (*sahih*) all the way down to a report with deservedly blameworthy reporters (*da'if*). The other scale attends to the connectability of the chain of reporters from known and connected (*musnad*) to a report whose authorities are not even fully identified (*mursal*) (pp. 7–9).

Suyuri then addresses the different classes of legal reports and views. Pointers to favorable evaluation of one report or view over the other are indicated by language such as "*al-ashhar*" (ie, the more common report), "*al-azhar*" (the view more accepted as an answer/*fatwa* delivered to questioners), "*al-ashbah*" (more consistent with other school doctrines), "*al-ahwat*" (the safer choice to satisfy or remove personal responsibility), "*al-akthar*" (more common among jurists), "*al-ansab*" (a synonym for *al-ashbah*), and "*al-awla*" (decidedly superior view, based on a certain rationale). He then attends to the possibility of a gridlock or the presence of conflicting and equal arguments by introducing the term "*taraddud*" (p. 9). He finally makes it one of the tasks of his commentary to spell out juristic disagreements and the manner in which one report or view may be seen as superior over the other (*wajh al-azhariyya wa al-ashbahiyya*

Figure 3.2 Al-Karaouine University (Al-Qarawiyyin) in the city of Fes, Morocco. Author: Anderson Sady. Image accessed via Wikimedia.

wa al-asahhiyya) and the reasons jurists may encounter cases where deciding who is right remains unattainable (*manatiq al-taraddud*) (p. 10).

One of the three options to reconcile conflicting arguments is to assign the conflicting laws they produce to different times or temporal frameworks. This applies particularly in the area of texts. The assumption is that a new text cancels out an earlier text. The Qur'anic texts themselves bear the possibility of abrogation, but abrogation is applicable in *Sunna* texts more frequently and abundantly.

This is one area where medieval Islamic law's theorization of superior argument finds a near-exact equivalent in modern laws and may thus serve as a segue to modern applications of the idea of superior argument. The essence of abrogation, as noted, is that texts of later temporal provenance cancel out texts of earlier provenance. Whether it is the Prophet's law or a modern legislative body's laws, the idea is the same. Sunni jurists, for example, acknowledge that temporary marriage used to be allowed at an early stage in the history of the Muslim community. Sunnis believe that this permission was abrogated, but Ja'fari jurists do not agree. In modern national laws, Islamic law itself becomes one contender, one argument among many, in the judge's search for the correct law.

3.4 Arguments equal in power, opposite in conclusion

Legal theorists also ask: Could two arguments be totally equal in strength? Karkhi (d. 410/1020) says no, but others think it possible. If it *is* possible, then the jurist simply picks one—so said Baqillani (d. 402/1013) and the two Jubba'is, Abu Ali (d. 303/916) and Abu Hashim (d. 321/933)—or both arguments cancel each other out. According to the first view, when a judge applies one of the competing arguments in one of his rulings, he could not use the other position and arguments in a new but identical case. In other words, he cannot swerve back and forth between the two equal arguments. The Prophet is reported to have instructed Abu Bakr al-Siddiq (d. 13/634) to not rule differently on what is in fact one matter.

The question at the beginning, then, is whether such a condition is possible. If you believe that jurists are searching for one law, God's law, would not there have to be a successful set of arguments by which to arrive at this law? Isnawi (d. 772/1370) takes it from here, explaining that the discussion falls under four queries, three on equal but conflicting arguments and one on determining what superior argument is. The three queries on equal argument address the presence of conflicting sources of the law that could not be eliminated or sidestepped, to viz. the Quran and juristic consensus. Two Qur'anic verses in ostensible conflict will turn out, upon reflection, to be reconciled: An instance of "particular" language will be identified in one verse and "general" language in another, or an instance of abrogation, where a subsequent verse cancels an earlier one. Juristic consensuses, similarly, do not genuinely clash. Both the Prophet Muhammad's reports and reasoning based on analogy, by contrast, are subject to determining which is superior and which inferior. These are the proper subject of *superior argument*.

Isnawi then inserts a note of clarification, removing what appears to be the requirement of the fulfillment of an insurmountable task. There is no denial that arguments leading to certainty cannot conflict; nor can an argument leading to likelihood or high confidence truly conflict with one leading to certainty. What is at stake is a conflict between two arguments that yield a position which one may hold with high confidence, rather than certainty.

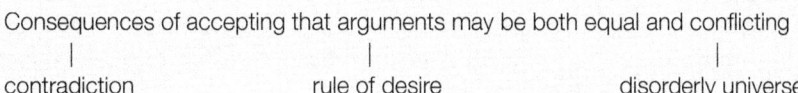

Contrasting with the view attributed to Karkhi, the majority of legal theorists say these equal-cum-conflicting arguments do exist. They appear to see things differently and, in a way, more simply and realistically. This is reported by Razi (d. 606/1209), Amidi (d. 631/1233), and Ibn al-Hajib (d. 646/1248). It is not difficult to imagine, so goes the argument, that two upright reporters of what the Prophet said or did would diverge, one reporting the presence of an event or statement and the other reporting its absence. This group of theorists then attacked the view of those who rejected equality and conflict in arguments. They said the logical division the rejecters consider is missing an important possibility, the very simple possibility that the conflicting arguments be reconcilable—that is to say that the conflicting arguments be considered as elements or components of one and the same argument. The jurist must, ultimately, apply his reasoning to this condition, preferring one element of the argument to another or simply declining to rule on the matter. In any case, one may acknowledge all this and refuse to say that the conflicting elements of an argument should all be abandoned, if they seem to lead the jurist in different directions.

A disorderly universe must be posited, if conflicting indicators of seemingly equal power present themselves to the mind. Isnawi states that this idea originates from the Mu'tazili *tahsin/taqbih* doctrine. This doctrine assumes that the human mind, being able to detect the qualities that make an act "good" or "bad," should not find itself at an impasse where conflicting indications of what is good or bad are available. There simply must be a way to decide the goodness and badness of good and bad; otherwise, this tool—the human mind—is not what we assumed it was. Isnawi gives this quick identification of the argument's source without a comment. His reader will take Isnawi's silence as a kind of sneering, given that by now, the reader will have encountered multiple instances of Isnawi attacking Mu'tazili doctrines, including instances of attack on this very skeletal doctrine.

Amidi stipulates that *tarjih* is needed when two arguments satisfy two conditions. They each must be in conflict with the other (the *ta'arud* condition) and be capable of indicating a conclusion (*salahiya*). This excludes arguments that could not lead to a conclusion, but it does not set up the matter as an epistemological crisis per se. Conflicting indicators exist, and one may be evaluated more favorably over the other, but one need not acknowledge that a state of equality between the two arguments, however apparent or ostensible, is there. In other words, *tarjih*'s prerequisite is simply *ta'arud* (+ *salahiya*), not the potentially problematic *ta'adul*.

Staying with laws and legal conventions and setting logic aside, we now consider practical solutions to this condition when it seems to arise. The practical solutions are the ones we learned earlier: Some say that a pure act of choice of argument by the jurist will do. This is the view of Abu Bakr al-Baqillani and the Juba'is—uncle and nephew, whom Baydawi mentioned. Others say conflicting arguments cancel out each other, and the human act under consideration becomes permissible or neutral—the principal condition of human activities before the law. If what is under consideration is simply a private matter in the jurist's life, he or she gets to choose. If it concerns others, he or she gives the questioners all options. If it is a judicial matter, the judge must make a decision, since he cannot leave it up to conflicting adversaries. Once he takes a decision in one case, all similar cases must be decided similarly, because of the Prophet's instruction of Abu Bakr, which Baydawi cited.

4 Conclusions

Islamic law regulates human actions, and it does that based on a limited number of sources. Disagreement among jurists is bound to happen, but the majority agree on some important matters. As the Islamic legal traditions functioned in certain localities within the confines of one *madhhab* or school of law, constant disagreement and reconsideration of *what the law is* would be minimized.

There are also other detailed conclusions one may make. The first conclusion concerns the medieval Sunni tradition. The discursive legal space (in *fiqh*) that is occupied by conflicting-cum-equal arguments is larger than the legal theorists (in *usul al-fiqh*) have covered. Medieval *usul* theorists think that true conflict among equal arguments is limited to *Sunna* and *qiyas*. This is where a jurist has to work either to eliminate the equality or the conflict of the arguments. By showing that one report (*hadith*) or one analogy-based argument is superior to another, the equality is eliminated. By reconciling one with the other, the conflict is eliminated. In *fiqh* practice, every evaluation of conflicting arguments follows the same pattern. **When two arguments seem to be opposed in the conclusions to which each points, either their equality or conflict must be eliminated.** The Sunni legal theory of evaluating arguments provides a point of convergence and connection (a motherboard of sorts) for the rest of Islamic legal reasoning that attends to legal argument.

Second, while Shi'i juristic reasoning seems to differ significantly from its Sunni counterpart (eg, the presence of *tahsin/taqbih* arguments and the absence, in theory, of *qiyas* arguments), **something of the same picture is found as to how conflicting and equal arguments are addressed, especially when it comes to the negation of "equality" among arguments.** Since *qiyas* is either ignored or considered not authoritative, conflict in reports (*akhbar*) is the focus of *usul* treatments of conflicting, equal arguments, at least since al-'Allama al-Hilli (d. 726/1325). In practice, a broad battery of tools is found that assists the jurist to resolve conflicts-in-argument that may lead to legal indecisiveness. This process also takes an intergenerational form. That is, some arguments that made it to older works of jurisprudence are weeded out in later sources by showing that these arguments did not stand up to scrutiny. This exercise is especially true of later (Hilli and 'Amili) Ja'fari authorities, such as Miqdad al-Suyuri al-Hilli (d. 826/1423) and the First and Second Martyrs, Jamal al-Din Makki al-'Amili (d. 786/1385) and Zayn al-Din al-'Amili (d. 965/1558). This process continues to operate until the modern centuries. In the nineteenth century, when Murteza Ansari wrote his *Fara'id al-Usul*, Ja'fari *usul al-fiqh* continued to offer the limited discussion on the conflict of *akhbar*, while the practice continued to cover the same broad scope, and a process of revising Ja'fari doctrines has continued up to the present day.

We will now move to some details of the laws of the shari'a. Separating the social, personal, national, transnational sides of the shari'a (the subjects of Units 4–7) is done only to make the study course possible. You will keep noting overlaps and fuzzy areas lying amidst two or more of these areas, just as you see in most systems of legal and moral reasoning where questions about what the law is and what morality is are decided based on some kind of "sleight of hand" or institutional divisions external to the queries themselves.

Review III

- In most schools of Islamic law, human actions fall under five categories: obligatory; recommended; permissible; reprehensible; and prohibited.
- The substantive law in Islam comes from reasoning that takes into account the Qur'an, the Prophet Muhammad's *Sunna*, and juristic consensus.
- A Muslim lawmaker or shari'a scholar's **goal** is to provide descriptions of actions on a spectrum of most "desirable" to most "undesirable." The scholar starts from a logical assumption that the teachings of God and the Prophet assume priorities among actions. The list of **sources** of Islamic law are the Qur'an, *Sunna*, consensus, reasoning from a standard or an exception to rule in a case, and reasoning based on utility that is worthy of consideration.
- The jurists of Islam disagreed as to the weight of local social standards in shaping the law, with Zaydi, Hanafi, and Maliki, and later Ja'fari, jurists as the most appreciative of it.

Exercises III

- Equipped with the above discussion about consensus and disagreement, search on YouTube for speeches (in English) by scholars of Islamic law. Type in the names "Hamza Yusuf," "Sherman Jackson," "Ovamir Anjum," and "Yasir al Qadi." Look for relevant videos. Try to identify sources of disagreement in the views you hear. Which schools of law are mentioned? Which issues seem to generate more controversy? Are all these disagreements inherited? Do some of them have a distinctly modern flavor?

Tips

- When you describe the theory of human actions in Islamic law, make it clear that Hanafi jurists added a distinction between two different kinds of obligation and prohibition based on the *certainty* of the source of the prohibition or obligation, not its *degree*.

Analyze this

- Jamil b. Khamis al-Sa'di (Ibadi scholar, active in 1840, see excerpts from this source in "primary source material" unit after Unit 5) says that an agreement of all jurists does not necessarily mean that there is a binding consensus. He says that if all Muslim jurists were to agree that a loud laughter during the prayer necessitates a redoing of the ablution (which is the Hanafi view) or agree that coffee was prohibited, this would only be an agreement but not a *consensus*. He means to say that the agreement in these cases is accidental, not based on any textual foundation. Is it really true then that Islamic law is Qur'anic or Prophetic law, after all?
- In medicine, **anatomy** looks into the structure of the body's systems (digestive, respiratory, etc.) and organs and their positions; **physiology** looks into the functions of organs; and **pathology** looks into the dysfunctionality of organs that leads to disease. With an admitted degree of license in the analogies, what would an anatomy,

physiology, and pathology of the Islamic legal systems as presented be like? Hints: anatomy (human reason, revelation, human actions); physiology (*qiyas*, '*aql* usage); pathology (counter analogy, arguments of equal power that diverge in conclusions, disintegration of legal argument).

Primary source material I

Theoretical Jurisprudence

Source: Qarafi (d. 684/1285), *Nafa'is al-Usul fi Sharh al-Mahsul* (The Jewels of Legal Theory, A Commentary on the text of Mahsul [by Razi (d. 606/1209). This is an eight-volume commentary. Selections from Vol. 5, pp. 2338–9.

THE PROPHET'S ACTIONS

Qarafi: The Prophet's actions must fall into three categories: that which is obligatory, that is which is recommended, and that which is simply permissible.

The Prophet is incapable of falling into illegal actions; his reason made him refrain from many things that are permissible, let alone those that are reprehensible. This leaves only the categories stated here.

If one objects: He is reported to have lost focus in the prayers. This is outside of [even all] all five [not only the three] categories of actions [mentioned]. It is like forgetfulness, making an unintentional mistake, or being coerced. It is, rather, like the actions of those asleep, or those of inanimate bodies, and the wind. It is outside of all of the five categories.

I reply: By actions here is meant actions he took, which we are supposed to "follow." This does not include missing the correct practice for being unfocused (*sahw*). We are not supposed to follow him when he loses focus. We simply follow him in correcting our own instances of erring because of lack of focus in the way he himself corrected his lack of focus. [That is to say, the compensatory prostration that is reported in these cases.]

Exercise

Write a 1,000-word report/essay explaining this text based on what you learned in Units 2 and 3.

4 The Social Shari'a

There are forms of social life in the Muslim world that are governed by complex hybrids of *medieval* and *modern* elements. In Unit 6, we will explain the foundation of these forms. This unit attempts to give a broad outline of social life in a Muslim society that *may diverge from recognizable modern norms*. This includes some of the historical institutions that do not have direct applications in national laws but may be found in Muslim communities across the world, if one looks for them.

After an introduction on jurists' discussions of generalizations and exceptions and a word on equity and nature in Islamic social justice, we will move to the core of the topic, which covers three aspects: authority in the social world; social standards; and the family.

Generalizations and exceptions

With Unit 3 still fresh in your mind, consider this. Sunni jurists state that five of the commonly discussed legal maxims of Islamic law govern most of its cases. The five maxims are:

1. *purpose governs action*;
2. *harm (or its source) is to be removed* (further explained by the subprinciple that lesser harms are incurred to avoid larger harms);
3. *customs and social standards affect the law*;
4. *doubt cannot remove certainty*, and
5. *hardship begets ease*.

Similar maxims are also found in Shi'i law.

Aside from the *madhhabs* we considered, these legal abstractions served as the macro-forces that shaped mature Islamic legal reasoning. Each one of these maxims has many applications in social laws. You may remember applications for this last and fifth maxim (*hardship begets ease*) in religious licenses we considered in Unit 1 (section 2.1.2). In more complex social laws, maxims 1, 2, and 3 are indicative of the direction jurists take in standard solutions to cases. The maxims are supposed to be "subsequent" to laws—that is, they are abstractions from actual laws or ways to describe considerations latent in legal reasoning, which operated in making the laws. But the maxims are also used to train newcomers to the field, usually with many caveats and elaborations of *rulings in actual cases* to illustrate applications; otherwise, the maxims are often misunderstood and misapplied.

Take the first maxim. *Purpose governs action* does not mean one may steal as long as one has a good purpose in mind (that you will build better hospitals or better schools for public benefit, for example); it does not even mean that good intentions allow one to be forgiven for an unintended mistake. It has the specific sense, albeit wide in application, that the *mufti* and the judge must consider the intention of actors as s/he rules on their actions, such as sales, gifts, proposals of marriage, divorce, assignment of desert in wills. Keep in mind that intentions must be demonstrated, not simply claimed. This maxim also has applications in addressing certain conflicts. In one application, if a man places a large container to capture rainwater *with the intention* of owning it (for personal use or to transfer to others), he owns the water. Someone who wastes or appropriates the water is not immune to suit. When the container is placed *without that intention*, the water is still in the public domain. (Again, evidence of the intention is required here, such as showing that water-collection has been done before by the same person.) Here is another legal scenario governed by this maxim (from the simple, communitarian laws of the past). If a person picks up an item of lost property with the intention of searching for its owner, and the property is destroyed without negligence, then the finder would not be liable for paying compensation to the owner; if the intention had been to keep it for himself, though, the finder *would* be liable and triable. (Ahmad al-Zarqa, *Sharh al-Qawa id al-Fiqhiyya* (Damascus: Dar al-Qalam, 1993), pp. 49–50.) If you follow applications of this maxim through cases and everyday scenarios, you will notice that in practical terms, intentions are not ascertainable in many cases, and the actual number of cases where the judge is able to consider the intentions is slim. This does not change the fact that it is an important consideration in understanding how laws operate, however.

Maxims do have exceptions, which arise either as a result of other maxims in the area of application or from a specific condition. Here is one general example. In social laws, the presumption of non-liability and continued legitimacy of the current condition applies overall (Arabic: *al-asl baqa' ma kan 'ala ma kan*) entails that any claim that is not supported by evidence leaves us uncertain about the claim; all conditions preceding the claim, hence, remain unchallenged. One exception is that a woman is presumed truthful in reporting the end of her waiting period (of three menstruation cycles after divorce) within the shortest possible period where the waiting period may have ended. In practical terms, she is allowed to get married within two months or less of her divorce, for example, as opposed to three, if the general presumption of juxtaposing one month to each menstruation is applied. The general maxim demands proof, and if we were attempting to ascertain the end of any other period (in debts, the delivery of any promised commodity in commerce, etc.), we would, based on the general principle, err on the side of *negating the change of an existing condition*. (That is: If we are not sure the debt is due, it is thus not due.) In the remarriage question, the condition is the "waiting," and the woman is here essentially trusted to end her commitment to waiting before remarriage. (Al-Zarqa, *Sharh al-Qawa id*, p. 93.) This is an exception, and the maxim remains operative in most cases. Other examples of a maxim, its application, and its exceptions are found after Unit 6.

Equity, equality, nature

Islamic social justice cannot be easily matched with an Aristotelian notion of justice, which centers on equality while paying attention to how *nature* equips humans to perform certain functions in society. Islamic social justice seems, in certain respects, to be closer to an Ulpian notion of justice (attributed to Ulpian or Ulpianus, Roman jurist, d. 228), which begins with the *nature* of an agent or member of society, and which then considers the *role* of that agent or member in society, and the *proper share* that ought to be assigned based on these two considerations. In Ulpian's world, no one can be said to be treated unjustly, if he or she asks for what he is given and seeks it. Let's modernize this notion for an example. Spending years to gain a bachelor's degree and a few more to gain to professional degree indicates that one seeks something different from working as a construction worker or bar tender. (For those whose appetites are whetted by this reference, check out books on the Justinian Institutes. The Justinian collection of legal opinions, 300 years after Ulpian, mention Ulpian by name more than any other Roman jurist.) In the early medieval Muslim world, in most rural and urban settings, people served functions in society, and their familial and work status determined their expectations in life.

Each time I speak of laws based on assumptions about human *nature*, try to suspend any sense you have of *modern* concepts of nature—put states of nature, Rousseau, Hobbes, or Locke to the back of your mind. (The state of nature any one of these modern guys yearns for or hates precedes the ordered society Muslim jurists attempt to regulate and govern.) Certainly the German idealists and their sense of a lofty (almost worship-worthy) nature, and their pre-established harmony between man and nature, are also out. Just think of basic biological qualities (physical differences between old and young; anatomical differences between men and women), social orientations and functions that become *second nature*, aided by basic notions of universal logic, addressing comparisons and contrasts among people and things, similar and dissimilar.

1 Authority in the social world

1.1 Global jurisdiction

Hanafi and Shafi'i jurists disagreed when they contemplated this question: Does Islamic law apply all over the world, or just in certain areas of it? One has to start with a context for the question. When this question arose, Muslims lived in areas where Islam was the religion of those in government but not the majority of the population, in areas where it was the religion of both those in government and the population, and in areas where it was the religion of neither. In certain areas Muslims also traveled or lived permanently under non-Muslim rule.

If you lived in the Arabian Peninsula (even before the Saudi state of the past century), the default religion was Islam, but in Egypt, the majority remained non-Muslim (for centuries after Islam's rise) while those in government were mostly Muslim. Muslims living as a minority under Muslim governments ruling a non-Muslim majority did not expect much support from Islamic social laws. It is apparent that whether or not the government was Muslim mattered more in the social arena.

The Shafi'i answer was that Islam was God's religion for all. Obviously non-Muslims did not and do not live by it, but this does not absolve Muslims living as a minority among non-Muslims from *their* duty to live by it. Hanafis said that law has a geographic and a personal jurisdiction. Muslims living in areas where usury is a common practice could not really be expected to refrain from dabbling in it, but they should abstain from what are considered unfair dealings by the standards of the community of which they are part.

There are interesting consequences for this disagreement, especially in times of large demographic shifts. Hanafi jurists have argued that even a rapid change in the demography or in political power should take into account the assumption that non-Muslim lands are not governed by what we may call public Islamic law. True, Muslims may fast and pray, even when they live as a minority, but they could not expect, for example, to apply Islamic criminal law among themselves. This is also true even when a Muslim commits a crime in a non-Muslim land then relocates to a Muslim land, even if the required evidentiary standard for establishing the crime was made available to a Muslim judge in what they call "the abode of Islam." (Compare how Saudi courts may look at the MMK case from Unit 1, based on Hanbali doctrines, which take Shafi'i's answer to the question of Islamic law's universal jurisdiction.)

Premodern Muslim jurists from both the Shafi'i and Hanafi sides of this theoretical divide regulated war and disagreed on many practical matters, including land taxes and re-appropriation, family breakups and reconstruction (after war), truces, peace treaties, commercial treaties across borders, migration from and to Muslim lands, term-limited international visits, and diplomatic relations. In lieu of multiple citizenships, all people in the world, as far as old Islamic law is concerned, belonged in one of four categories:

Muslim	*Dhimmi*	*Musta'man*	*Harbi*
	A non-Muslim living permanently in a Muslim land	A non-Muslim residing temporarily in a Muslim land	A non-Muslim with no agreement of residence with a Muslim government

The *harbi* is, in effect, of two types: one living in a non-Muslim land (which is the norm) or one found in a Muslim land, either in a time of peace or in a time of war. The *harbi*, in the Hanafi view, is protected by the laws that apply in his country and the agreements between

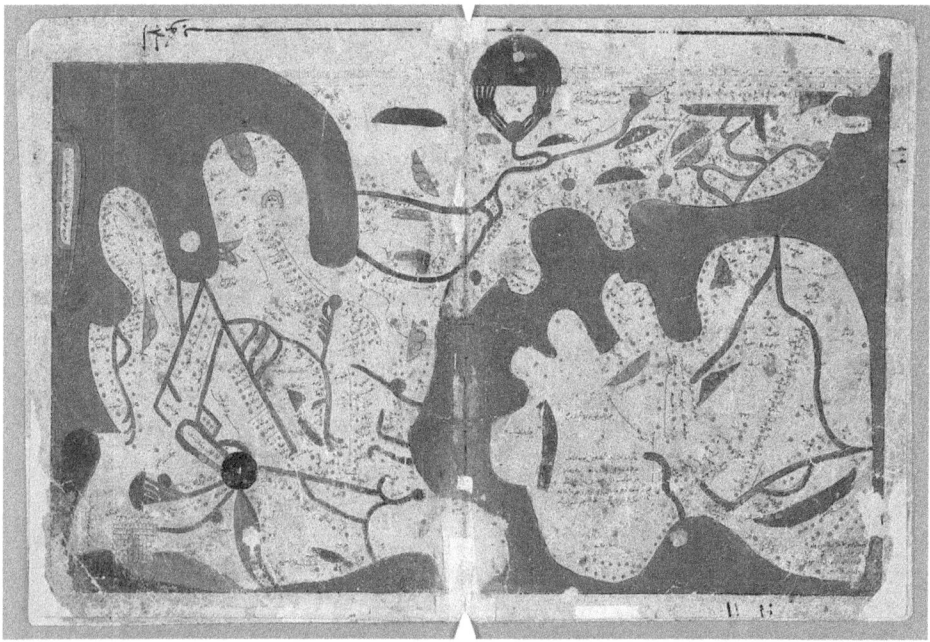

Figure 4.1 *Book of Curiosities of the Sciences and Marvels for the Eyes*, copy of manuscript originally written in the first half of the eleventh century.

his country and other Muslim countries. To receive the protection of a Muslim government, the *harbi* needs to update to a *musta'man* status. But when this person goes outside of his land and fails to seek a *musta'man* status, no Muslim government is expected to protect him or her. The Shafi'i view that the world is, in a sense, one piece, faces the most difficulty in regulating the status of the *harbi*.

In a novel type of jurisprudence, the shari'a's global scope is reconsidered in creative ways. (See Unit 7, section 4.)

1.2 Judgeships

Inside a Muslim society, Islamic law is adjudicated by judges and *muftis*, as we have learned. How formal is this job of a judge? It may just depend on when and where cases are heard. But here is one interesting disagreement to consider.

Centuries ago a dispute arose among jurists about whether judges should be allowed to charge for their services or work only as uncompensated volunteers. Alhough apparently carrying the hallmarks of earlier and simpler times, it is a remarkable disagreement, because no one now doubts that the knowledge and the dedication of one's time to this service must be compensated, and that it is unlikely that this service would be provided at a high level without a price (a salary). It still strikes many as odd that some held the view that jurists may be able to be both independently wealthy (in some cases, just ascetic) *and* willing to provide the service of adjudication for no charge.

A Muslim judge, one may say, acts like a *mufti* with a specific case that involves two adversaries, and is backed by a force that will support his ruling. In this simplified analogy, he is a community leader not unlike the *mufti*. He is also providing a religious service, again not unlike a Qur'an reciter or teacher. The judge and the Qur'an reciter are actually just practicing their religion when they do what they do. Can the judge or the Qur'an reciter charge money for practicing his religion?

Abu Hanifa thought no one should charge for a ritual, and in his view reciting the Qur'an was a ritual. Within a generation, Abu Hanifa's two students disagreed with him, saying that knowledge of the Qur'an and the religious sciences would simply disappear without specialized attention and dedication, which demanded compensation.

In modern law, judges are asked to apply statutes. Some judges believe their duty to interpret the laws allows them to create rules of law out of the existing rules of law in statutory or constitutional laws. Some judges, especially unelected ones, think that because they have not been elected to their position via a democratic process, they should not make laws from the judicial bench. A Muslim judge, especially in the later centuries, is usually restricted by a *madhhab*, not statutes, and must be from the population within which he works, so as to understand the environment in which the cases arise—not unlike the *mufti* in all these matters.

Let us now move to non-judicial social-legal authority.

> Shurayh, Ibn Sirin, Shafi'i and the majority of jurists allow judges to charge for their services . . . Abu al-Khattab [d. 510/1116) says: If he needs the salary, then yes; otherwise, there is a disagreement . . . Ahmad (Ibn Hanbal) did not approve of charging for the service of providing justice.
>
> Ibn Qudama, *al-Mughni*, Vol. 14, pp. 9–10

1.3 Fatwas and muftis

In a momentously valuable introduction to a long legal commentary he did not live to finish, the great Shafi'i jurist Nawawi (d. 676/1277) starts a section on fatwas by stating that muftis, scholars who deliver fatwas, are fallible representatives of God. He thus acknowledges the imperfect knowledge humans will acquire, in any fatwa case, of their religious obligations. But this seems to require no apology. He takes the opportunity to warn scholars to never take their work lightly, given their unique position, and proceeds to tell anecdotes of experts refraining from giving their opinions when they were not certain how to answer a question posed to them.

Since muftis disagree, and in some cases they consider one another to be wrong, even egregiously so, accusations by one scholar of another being "wrong" or "too lenient" do not simply disqualify a mufti from exercising his legal and moral role, as long as he or she is a scholar of acknowledged authority. Muftis are either "independent" or followers of a particular madhhab (school of law). In the first instance, they must command thorough knowledge of original arguments to arrive at their conclusions. They cannot be independent if they do not understand all the basic tools required here, including language, the history of the Prophet, and the history of juristic debates (consensuses and disagreements).

If the mufti chooses to take the less taxing path and follow an existing madhhab, however, he or she must master the methods of legal reasoning within that school of law. Whether independent or affiliates of schools, muftis do inevitably vary in quality and "rank." That is, some of them are going to be better masters of their traditions or argumentation method than others. The ranks are a bit of an obsession for scholars who write about ifta' theory. At the highest ranks, essentially revising and clarifying school doctrine is one thing a jurist may do, among other tasks, and at the lowest, consumption of older legal tradition and explaining them to questioners is all one is able to do.

Here is a short miscellany of principles that govern ifta' or fatwa.

1 Because solving inheritance questions depends on it, according to Nawawi, the mufti must have a working knowledge of mathematics—he means mostly arithmetic and pre-algebra—in order to understand how to deal with fractions that exceed the full amount (100 percent) in an inheritance question, when of course only 100 percent of an inheritance can be distributed. (This is essentially addressed to the way bankruptcy debts are covered, with a pro-rated loss to be shared equitably by all inheritors. A simple case is when inheritors expect to collect one-third + one-sixth + one-sixth + a half, respectively (requiring seven-sixths), wherein they will each have to lose a proportional amount of their share, collecting two-sevenths, one-seventh, one-seventh, and three-sevenths, respectively. The term of art for this procedure is 'awl—"share-overflow coverage.")

2 A qualified mufti in a town that lacks other appropriately experienced muftis may not refrain from offering solutions to cases that are given to him.

3 In contrast with #2, even a qualified mufti should refrain from offering an opinion or a solution to a case when under time or health constraints, or in similar conditions that may affect the quality of his reflection or possible research.

4 Questions that involve a linguistic element and knowledge of a certain dialect require a mufti who has mastered this dialect. (This is particularly important in questions involving contracts, vows, and promises.)

> That which you consider authoritative and apply in your worship and life affairs, of transmitting the view of dead authorities in legal matters . . . and take to be valid, and employ in your fatwas and rulings in the matters of property, marriage and other affairs . . . is unrecognizable to us, and no Imami scholar takes seriously . . . and this practice is invalid and no consequences ensue from it, even if a correct answer came out of it.
>
> Rasa'il al-Shahid al-Thani (d. 965/1558), Vol. 1, p. 6

In terms of etiquette, the questioner is expected to be clear and show reverence to the *mufti*, and the scholar/*mufti* is expected to be concise, decisive, and considerate of the questioner's limitations. The scholar may not simply relate juristic disagreements and leave it up to the questioner to choose the way forward. However, it is understood that the opinions of early authorities (dead authorities) are the foundation of answers to new questions, even as the new answers are constantly adapted to fit today's conditions and questions.

Ja'fari law has developed a more nuanced and interesting doctrine on the question of dead authorities. They hold that transmitting the views of deceased authorities, even for adaptation in new circumstances, is not acceptable. The study of texts is supposed to be a way for scholars to be trained, rather than for laypeople to learn what the law is or how to fit old views into new circumstances. The emulation of dead authorities, in what seems to be a simple format as Nawawi describes, is out of the question for Ja'fari jurists.

In practice, both Sunni and Shi'i authorities act in relatively similar manners. The *mufti* is supposed to be qualified to take responsibility for answering the questions of his contemporaries, and his studies always involve the study of dead authorities.

2 Social standards

In this section we will take a brief and broad sweep that takes in multiple aspects of social life, specifically: contracts, crime and punishment; charity (in this case, confusingly obligatory charity or alms). The following sub-unit (3) will address the family.

In European history one learns as a rule of thumb to distinguish a village or small town from a large city in that the village or town has *smaller streets*, operates with more *barter* (eg, exchanging vegetables for a piece of clothing) than currency-based trade, has *transient markets on given days* (the Wednesday market, not there on Thursday), as opposed to established, permanent shops, and that the town is home to people who know someone who knows someone . . . who knows you. Not all historical Muslim societies were small, though. People did not always know one another; when they did, this allowed a higher chance for the enforcement of public mores and acceptable good standards without the need for police or resorting to a court of law. Medieval Muslim cities were thus partly societies of strangers. Islamic law operated in both (urban and rural) settings. This is why it is untenable to pretend that all medieval Muslim societies were societies of virtue in a stereotypical European Christian villager's sense.

Premodern societies were certainly slower than modern ones. Traditional distinctions between male *v.* female, adult *v.* non-adult, and then robust adult *v.* ailing or "older" adult, those capable of good reasoning v. the mentally impaired or challenged—all certainly seemed so natural. *Their opposites seemed unnatural.* The consequences of these distinctions will appear in substantive laws addressing human interaction, marriage, divorce, child custody, inheritance, and even alms—or charity laws and market dealings.

Today there is still no dispute about rejecting the equality of those capable of reasoning and those who are not. Interdiction, an act that allows imposing the will of a person over his senile mother or father, is acceptable in modern moral and legal systems. Distinctions between young and old also seem to work universally. There will always be laws restricting the young from owning and disposing of property, from getting married and claiming parental rights over their children, even from driving mechanically operated vehicles and from drinking certain liquids when under a certain age. Bringing male/female distinctions to this discussion, by contrast, would be offensive.

From what modern people see as unnecessary restrictions on male–female interactions and a slow pace of life you will find that Muslim jurists have (in years gone by) developed theories of human nature that operate in their jurisprudence. This is the context for the laws that some modern Muslims themselves find in need of reflection and reconsideration today. For example, a jurist might argue that (in his view) women's natures means that they are more comfortable being at home than at work. Some might say that this is still true to a much larger extent in our modern societies than certain contemporaries want to think. It was a fact of life to a larger extent in the past, and it led to assertions about human *nature* as it applied to social life and standards.

Medieval Muslim jurists say that "silk" and "gold" are an inappropriate clothing choice and/or accessory for males. A Shafi'i (also a Mu'tazili) jurist named Shashi (d. 365/976) explains that this is what *nature* prescribes. Shashi objects to views that extend the logic of this idea and prohibit men from wearing clothes of certain colors that are said to be appropriate only for women (saying, for example, that it is reprehensible for men to wear yellow paisley or similar, colored patterns). Shashi (an Uzbek) says that social custom differs from one land to another and hence no prohibition may be justified beyond the prohibition of gold and silk. Gold seems to lend itself to use as jewelry (and currency), and silk is a material appropriate for women's garments (*Mahasin al-Shari'a*, pp. 235–40 (Beirut: Dar al-Kutub al-Ilmiyya, 2007), pp. 616). By the same token, more of women's bodies are often covered, he says, than men's, because male bodies are not apparent objects of desire. Women are not expected to serve in the army (and the *duty* to fight and the *prohibition* of retreating in the three cases of assignment by the authorities, a foreign invasion, and at the time of the battle itself) all apply only to male Muslims (Ibn Qudama, *al-Mughni*, Vol. 13, pp. 8–10.) Arguments of *nature*, in short, should not confuse *nature* with *nurture or social conventions*, as he understands the borders between these two realms.

The same type of reasoning is at work when nature tells Muslim jurists that a human being is an adult when physical signs of puberty are visible or otherwise detectable along with new physiological functions. It is puberty that distinguishes an adult from non-adult, rather than an age estimated by a number of lunar or solar years, be it 16, 17, 18, or 21. These jurists certainly recognized the existence of exceptions and labored to regulate exceptions. The yardstick remained physical and medical (more emphasis on the functional, *physiological*, and less emphasis on the *psychological* aspect of medicine). Many matters of civil and criminal law are directly affected by considering an individual to be an adult, such as adults' freedom to sell their house or competence to stand trial that might result in the death penalty. Questions such as underage marriage and the prohibition of same-sex relations fall under the category of reasoning toward prohibition from nature's imperatives, too.

> Call this the first law of the medieval social shari'a: *Equality among naturally unequal persons leads to injustice.*

The way people treat each other is also relevant to how a social shari'a is structured. In a traditional Muslim society, an individual is freer than a modern individual to *raise their children and arrange their household matters as they wish*. In the modern world, much of this has become matters of state jurisdiction and supervision. Children could enjoy free-range public presence in traditional societies. Again, some of these societies, while declining worldwide, have existed and continue to exist, including in the United States. This accounts for the persistence of arguments of this type to our day.

Claims of "*freedom*" are countered also by claims of "*freedom*," and claims of "*protection for the vulnerable*" are countered by claims of "*protection for the vulnerable*." What one person sees as freedom/protection for the vulnerable, another person may see as the exact opposite. To defend a traditional arrangement, you will hear those who speak of the freedom of parents to raise their children in a manner of which they approve, the freedom of children to roam around in the midst of the warm and supporting eyes of neighbors and the freedom of women to respond to their nature and refuse to be part of the rat race—all in traditional societies. Such claims might be countered by saying that cosmopolitan societies free women and children from their oppressive families and guardians. Traditional Muslim societies will also see themselves as sites of care and protection by the community for its individuals, especially the weak (eg, those taken advantage of in deals including duress, usury, or other forms of exploitation unaddressed in a system that trusts the free market to allow all supposedly informed agents to engage in free commercial and personal exchanges). Modern societies think they provide, via laws, better protection for all the classes that need protection.

2.1 Contracts

Medieval jurists disagree considerably on many points in contract law. There are contracts that include intolerable degrees of "absent" or "missing" information (Arabic: *jahala*), which render the contract invalid for some jurists, while others find ways to correct this absence either by reference to social customs or by demanding that the information be provided. There are disagreements about what constitutes usury in different kinds of sale deals, deferred or immediate, and currency exchange. But one cannot help but note repeated patterns and habits of legal reasoning, and these are shared by Sunni and Shi'i jurists.

These principles include first of all an acceptance of "*orality*" as (at least) a possible quality in contracts. Some contracts are documented in writing, and the Qur'anic verse (2/282) is emphatic about preferring noting all "debts and dues" regardless of size, but writing a contract is not a requirement. Another point of reference is *deferring to market and social standards* and what is familiar to merchants in the markets in which a case or a legal scenario arises. So-called "cash endowments," which are asset-less trusts that are based on continuous market activities and exchanges (*waqf al-nuqud*) were allowed in Syria but not in Egypt under later Ottoman law, because local custom had allowed it and regulated it in the

Syrian markets but not in the Egyptian environment. Non-Hanafi jurists also allow the reliance on customs and social standards in interpreting contracts and judging some of them to be valid or invalid. A third quality is *near-unlimited* freedom of contract. Since it is only near-unlimited, of course, it follows that there must be *some* limits, and these stem from prohibitions on injustice to which one party is definitely or more likely exposed (usury; *riba*) and injustice to which both parties may be subjected (ambiguity; *gharar* or *jahala*). Consent, in other words, is sufficient to enter into contract, unless there is *missing information* or the two parties *are not in equal positions*. Contracts unknown or undescribed in early legal literature (*ghayr musammah*) must be subjected to the same test of "justice" as early contracts if they are to be considered lawful sales, tenancies, partnerships, or industrial investments.

2.2 Consent, take one

A shared principle among the different *madhhabs* is that "silence" by an agent or individual cannot be considered a position, but silence in a situation that demands a statement possesses a legal value. This has significant implications for those areas of consent needed to consider contracts effective. In Hanafi law, if a man is silent as he witnesses the sale of property he owns, this is not indicative of approval, but if he is silent at the time of the delivery of the property to another person (who is then presumed to be a buyer or a debt-collector), the silence *is* indicative of approval. This principle is qualified by social customs, which may consider one's silence indicative of approval, regardless of whether this is argued to be the context for approval or not. (Ahmad al-Zarqa, *Sharh al-Qawa id al-Fiqhiyya* (Damascus: Dar al-Qalam, 1993), pp. 337–44).

In Unit 7 (2.2), we will revisit consent to cover revoking transactions based on Islamic law. These contrast to a degree with capitalist assumptions about the freedom of the parties, and the corresponding high degree of liability on their part.

2.3 *Zakah/zakat*:* The social and the economics

Tax systems are most developed in nations that have been to war frequently. This seems to be a principle one learns from European history: ancient, medieval, and modern. Islam's history, on the other hand, shows a consistent lack of standing professional armies and complex tax systems.

Following a seminal treatise on the topic that appeared in print in 1973, many modern Muslim jurists wanted to claim that *zakah* or *zakat* was a comprehensive tax system. The *zakah* is actually relatively simple, although its history is long, and its collection was relegated on occasions to the state. Islam is built on five pillars: a statement of the faith; five daily prayers; fasting during Ramadan; pilgrimage; and something called *zakah*. Now let us consider how this final pillar, which can be understood as almsgiving or obligatory charitable donations, is seen by Muslim jurists in both economic and social perspectives.

---

* Both "*zakah*" and "*zakat*" are used; *Zakah* is more correct and common, but "*zakat*" facilitates applying to money or property the adjective "*zakatable*"—comparable to "taxable."

In religious Islamic literature, you will read that both fasting and *zakat* bring poor and rich together. When you fast, you experience what the poor experience, and when you make a charitable financial donation (obligatory or supererogatory), you remember the poor and the needy. The poor are exempted from payment of *zakat,* but if physically capable, they fast.

One must have owned the property that is subjected to *zakat* for a full lunar year before the *zakah* is collectable, and the property needs to reach a minimum limit to be liable for *zakat* (taxable, in broad terms; we could use the term "*zakatable*"), and remain at least at that minimum for the whole year. When you pay *zakat,* you hand over a percentage of money you did not need. If likened to a tax system, it is a "surplus" tax or a *savings*-tax, rather than an income tax.

Money employed for business or commercial activities is also liable for *zakat*. In commercial activities, one may keep exchanging commercial property for another, and only when new "money" is generated does one start counting the year at the end of which the new money is subjected to *zakat*. The ownership of the property or commercial interests has to be complete, which is why jurists disagree about whether one owes *zakat* on property one lent or pawned, if the chances of the property being recovered are genuinely threatened. (Modern jurists broadly agree that *zakat* is collectable from money kept in standard banks.)

Now, what distinguishes alms (*zakat*) from supererogatory charity is that *zakat* is due in specific amounts, when the property hits a certain threshold. The simplest way to understand *zakat* amounts is to think of two financial regimes for it:

1. 2.5 percent for the value of items that correspond to gold and silver; in principle, any property other than animals and crops. The minimum counted in gold used to be 3 ounces or a little under 88 grams. This was estimated in 2015 by the Islamic Relief Fund (http://www.islamic-relief.org/zakat/nisab/) at about US$3,731. The Algerian Ministry of Religious Affairs suggested a sum of 395,250 Algerian Dinar (roughly US$3,754) for 2015. (Yes, if you have $4,000 sitting in the bank for a whole year, you would be paying $100 to the poor at the end of that year.) The silver standard hasn't been in use for centuries, given the excessive inflation it faced over time. The 2.5 percent is also the rate of *zakat* for commercial activities. As long as the "property" can be traded (currency, land, houses, animals, etc.), the *zakat* is paid at the end of the year.

2. 5 percent and 10 percent for the value of land harvest and crops, depending on used cultivation schemes: 5 percent for those who dedicate their own resources to irrigation and 10 percent for those who use natural, accessible water.

Animal owners have to follow more complicated schemes to pay their *zakat* that factor in the age, gender, and type of the animal. Their levies are normally close to (if not lower than the 2.5 percent level), and they typically pay in kind, usually from the same type of animal (eg, one sheep per flock of forty). Sometimes, though, lesser quantities of large animals are assigned a *zakat* value from smaller animals (one sheep per five camels, for example); in such cases the *zakat* is paid in camels when the owner's herd reaches twenty-five in number. Larger herds yield older, heavier animals in *zakat*. Disagreement can arise with regard to working animals (working camels, for example), with the majority excluding these animals from *zakat* calculations. This shows that the standard stipulation of animal *zakat* is that the beasts graze freely, and may be consumed or exchanged for another value.

The second law of the medieval social shari'a could be phrased in this way: *wealth should not be concentrated within a certain class of families (as in "those who normally have money to lend," but may be inherited from one generation to the next*. We'll get a clearer idea of this when we discuss inheritance later in this unit.

The collection of *zakat* in combination with state taxes has followed a range of patterns across different Muslim societies. In modern times, Muslim jurists have attempted to incorporate the discussions on *zakat* with taxes, thinking of the two as elements that serve an ultimately unified purpose. Modern re-articulations of *the philosophy of zakat,* as it came to be called, have arrived at the following principles:

1. For a certain property to be considered *zakatable*, it must be **subject to growth**. Jewelry used only as ornaments is not *zakatable*, for example, but should the same pieces be rented, they become *zakatable*.

2. The **actual growth** of the property is what determines the amount of *zakat* to be paid. This applies to house rentals, land crops, animal reproduction, and any other products of value in the market. An apartment that is sitting empty is not *zakatable* except for its value (since it would exceed the minimum required for *zakat*); the potential rent the landlord may collect if it were to be leased is not taken into account. (Good students will remember this as they read Unit 7 (section 1.4).)

3. A sizable amount of gain must be attained, and a full lunar year must pass *with this gain being intact* for *zakat* to be levied. As noted, *zakat* is basically a surplus or a *savings*-tax scheme, not an *income* tax system.

To get a sense of how some of the premodern assumptions are reconsidered today, take the example of *zakat* payable on agricultural yield or crops compared to merchandise-related *zakat*. Crops have been seen as *zakatable* at a rate of (5–10 percent). This is clearly higher than the *zakat* rate of merchandise (2.5 percent), because crops were seen as something of a divine gift, and were thus regarded as requiring less human work and intervention. A merchant sells goods and may have to travel to acquire them, while a farmer attends to a piece of land that he knows very well. In the modern world, this effort-estimate has been questioned, and even the lines between trade and agriculture have become blurred. A blueberry farmer from Bosnia argued in a question he posed to an *imam* in an Islamic center that he was essentially a merchant because he has to find a buyer for his crop with refrigerated vehicles so that it can be moved immediately upon harvesting; otherwise, the blueberries would be spoiled and be of no commercial value. Such questions have led to new views on how to calculate the *zakat* of these products.

The doctrines of *zakat* go hand in hand with the prohibition of exploitation through usury or contractual ambiguity. One must share his or her wealth when it is abundant (*zakat*), while one may not exploit others by offering them loans at interest (usury) or because he or she has a better grasp of how business dealings may turn out (exploiting ambiguity or shortage of information). In a Muslim society, government plays a role here; a Muslim judge will invalidate any contract that involves usurious elements or exploitation.

In this vein, we gain an insight into the prohibition on "selling to newcomers to town." The Arabic term is *talaqqi al-rukban*—literally *meeting those who just ended their trip*. The prohibition means that merchants in a certain town must not sell goods to visitors *until* the visitors have become familiar with the town's market prices. The idea is that the visitors, unaware of prevailing pricing trends, may over-pay for merchandise. On the modern assumption that all market agents are free, and unless demonstrably deceived, their sales are binding, this prohibition makes little sense. Its rationale in premodern Muslim markets, however, was to afford protection for those unaware of all the negotiating positions open to them.

> The second law of the medieval social shari'a: Wealth should not be concentrated but may be inherited from one generation to the next.

The discussion within medieval Muslim jurists on *government's ability to impose taxes and to what extent* complicates this picture. Some jurists simply assumed that governments did not have the right to ask its people to pay more than the obligatory *zakat*, citing a report in which the Prophet Muhammad states that "No sum may be taken from a property, except *zakat*." Most jurists disagreed with this broad prohibition but got on with a discussion on reasonable and unreasonable amounts of taxes. Their ceiling of what was "reasonable" tends to be way below modern tax schemes, but one must also note that the reach of government services in medieval times was not as extensive as that enjoyed by modern governments.

Modern interpretations of these doctrines remain fluid. This may, in part, be due to the volatility of current financial market activities and the lack of clarity on what qualifies as "value" in the current context. An aspect of *zakat* remains a local, piety-driven, and hard to regulate activity, except via the same simple rules that makes a farmer dedicate (in *zakat*) a heifer when he accumulates thirty cows.

2.4 Social standards, criminal law

Social laws include the criminal arena, as outlined in Unit 1. Criminal law is one aspect of public law where government inserts itself and exercises influence. In exceptional cases, the separation of these three notions of private law, public law, and public policy is violated, but under normal conditions they are separate.

There is a case I want to introduce here to make a few points. Taj al-Din al-Subki, a fourteenth-century Shafi'i judge, applied an interpretation unavailable to him in his *madhhab* (according to Ibn Hajar al-Haytami, a fifteenth-century jurist) whose argument may have been borrowed from Maliki law to execute on the charge of apostasy a troublemaker who had caused turmoil in Cairo. Haytami argued this was an aberration, since a doctrine to execute as apostates those who hurled verbal abuse against the Prophet's two successors is unknown in Shafi'i law, and must not be used by those loyal to their school of law as a precedent. (For independent jurists, the lesson here is that each school of law has its own limitations.)

This case has several implications. First is that social peace is under the jurisdiction of judges. In Islamic legal theory and practice, judicial discretion is considerable, as most crimes fall under a category of "no assigned punishment." In crimes *with* assigned punishments, however, borrowing legal policies from one school or *madhhab* to another can sometimes occur, especially where public policy and public interest is taken into account.

The second point is that this was a case where the explicit doctrine of the *madhhab* or school of law was seen as not serving an important objective that needed to be observed in this particular case, that is to say, addressing what seemed to be an epidemic of inappropriate attacks on the symbols of piety and authority in Islam at the time. This became a principle that (broadly speaking) still operates in modern times. The charge against this line of thinking is that it allows for casuistic and haphazard thinking. In point of fact, so-called "forum shopping" and casuistic reasoning can be done in many different ways. In the medieval tradition, the *madhhabs* were certainly more powerful than they became in subsequent centuries, but they were not the sacred cows some historians make them to be. Scholars did shift from one *madhhab* to another on occasions, and even within the same *madhhab* legal borrowing happened more frequently than is presumed. It is true that such forum shopping and changing could not be done frequently and on a whim, as it might mean that the consistency of the law was adversely affected. An explanation was always required, and an explanation that carried the day in one generation may not have been acceptable to later authorities. The predictability of the law, in any case, is a matter for other jurists to handle rather than an issue of what individuals expect the law to be.

3 Marriage, divorce, and the rest

For many Muslim jurists, women—especially adult women who run their families' financial affairs and control young children's education—have been presumed to be good with money. They are good negotiators, good planners, and possess good financial minds. This presumption has consequences; for example, women can be judges in civil matters or matters of property and contracts, as opposed to criminal matters, and have an independent financial legal personality from their husbands (hence their inheritance from their parents does not lie under the husband's jurisdiction). This is a factual rebuttable presumption, however. In other words, in reality, not all women are good with money (nor are all men, for that matter). Thus, in some cases (and we are back to medieval assumptions about women in their families) it may be demonstrated that a given adult female, even a mother or a grandmother with long experience in running her household, is unfit to run her own financial affairs. This requires additional rules, rules of exception, allowing, for example, procedures to carry out "interdictions" against them.

Standing in an ostensible contradiction with this is a presumption in medieval Islamic family law that women were not expected to "earn" the money they manage. Although they could work, they were not expected to. Women were also presumed to be the custodian of choice for young children, and since traditional families typically had a larger number of offspring than many modern families, a wife and mother might have struggled to lead two simultaneous lives whereby she worked *and* cared for multiple children at different stages of their lives.

The marriage contract was essentially configured with these elements in mind. In the simplest form, the contract had to be seen, like any other contract, as an instance of mutual compensation or exchange. Though marriage is "against the presumed original position of *being free* in human beings," the Hanafi jurist Sarakhsi (d. circa 500/1106) says, it is a good thing, all things considered. The benefits outweigh the harm. It is justified, as regulated in Islam, based on a confluence of many elements:

1 the nature of females makes them, as a rule, incapable of earning and supporting their children (according to medieval mores);

2   the need to fulfill human sexual desire;

3   the need to populate the earth and perpetuate the human race;

4   the need to do all that without a confusion of children's attribution to families or conflict between men and women, leading to conflict over sexual partners. There is not a clear alternative that fulfills all these goals.

The fact that marriages were built and kept alive based on emotions and attachment to children was not denied by jurists, but given that emotions are hardly a measurable standard, they were considered only in the context of marriage counseling, rather as concepts key to the contractual obligations side of marriage.

The marriage contract makes two obligations the responsibility of the husband: a dowry at the start of the marriage and continuous financial support during it. Against these the marriage contract establishes one duty that is divided into two for the wife: sexual availability (to go in the first instance against the dowry—in other words, be paid for by the dowry); and a continuous acceptance of fulfilling the husband's sexual needs for the duration of the marriage. This crude analogizing of marriage as contracts of exchange will come in handy as fuel for attack against medieval jurists when modernists and reformists such as Muhammad 'Abdu and Qasim Amin arrive on the scene in the nineteenth century.

Men are then presumed to be responsible for working in order to support their wives. A man is expected to provide housing, basic expenses, and in the language of Shafi'i jurists, he must provide his wife with the "self-care" tools she needs to maintain her appearance (oil, combs, etc.) Again, in reality, men were not always able to support their wives. Some were poor and married rich wives. In some cases, the marriages dissolved, when a man failed to support his wife and she failed to pick up the slack. The standard presumption, though, remained the starting point.

3.1 Contractual vagaries

As we have seen, in many Muslim societies, marriage was a contract whereby a man provided for his family and the woman took care of the house and the children. This built a relationship of equivalent compensation between a husband's provision of housing and expenses and a woman's domestic, sexual role. As noted, the husband was expected to offer a dowry at the start of the contract. Some jurists allowed it to be a symbolic gesture or service (eg, teach the wife something she did not know), but Hanafi jurists stipulated that the dowry be monetary. As the dowry questions spelled out above show, there is a presumed equivalence between half of the dowry and the limited access a marriage contract gives a husband and between the full amount of a contract and full sexual access (upon consummation). The double equivalence of sexual intercourse (vis-à-vis both dowry and regular, long-term provision for the family) has been a weakness in Islamic legal reasoning on this issue. This is despite assertions by major Hanafi jurists that the dowry is matched up against the first instance of sexual access (which is often coupled with discussions of virginity in many cases), and the continued, long-term financial support is measured up against continued availability after that first instance (Ibn 'Abidin, *Hashiya* (Beirut: Dar al-Fikr, 1987; a copy of Cairo edition), Vol. 2, pp. 329, 359).

To complicate this picture a little further, Muslim jurists did not require a woman to work at home for her husband (cook or do chores). She simply had to be "available" for her husband. This phrasing has some interesting implications in legal terms. It means that the husband provides sexual pleasure to his wife for free, but she provides this pleasure in exchange for a compensation of financial support. Hanafi jurists go back and forth on the limits of this arrangement. In the school doctrine, the husband may have a religious but not a legal duty to fulfill his wife's sexual needs (Ibn 'Abidin, *Hashiya* (Beirut: Dar al-Fikr, 1987; a copy of Cairo edition), Vol. 2, p. 259). This is based on a distinction between the contractual obligation, which places financial duties into his side of the obligation, and service or availability obligations on her side, but not vice versa: The wife is never obliged to support her husband financially (unless you follow an aberrative view by the Spanish Zahiri scholar, Ibn Hazm), and the husband is never responsible to provide sex on demand to his wife, although she could take him to court if he makes a verbal statement of abstention (*zihar*) from having a normal sexual relationship with her. Married women, then, may demand that their husbands not deprive them of sexual pleasure. Women are also able to nullify their marriage contracts if the man turns out to be impotent. One more anomaly: When a husband has multiple wives, he must be equitable in his sexual availability (the so-called *qasm* or *division* of availability at night) to his spouses. Hanbali jurists prohibit a man from being available at night with the "wrong" wife (Ibn Qudama, *al-Mughni* (Vol. 10, pp. 242–5)).

When Hanafi jurists found that many families did not find this model acceptable—women were, in fact, working outside of the house—they disagreed as to whether the man was still responsible for financial support. One of these jurists (al-Ghazmini) said that in such cases a man did *not* need to support a working wife, while others insisted that breaking the contract model based on exceptions was not a good idea.

Inevitably this issue became more difficult to regulate as time went on. Again, the simple legal presumption had it that a husband's financial support for his wife, covering housing and expenses as needed, was the husband's main contractual obligation, and the wife's availability was her equivalent obligation. This is what led to the disagreement about whether a working wife must be financially supported by her husband. According to this view, the dowry is nothing but an uncompensated gift by the husband to his wife. Later Hanafi jurists acknowledged that the dowry *was* seen as a compensation for sexual availability.

Things got even worse when a subsequent social custom (around the seventeenth century) held that a man paid a dowry while expecting the bride's father to provide furniture for the marital domicile, which he (the prospective husband) bought. This means that the furniture stood as a compensation against the dowry, which suggests that one element (the dowry) was compensated twice. A strong argument against this, however, is that the bride both owns her furniture and may take it with her should the couple divorce (Ibn 'Abidin, *Hashiya* (Beirut: Dar al-Fikr, 1987; a copy of Cairo edition), Vol. 2, p. 651).

Regulating marriage as an exchange between husband and wife has been subjected to the harshest criticism and been caricatured by modern Muslim reformers. And subsequent shifts in modern life have led modern Muslim nations to change the laws that are based on this "exchange" assumption. Yet the old institution has not gone completely. In their quest for change, modern Muslim jurists started with laws that assumed that a husband has supervision rights over his wife. Domestic abuse, they said, resulted. But we would be wrong to assume that domestic abuse was habitually condoned by medieval Muslim judges because these jurists were (normally) male. It was a hard balance for all involved. In the modern context, the model for a marital contract is still by no means perfect, and has raised some interesting questions about the rules based on it regarding issues such as inheritance and child custody.

The old inheritance system assumed that a male's financial responsibility bred financial gains in the case of inheritance, although, as noted, gender was only one factor in inheritance laws. Men were responsible for supporting their wives. If a brother and a sister were to inherit the same amount from their father, while the brother is expected to support his wife, while the sister is expected to be supported by her husband, giving the brother and sister the same amount of inheritance from their deceased father would be unfair. If a father dies, then, leaving two sons and four daughters, each son one-quarter (0.25), and each daughter also just one-eighth (0.125) of the inheritance. Cases like these, regardless of claims to the contrary, continue to give the impression that a man is always worth twice as much as a woman. The system is thought to date back to tribal times where men also bore the responsibility of paying "blood money" (money owed for the killing, intentional or otherwise) of relatives. There are, however, many irregularities in the inheritance scheme (cases where females collect more of the inheritance than male relatives), but the reasoning that men's higher inheritance gain is there to offset their higher financial burdens can be found (as a good-enough explanation of the majority of cases) in medieval and modern literature.

According to the same system, divorce leads women to be the presumptive custodian of their "younger" children and the men the presumptive custodian of the "older" ones. If there are young children, the male divorcee supports his divorced wife and her children. He also supports the old children in his custody until they are independent. What actually constitutes "younger" or "older" in this situations is still moot. Again, gauging standards of who is old and what a child is raised many problems for these laws in the modern context—the age of two indicated lack of need for motherly nursing, seven was considered an age of early distinction, and fourteen a presumptive age of puberty.

Just as it is wrong to assume that laws applied many centuries ago can apply in modern Muslim cities, it is also wrong to assume that these arrangements are purely historical and do not exist today. It is still true that inheritance and child custody laws are the fallback standard for lawmakers in Muslim countries (and not just in Saudi Arabia). They are also the standards by which many family disputes are resolved extra-judicially or away from the courts, normally with religious advice by someone who claims some knowledge of the religious law.

Ja'fari (Shi'i) law presents some interesting anomalies. It allows temporary marriage, for example. This is called *mut'ah* marriage, although some call it colloquially by other names (*sighah*). This institution made Ja'fari (Shi'i) law a target of attacks by Sunni scholars but was probably practiced by many individuals in what would be considered Sunni law and came, in modern times, to represent a solution to some new social problems, such as Muslim males' interim residence in a foreign land. Ja'fari scholars allow women to stipulate in temporary marriages that men support their wives, but its default is an agreement of temporary companionship, where the man is still financially liable for a dowry. Ja'fari scholars have always been, and are now even more, reluctant to allow this arrangement on a large scale.

> Q: If in the *mukallaf*'s [responsible human agent] country/city the common view considers *mut'ah* marriage as a slander or accusation in such a way that a believer is accused of being not religious and having illegal relations or even despised if he/she does it, what is the ruling, then?
>
> A: Although *mut'ah* marriage is permissible, or rather *mustahabb* (recommended) in our view, it is not obligatory in shar'. Therefore, if it leads to conflict, accusation or vile consequences matters that are not acceptable by the Divine Legislator, it is rendered impermissible for the *mukallaf* [responsible human] to be indulged in such a marriage.
>
> http://www.leader.ir/tree/index.php?catid=72 (retr. 9/8/15 at 1.43 pm Pacific)

The textbox includes an answer by Iran's Supreme Leader, Ayatullah Khame'ni, amounting to the doctrine that this practice may occur only in a social context that accepts it and understands its objectives. It has to be done in a Ja'fari (Shi'i) society, essentially.

3.2 Marriage and religion

The freedom to change one's religion is broader in Islamic law than the freedom to choose marital partners without regard to their faith. (There are in fact ways to get around the charge of apostasy and move from Islam to another religion, with or without immigrating from one's land, but it is harder to keep a marriage that violates the religious links between husband and wife.)

Marriages are restricted based on the religion of the spouses in two directions. First, a Muslim man is not allowed to marry a "non-scriptuary;" he may only marry a Jewish or Christian woman (or any other female of known scriptural religion), if he cannot or does not want to marry a Muslim. Second, a man owes half of the dowry to a woman he marries but divorces *before* consummating the marriage; following consummation, he owes her the whole amount.

In a major text in Hanbali and comparative law (*Mughni*, Vol. 10, pp. 5–11), the following scenarios are discussed. When a non-Muslim who is married to four non-Muslim women converts to Islam, assuming none of the marriages was consummated, the man owes each wife half of her dowry and the marriages are all dissolved. He, now as a Muslim, owes half of the dowry, which is due upon the contract, even before the consummation of the marriage. But the marriage cannot survive, because of the difference in religion.

Now, if one or more of the women converts to Islam after the marriage is contracted but not consummated, and the husband stays a non-believer, this marriage dissolves but the man owes nothing. You may have already guessed why. A Muslim woman could not marry someone of a different faith. And a non-Muslim man is not required to pay dowry if his religion or custom does not require it.

Hanafi jurists, however, are very clear that a non-Muslim woman who does not expect (based on her religion) to receive a dowry from her husband does not gain the right to a dowry by converting to Islam after the contract (Ibn 'Abidin, *Hashiya* (Beirut: Dar al-Fikr, 1987; a copy of Cairo edition), Vol. 2, p. 361). The disagreement is caused by whether one should only consider the party that has an obligation or whether the other party's expectation is also relevant.

When conversion happens during the marriage—that is, after it has been consummated—the marriage also dissolves and sexual relations must be stopped. Dowry is not an issue here, because it would be governed by the laws regulating the lives of non-Muslims (because they were so before and after the marriage was consummated). This leaves the possibility that all convert to Islam together, which is an easy transition into a condition governed by all the rules available to a Muslim *mufti* or judge.

Jurists disagree as to whether a waiting period should be given to the non-convert spouse to consider the implications of the change caused by the conversion. Many revert to employing the normal waiting period for a divorce, which is a period of three months (or three menstrual cycles), with an assumption that sexual relations are severed during this period. Some Muslim jurists may be happy to see the non-Muslim spouse convert and join the Muslim spouse, but they are also realistic and note that this waiting could be in vain. The legal imperative of deciding the rights and responsibilities of the partners in the marriage takes precedence over any "marriage counseling" considerations.

3.3 Family ties

In the MMK case described in Unit 1, we learned that natural and contractual bonds forming families lead to a cementing of the status of individuals vis-à-vis others. Some ties are temporary and others are permanent. When a man (X) is married to a woman (Y), he may not simultaneously be married to her sister (Z). But this prohibition expires when the marriage of X and Y expires. But when a man (A) marries a woman (B), her mother (C) may not be his wife at any point in the future.

We learned that fifteen categories of females are considered prohibited for men to marry. One of these is when two infants share a breastfeeding "*mother*"; this is an example of permanent prohibition. There are interesting extensions of this idea, but not all jurists agree about the extension. Hanafi jurists, for example, prohibit two infants who nursed on two different women who were simultaneously married to the same man. That is, when man (X) marries both Y and Z simultaneously, and both women breastfeed two infants (even without both infants breastfeeding on both mothers), those children are regarded as brother and sister and hence are unable to marry any time in the future.

3.4 Inheritance

Many would consider any legal system's willingness to allow individuals to bequeath their property to their relatives a way of perpetuating wealth within certain families. If one adds to this the fact that *professions* were also inherited in many areas in the Muslim world—where the carpenter's son is a carpenter and the doctor's son grows up to be a doctor—the prejudice that social mobility was basically not allowed in traditional Muslim societies is strengthened.

The inheriting of professions is not the norm Muslim cities. But it remains true that against the limited distribution of wealth allowed by the *zakah* system, there is a circulation of wealth within the family. Indeed inheritance by family members was still seen as the fairest way to transfer the property of a deceased person.

The Arabian society that witnessed the rise of Islam was a tribal one that believed in distributing liability of action among clan members. In cases of manslaughter (inadvertent killing) the victim's clan expected compensation (the blood money referred to above) from the

wife mother grandmother
full-sister paternal-sister
maternal-sister daughter
son's daughter husband
father grandfather
maternal sibling

SHARE-CARRIERS IN INHERITANCE

transgressor's clan, which was collected not only from the killers themselves, but also from their agnate relatives (son, father, brother, uncle, cousin, etc). When inheritance is distributed, this responsibility is taken into account. In Islam, as you learned, the responsibility to support one's family financially falls to men (husbands, fathers). These two considerations affect the laws of inheritance in Islamic law. One may say these conditions do not affect the system enough, and many female close relatives end up with higher shares that they would have, if the inheritance system were a strictly agnate-centered system (as opposed to enate—via the female side—or cognate—via both sides). In other words, Islamic inheritance laws as they stand seem to favor males over equivalent females (son and daughter of the deceased, for example) but don't do that consistently.

The Qur'an identified twelve inheritors as share-carriers in the inheritance: eight women and four men. In any inheritance case, there can be representatives from only eleven of these twelve categories, because one of them is the husband and one the wife, and the deceased has either a husband or a wife, depending on whether they are male or female (note that even though the deceased may have more than one wife, all such spouses must share in the funds allocated to the "wife" between them).

There are multiple ways to teach this subject based on a simple mathematical model, where one asks a series of questions about who are the inheritors, moving from those who payments are never blocked, to those whose shares diminish in the presence of other inheritors, to those who rarely collect any share. I will give you a simple formula that explains many cases. Look for daughters first. One daughter gets half of the inheritance, and two share two-thirds. Then move to spouses. With the daughter, a wife gets one-eighth and the husband a quarter. (If there is/are no daughter/daughters, the wife receives a quarter, and the husband a half.) Now look for parents. With two daughters receiving two-thirds between them and the wife one-eighth, the father of the deceased receives one-sixth and then collect the rest as if they were a male agnate (such as brothers and male cousins); a mother gets one-sixth. If there is a son, he gets twice the share of the daughter (or each daughter). The sisters and grandparents do not receive anything if they are added to the last case. The maternal brother or sister, an anomaly in the whole system, collects one-sixth notionally but is blocked by the father, receiving none of the inheritance.

Many will say: I don't get it. An example might help. The following case came before 'Umar b. al-Khattab, the Prophet's companion and second successor. A woman died, leaving her mother, husband, and one sister. The mother's share is a third of the inheritance in this case, because the deceased has no children; otherwise she would have ended up with one-sixth. The sister collects one-half, since the deceased had neither children nor brothers. (In many cases, the sister ends up with nothing.) The husband collects one-half when there are no children, and one-quarter if there are offspring. But hang on: one-half + one-half + one-third = more than 100 percent of the inheritance. Where will the surplus come from? Umar said: Suppose this was a loan that ended in bankruptcy. The debtors only get a percentage of what they are owed, based on what is available after bankruptcy is declared. Suppose, in other words, the deceased was a bankrupt merchant who owed an amount equal to a half of his inheritance to two people and an amount equal to one-third of his inheritance to a third debtor. What should they all receive? (*Qamus al-Shari'a*, Jamil b. Khamis al-Sa'di (d. 1840), pp. 244–5). The answer is that each debtor *loses* an equal percentage of his share. To apply this in the above example, the husband and the sister each get three-eighths instead of one-half (four-eighths), while the mother receives two-eighths or one-quarter (instead of two-sixths). Each share out of six becomes a share out of eight, and each heir *loses* an equal percentage of their inheritance.

Ja'fari jurisprudence has two interesting peculiarities that distinguished their inheritance laws from the majority. First, they allow the deceased to extract some of his possessions (normally his ring, or sword, or some of his personal clothes) out of the inheritance and give them to his oldest son. Second, they prohibit the wife from inheriting any land or house that belonged to the husband, *but* they offer her compensation equal to its value. In other words, she gets to collect the price of the house, but not the house itself.

If whoever outlives the deceased of the above twelve share-carriers are given their shares and the inheritance is not exhausted, the male agnates collect the rest. So, an uncle or a nephew receives what is left of the inheritance. Suppose a man died, leaving a wife and a full sister. The sister collects one-third of the inheritance, and the wife one-quarter of it. This leaves a little less than half of the inheritance for the male agnates. If there is still money left after the male agnates have taken their cut, we then move on to other relatives, and if none is found, the inheritance ultimately goes to the treasury.

Before dying, one can manipulate only a third of his (future) inheritance (directing it to a charity, for example), and this he or she can only give as a gift to those other than his share-carriers. Thus one might give one-third of one's money to a chosen hospital or a school, but one cannot make give a favorite daughter more than she is officially due from inheritance. This is true in Sunni law, as we said, and the exception in Shi'i law is stated earlier.

Online inheritance law tables and calculators are available online. For example:

1 http://www.saaid.net/book/11/3993.pdf or (Arabic version) http://www.saaid.net/book/9/2203.jpg
2 http://www.jdsupra.com/legalnews/table-of-inheritence-muslim-sunni-law-75662/
3 http://www.lubnaa.com/money/InheritCalc.php

3.5 Decency and entertainment

One of the striking aspects of Islamic law that persists with confidence into modern contexts is an emphasis on a notion of decency. This emphasis, in its extreme form, is employed to restrict entertainment to a minimum. Ibn 'Abidin's (d. 1836) treatment of the issue of moderation in food and dress shows a degree of relaxation unknown to the strict Islamic public mores regimes prevalent in the twentieth century, but he still thinks that entertainment is a subsidiary to serious actions, rather than a norm of equal value. You do not have to look for extreme opinions to find discussions of the prohibition of inappropriate looks (by men) and the prohibition of relaxed dress (by women). The same assumption that nature distinguished these two genders operates comfortably in legal and moral reasoning here.

Though a modern question, there is no disagreement that pornography is prohibited, according to those who speak on the authority of Islamic law. What remains of this prohibition in US law, by contrast, are elements such as the filmed sexual abuse and exploitation of children, as well as public display conditions. The notions of obscenity and even prurience struggle to find an area in which to operate. The arguments regulating propriety in areas of decent and indecent exposure and interaction have squarely shifted away from a simple emphasis on decency and are more emphatic on considerations of consent. In recent European and American history, access to pornography was restricted to the upper class, which was believed to be able to "cope" with such material, according to Christian Person (Christoph Knill et al., *On the Road to Permissiveness?* (Oxford, 2015), p. 103). This changed over time, as all know. A shift in this conversation in the United States was facilitated by the US Supreme Court decision (*Hustler Magazine, Inc. v. Falwell*, 485 U.S. 46 (1988)) that considered pornography to be protected speech, since images may be taken as speech according to a broad definition of it. The decision has made the Court an easy target of legal amusement, but it may simply be the case that societies without this First Amendment protection of images as speech have arrived at similar conclusions by other means.

Entertainment-prohibiting laws manifest themselves in *fatwas* or non-binding opinions and are not enforced in any meaningful manner. Abiding by them in practice, however, depends on the individual's piety. The next unit takes us to other personal aspects of the shari'a.

4 Conclusion

Laws #1 and 2 of the medieval social shari'a are: Equality among naturally unequal persons leads to injustice; and wealth should not be concentrated but may be inherited from one generation to the next. Reform-minded Muslim jurists who share these assumptions simply believe that the medieval jurisprudence stretched these laws, which are true in themselves, beyond reasonable limits. In its medieval version, the social shari'a deliberated on the following doctrines:

1. Men and women could not be expected to perform the same functions in society. Hence, men, in principle, work and support their families, and women take care of the home.
2. According to doctrine 1, men must support their wives financially.
3. According to 1 and 2, males may end up with larger shares of inheritance than female relatives—although this is not always true.
4. Men are in public spaces more regularly than women; hence, their testimony is expected in criminal cases, where exposure to criminal behavior allows them to understand it better.
5. Men are expected to be leaders in the community, but women are not.
6. Women may be teachers and *muftis*, because these functions do not require the same exposure to public spaces. (There is a degree of inconsistency in allowing women to be *muftis*, who are expected to have a good amount of social knowledge to provide solid legal opinions.)
7. Women from certain families may be merchants (the Prophet Muhammad's wife Khadija continued to be a merchant even after they married), patrons of scholars, etc. Regulating from this margin, however, is not done as a matter of standard thinking by Sunni jurists.

Review and reflections IV

- Family used to be a partnership based on men and women performing different functions in society. If men and women must perform similar or more similar than dissimilar functions, but men and women still want to procreate, which principles of old legal reasoning survive and which must be abandoned? Think about inheritance laws. Think about the laws of alimony and financial support by men for the benefit of their former female spouses.
- A Copernican or Newtonian revolution in family and financial affairs in society is not complete yet. Modern families still resemble premodern families in many ways. Review the elements that show the similarities. Can you state where families today are in comparison to the families of the past—if all is governed by Islamic laws? Think about care for children, concepts of adulthood, and rights of supervision over children.
- Do you think a Muslim state should be in the business of collecting and distributing *zakah* money? Why?
- Ambiguity in religious faith is not a new or modern phenomenon. Think of scenarios across different times and places where hybrid families may have coped with the potential for judicial and *fatwa* reasoning that may affect their lives based on the maxims and cases you learned here.

The midterm review sheet

The prospect of MMK's losing custody of her son or living as a pariah in her society may be specific to Saudi society. But in Islamic law, sex outside of the family is not allowed. There are, in fact, principles that most Sunni and/or Shi'i varieties of the Islamic legal system agree to protect. Review the sheet below and think of the general principles it states. Some of these principles will be followed without qualification, while some must be reconciled with other important principles. The principles take different forms and, depending on the argument a jurist makes, may take a broad or a narrow form. The essence of most of these principles revolve around a few basic and simple ideas.

In this sheet, some of the principles and maxims are stated in the format of an "imperative." For example, under "family" you will read "preserve female and male roles in the family" and "protect legitimate natural dispositions." You already know that many of the assumptions about nature here are socially constructed, but the jurists think of them as responding to a more original or simpler human nature.

There are other generalizations in this sheet that will allow you to recall the different modes of legal reasoning. Shafi'i, the founder of one of the four Sunni schools, thinks that reasoning from analogy is the most important mechanism for generating laws. He thought that *ijtihad* and *qiyas* may be interchangeable in many contexts. Other views that differ are also stated in economic language here.

Now, try to remember the cases that fall under or are associated with these legal generations and guidelines. Before you take your midterm, write yourself notes and references to the previous four units that go with these principles. The new material in Units 5–8 will crowd your mind with more information and make it harder to remember the details you've covered already. Don't delay this review until the end.

Family

- Preserve female and male roles in the family.
- Protect legitimate natural dispositions (eg, sex within a heterosexual family) and prohibit deviant ones [more on "law and medicine" in Unit 5].

Markets

- Avoiding contractual ambiguity (reconcile with) fulfill commercial needs.
- Avoid profit without investment (= no usury) [more in Unit 7].
- Protect those susceptible to deception (= no contractual ambiguity, no sale to those uninformed about the market).

Society

- The poor collect a small share in cumulative, saved wealth (*zakat*).
- Equating those naturally unequal is unjust.

Vacuum in law

- All human actions must qualify as good, bad, or neutral—that is, simply permissible.

Nature in law

- Keep natural bodies untampered with (reconcile with) allow needed medical treatment [more in Units 5 and 6].

Reasoning

- The essence of law is reasoning from analogy (Shafi'i view); law allows reasoning from and against analogy (Hanafi view); law judges actions based on inherent qualities (Shi'i view); law is texts (Zahiri view).

Rights of God

- Responsibilities toward God beyond the normal capacity of humans are to be forgiven [Unit 5].

5 The Personal Shariʻa

There are two qualities in Islamic legal reasoning that apply to the personal side of the shariʻa, one confirming *the limits* of the personal laws (in relation to social laws) and the other the *power and comprehensive nature of* personal laws.

Therefore, on the one hand . . .

John Stuart Mill, whom you may or may not have read, quotes from the Roman historian Tacitus as follows: *Deorum injuriae Diis curae* (offenses to the gods should be compensated only by the gods). In an Islamic context, the law is concerned with remedies for offenses against God. In other words, these are not to be ignored or left to God Himself to compensate. Not only that: In Islamic legal reasoning, the rights of God compete with the rights of humans. But something important remains of the spirit of the Latin saying in the Islamic juristic tradition, which is that: first, a degree of "forgiveness" is applied when pure rights of God (eg, prayers and fasting) are violated; and second, the rights of humans are given priority over the rights of God (*huquq Allah mabniyya ʻala al-tasamuh*—a statement that comes up when God's rights and human rights compete). Hence, making up for obligations regarding prayers or fasting that have been unfulfilled or ignored for years, and which may simply be too burdensome to fulfill, is not required; debts to humans take priority over a vow to pay a large sum in charity; and so on.

. . . and on the other hand

The most difficult thing in assigning God's rights the status of being "supererogatory" or secondary all the time is that these rights overlap too much with human rights. As you learned in Unit 3 (section 1.1), Islamic legal reasoning aims at regulating "actions," and human *actions*, rather than human rights, are the proper subject of the law. But Muslim jurists understand and think deeply about rights and have classified these into rights of God and rights of *His* (that is *God*'s) servants. The classification is analytically, and in some cases practically, helpful (eg, the fact that the inheritors of a murder victim get to forgive and spare the life of their relative's killer shows that their right trumps God's rights), but it does not work all the time. Hence, a good human being is simply unable to trivialize God's rights and be simultaneously kind to humans. This overlap strengthens God's rights in some cases, just as its absence diminishes them in others.

There are aspects of the shariʻa that would apply in a Muslim's life, even if s/he were to live on an island, like the main character in Tom Hanks' movie *Cast Away*. And these are not necessarily always less or more important than the rest of the law—especially on the level of popular opinion among practicing Muslims. Some Muslims may argue that the four principal rituals of Islam—prayers, fasting, alms, and pilgrimage—are the most important of all religious obligations, because they are seen to account for four of the five pillars of the religion. Some may also believe that dietary laws, such as the abstention from drinking wine and eating carrion (improperly slaughtered, otherwise lawful to consume, animals) and the flesh and fat of pigs, are among the most distinctive of Muslim practices. While these assumptions are disputed, no one would deny the importance of these personal aspects of the shari'a. Vows are also crucial; these are contracts with God, in a manner of speaking. These obligations are important, but as we learned earlier, they must be balanced against other obligations.

Come modernity

Personal laws today must operate in two areas. The first is where the national laws are *silent or indifferent*. Modern national laws will not, in principle, care where you send your children to school. They may not care how you invest your money either. As long as one lives within the limits drawn by the national laws, one may impose on herself or himself additional personal laws. The second area where personal laws operate somewhat unimpeded is where *national laws themselves attempt to accommodate religious beliefs and practices that arise out of these beliefs*, as we learned in Unit 1 (sections 2.1–2.5). Again then, the

Figure 5.1 The Sultan Hassan Mosque. Author: Ahmed Al.Badawy. Image accessed via Wikimedia.

personal shari'a has both a broad potential, emanating from its comprehensive scope, and an inherent weakness, emanating from its vulnerability to being trumped by the social side. We will see that personal laws have a way of benefiting from many gray areas in our lives today and a way of being submerged under pressing social considerations.

1 Legal but unlawful

Let us be explicit about the scope of this personal side of the shari'a. National laws or humanitarian international laws may simply accommodate or defend religious laws. In these cases personal law is given a space to operate, unimpeded and unaffected by other laws. We have already seen applications of this general point.

National and international laws may also explicitly grant rights or privileges to an individual, such as *the right to ownership or title*, but the option of relinquishing the right or title is also available to that individual. This may happen when someone follows a religious law that prohibits this ownership. A man may not be legally required to provide financial *support for his mother,* but he feels bound to do that by the religious law. Modern law may consider a certain transaction "legal" but a religious Muslim will avoid it because it is "usurious." *No-fault insurance* contracts may award a Muslim individual compensation, but he will hesitate to take it, because (for example) it was given to him for a malfunction of a fully parked car next to his, which moved and hit his car through no fault of its owner. A Muslim woman may be legally (based on national laws) free to rent her womb to another (in a surrogacy arrangement), buy another female's egg, artificially inseminate herself, sell a kidney, or give up her child for adoption, *but she remains restricted and unable to carry out any of these actions, owing to religious prohibitions*. A Muslim may avoid commercially available and legal food products, such as meat *improperly slaughtered*, because it is against her or his religious conscience. All these are real, rather than imaginary, situations. Islamic centers in the United States, Canada, Australia, Europe, and South Africa, amongst other locations, deal with questions such as these all the time. Personal laws do operate in many of these and similar areas, which are reductively seen as "ethical" matters.

There are, in short, scenarios and cases where an action may be legal from a national or international law standpoint, but which remains unlawful from Islamic law's point of view.

Modern laws do not comprehensively negate the category of "obligation arising out of 'natural'," as opposed to "legal" commitments. For example, contemporary French law states that if someone pays what he or she thinks is a debt they owed (which legal evidence does not consider to be an obligation), he or she cannot subsequently demand a return of their payment. According to Sanhuri, some French jurists understood this institution to appeal to a Roman law institution, which acknowledged that natural obligations (based on affinities between father and child, master and slave, and the like) are too important to ignore in cases when the formalities of the law would mean these obligations are considered to be non-existent. Some French jurists, Sanhuri also contends, understood this institution in Christian and ecclesiastical terms and hence more broadly. Modern civil law in Egypt, Libya, Lebanon, and Syria acknowledged natural obligations but allowed judges a high degree of discretion in supervising the fulfillment of them ('Abd al-Razzaq al-Sanhuri, *al-Wasit fi al-Qanun al-Madani*, vol. 2: Nazariyyat al-Iltizam, pp. 722–56).

1.1 Unlawful marriage, unlawful dowry

For Hanafi jurists, laws follow geography: In Muslim lands, Islamic laws are enforceable, but these laws are not enforced in non-Muslim lands. This is what Hanafis call "abodes theory" (*ikhtilaf al-ahkam bi-ikhtilaf al-dur*)—the governing principle being that many of the laws of Islam apply only within the abode of Islam.

So what happens when unlawful marriages take place among non-Muslims in a non-Muslim land? These marriages are valid if they are valid in the land where they take place. What happens when a man takes five wives? If the law of the land where he lives allows it, it is allowed. What happens if the dowry he offers to his wife is an object of no value in Muslim lands—say a company that produces narcotics or harmful objects? If this is acceptable in the land where they reside, there is no problem. But what happens if one of these individuals *converts to Islam and moves to the abode of Islam*? Calculations must be made.

A dowry that would be invalid in Islamic law, since it was accepted at the time of the contract according to laws dominant in its land, is deemed valid and will have satisfied its purpose at the time. This is true even if the couple converts; neither renewal of the contract nor a new dowry is needed. Having five wives, however, will not work out. If, as is usually the case, each marriage is separate from the rest, the first four marriages are valid, but the fifth marriage is invalidated. But what if the five marriages were conducted simultaneously, with one contract statement? The answer is that they *all* become invalid, and those involved in these marriages have to start over, as if they were never married. The same is true if a man married two sisters simultaneously, with one and the same contract statement, since marrying two sisters simultaneously is prohibited (Muhammad ibn al-Hasan al-Shaybani, *al-Asl,* Vol. 7, p. 486).

Another principle operating here, besides the geographic jurisdiction of laws, is that "consent" is carried over and has consequences, even after a move to the abode of Islam, *unless* the conditions it creates are physical and material conditions repugnant to Islamic laws. Being married to five wives or two sisters simultaneously is a state that persists after the move to the abode of Islam, which could not be tolerated. This is not true of contractual agreements that were concluded with proper consent and do not include a persistent condition that is abhorrent to Islamic laws. If all contracts concluded in a non-Muslim abode were questioned based on Islamic legal principles, too many of them would be invalid—an undesirable and unworkable end. This is why only the unacceptable conditions that persist after the initial consent are rejected once the matter falls under Islamic law's jurisdiction.

In all Sunni schools, a man cannot marry a woman and her mother. Hanafis stipulate that extramarital sexual intercourse with a female makes her mother and daughter unaccessible to marry for the man who performed this act. What happens if they all—that is, a man, his sexual partner, her mother, and her daughter—convert to Islam? This condition was considered so repugnant by Muhammad al-Shaybani that he equated it with marrying two sisters or marrying a mother and a daughter. It just can't happen.

An anomaly in this area reportedly took place when the Mongol emperor, Ghazan (also known as *Mahmud*), grandson of Hulagu and Genghis Khan, converted to Islam in the year 694/1295. Though Ghazan was known to be a believer who cherished rituals, such as the prayers and the fasting in Ramadan, he stumbled over one aspect of conversion. *Mahmud* inherited one of his father's wives after his death as his own wife, and he was fond of this wife. He was told he had to divorce her, because one could not marry one's father's wife after his death. He expressed consternation and, it seems, reconsidered his decision to convert to Islam. One of the jurists found the solution in some kind of parsing. He said that his father's marriage to this woman was not a true marriage, because it was based on the false laws he followed. The Mongol king's conversion was thus completed, as he was able to reconcile his desire to become a Muslim with not being separated from his wife (Ibn Hajar al-'Asqalani (d. 854/1488), *Biography of Notables of the 8th Hijri Century = Al-Durar al-Kamina fi A'yan al-Mi'ah al-Thamina*, (Beirut: Dar Ihya' al-Turath, 1993), Vol. 3, pp. 212–13).

1.2 Keeping your side of the contract

Shaybani also believed that when a Muslim individual makes a commitment to a non-Muslim state, this commitment could not be breached by the same individual, even if the state itself violated it. The view stated here is not a matter of consensus, but let's explain Shaybani's logic. In questions of dealing with non-Muslims, whether state actors or individuals from another country, Shaybani always asked himself what would happen if the non-Muslim became Muslim, then reasoned backward. A series of questions went as follows. ("I" indicates the interlocutor and "MS" Muhammad al-Shaybani.)

- I: What if a Muslim's concubine is seized by an enemy, while its [Muslim] owner was allowed to visit this land as a merchant or based on some kind of agreement (*aman*), is he allowed to take her away [by force or trick]?
- MS: I would not recommend that (*akrah lahu dhalik*).
- I: And you would not allow him to cohabit with her?
- MS: Yes. I do not recommend it.
- I: Why?
- MS: Because they seized her.
- I: What if she was free, a mother (*umm walad*; a person who cannot be sold and is automatically freed upon the death of her owner) or stipulated to be freed upon his death (*mudabbara*) or even his wife?
- MS: In all these cases, he is allowed to take the woman (*kull shay' min hadha fa la ba'sa an yasriqahu*) . . . don't you see that if they [those who seized her] were to convert to Islam, they would keep the concubine, with no recourse to her owner, but the free and all those whose freedom is pending upon their owner's death are to be returned to their families?
    Muhammad ibn al-Hasan al-Shaybani, *al-Asl/al-Mabsut* (Vol. 7, pp. 455–6)

2 The personal realm

2.1 Religious equilibria

There is a side of legal reasoning that digresses into whether a balanced life must end up not being a life that skirts very close to violating the law without actually doing so. That is, not becoming a bad man who ostensibly follows the law all the time but comes close to breaking it; in other words, this is someone who follows the letter of the law but not its spirit. This "bad man theory of the law" is one of the treats of American (judicial) jurisprudence. In a famous speech titled "The Path to the Law," Justice Oliver Wendell Holmes (d. 1935) developed this theory to explain how the law works in real life and how people follow it. The way to predict the law, he thinks, is to avoid all talk of ethics and think about the bottom line (for bad men, it is staying out of jail and avoiding to pay a fine; their question of how to follow the law is then how could one behave and *stay away from trouble*).

Stratagems that kept Ghazan among the believers aside (section 1.1, above), Muslim jurists by and large do care about ethical behavior and even proper etiquette. In Hanafi texts, a chapter is titled either the chapter on "prohibitions and permission" or the chapter on "*istihsan*," a word that simply means seeking the right way. The content features diverse discussions about the limits of good behavior and where one may go wrong. If you remember (Unit 2, section 2.1; Unit 3, sections 2.2–2.5), *istihsan* was the mechanism by which exceptions to rules (derived in *qiyas* fashion) were made, and its applications certainly go beyond personal piety or balance. But as far as it overlaps with "prohibition and permission," the side of it that is relevant here is when an accountable Muslim may go wrong, too far or too short, of the correct mark.

What are examples of this balance? We all know that one must eat in order to survive. But how much and what kind of food? Islamic law, with limited prohibitions on pork, other dirty animals (such as chickens fed on trash), and wine, is overall a laissez-faire system. But should one be allowed to simply gorge themselves on good food? Muslim jurists would not go for that. Excess generates excess, and excess in eating may lead to excess in sleeping or abandonment of one's duties.

If you are not too tired of my invocation of nature in the previous unit, one more comes here. Should one need to drink something normally not permitted, and it had to be either wine or urine, the author of the *Taratkhaniyya* states that the first is the correct option. A mix of legal and psychological standards are at work. The same law of balance (about needed and excessive clothing) is stated (Ibn 'Abidin, *Radd al-Muhtar*, Vol. 6, pp. 338–9).

This notion of balance has broad applications. This may seem tedious in a postmodern, twenty-first-century world, but appears time and again in Islamic legal texts. Balance in clothing, and balance in entertainment, are desired. In Unit 4, we already hinted at the social aspect of this balance, where clothing for males and females differs, and where ornaments are seen as befitting a female more than a male (remember what we said about silk, gold, and precious stones.)

Etiquette also appears in some of the long legal commentaries. In the same source and the same chapter, readers learn that one is advised not to address one's father by his name directly, and the same goes for a wife addressing her husband. One is also advised to speak Arabic, unless another language is needed for communication, and not speak too much in the mosque, during a funeral, and during sexual intercourse. One is also advised not to put an ornament on a male child, or tell them stories that are absolute fantasies (compare Plato's dislike of epic poets for their ability to market the fanciful as real, which causes these two to be confused in some people's minds).

2.2 Privacy and contra-judicial religious personal law

Four witnesses must testify to the act of coition to establish the guilt in a fornication or adultery case. An individual's testimony for or against a close family member (especially parents and scions, ie, father, mother, son, daughter) is not heard in a court of law, according to many Sunni and Shi'i jurists. One may refrain from offering a testimony after a promise of confidentiality, according to some Hanafi jurists. These are social laws that make sense in a context where the court of law is run by those who are bound by Islamic legal doctrines, but they also institute personal laws of an important character. These and similar doctrines make a strong case that privacy is protected in principle, although there are notable exceptions.

The clashes of social and personal laws caused a stir among Sunni jurists. Shafi'i jurists argued that God's law does not change because a judge got a case wrong. The adversary who is forced to follow the wrong law, issued by a judge, may still follow the correct religious practice and reject the incorrect ruling. Hanafi jurists argue that the judge's decision reveals what God's law is in the case. The standard example in their debates is a woman who denies being married to a man even though two witnesses have established her marriage. A reported tradition had it that 'Ali ibn Abi Talib adjudicated a case of this sort based on available evidence, but the woman said *since she was not actually married to the man, despite the apparent evidence* (she believed the witnesses were lying), *'Ali should now marry her off*—so as to, at least, have her be with the man with a clear conscience. 'Ali said "your witnesses did marry you off."

Hanafi argued that presence of witnesses and the judge is all that is required for this marriage to have been seen as valid. If you want an extreme legal scenario making this point, take this one. A man, having caught his wife cheating, knows full well (as she does) that she is guilty of extramarital sexual intercourse. She denies it before a judge, however, who separates them (after the *li'an* procedure, which is beyond the scope of this unit). Afterwards, Shaybani says, they are separated, even though they both know that procedure did not bring up the correct facts (Shaybani, *al-Asl*, Vol. 12, p. 8). Hanafi jurists certainly require the "winner" in an adversity to refrain from receiving any advantages from a court decision he or she knows to be faulty. The loser, they think, has no choice. Shafi'is disagree and reprimand Hanafis for the implications of this appalling doctrine. Two models of reasoning came out of this debate, one side thinking that God's law is simply revealed through the judge's decision, and the latter continuing to state that personal and social laws may indeed conflict in one and the same case.

Re-read the sections on the possibility of conflicting and equal arguments in Unit 3 and compare these two debates. Do they overlap? After this unit, a translated text from an Ibadi source addresses whether God's law must be one and the same in each case or whether it could be multiple.

3 Rituals and dietary laws

As noted above, four key rituals in Islam are considered pillars of the religion. There are five pillars overall:

1. a "statement of faith" (No God but God and Muhammad is His last messenger);
2. five daily prayers;
3. fasting in Ramadan;
4. paying alms for significant amounts of savings arising from property that may enter into trade and acquire higher value (such as currency, livestock, crops); and
5. pilgrimage to Mecca, once in a lifetime, for those financially and physically capable.

Two facts must be noticed here: First, the rituals are important; and second, the rituals are regularized. All the social activities of a Muslim we discussed in Unit 4 may be important, but they are not pillars of the religion. And none of these activities, except the rituals, have the quality of occurring repeatedly. True, pilgrimage is a once in a lifetime requirement. But those physically and financially able may elect to do it more than once (although space would limit the number of people who can make it inside the precincts each year), and those who do not go to Mecca can participate from a distance in some of the activities by either making an offering (an animal) available to the poor or by receiving such an offering from affluent neighbors or family members. The regularity of alms and fasting (both annual), at least for those capable financially and physically, is obvious. And the regularity of the prayers for most Muslims is not in question.

Muslim jurists have agreed that anyone who denies that the five daily prayers are compulsory is a non-Muslim, ie, as good as an unbeliever. They have disagreed as to whether someone who concedes that they have failed to perform an obligation for whatever reason—laziness, lack of time, etc.—is or is not a Muslim. (Appendix I reproduces a version of a debate between Shafi'i (d. 204/820) and Ahmad Ibn Hanbal (d. 241/856), the eponymous founders of Shafi'i and Hanbali law about this matter. The argument attributed to Shafi'i is that if we encounter an unbeliever who professes the *shahada* or statement of faith in God and the Prophet Muhammad and who is considered an unbeliever for failing to perform a ritual, we must find a way for this person to become a Muslim, and neither repeating the statement of faith, nor actually doing the prayers, will serve that purpose. Shafi'i thus makes the case that this person is simply a Muslim.) In Unit 1 (sections 2.1–2.5), we saw an application of how conflicts between prayer times and work schedule can be resolved.

The prayers are also symbolic of dedication, and the ablution that is required before the prayer represents the (bodily and spiritual) cleanliness of the worshiper who performs the prayers. One may perform more than one prayer with the same ablution, unless it is breached by a list of acts, about which we need not worry too much here. But take it that, if one uses the bathroom, the ablution is breached. Here is an application of one of the maxims you read about in Unit 4. Remember *doubt cannot remove certainty*? One of its applications is that, when one is certain one had proper ablution for the prayer an hour ago but is not sure whether the ablution was breached [whether one went to the bathroom], one is presumed ready to conduct the prayer and does not need an additional ablution; if one was sure to have visited the bathroom an hour ago and cannot remember whether one has performed the ablution since, one is presumed in need of ablution.

Alms, or *zakah*, as we discussed in Unit 4, are collected annually or at the time of harvest. The point in imposing it annually is that a passing of one year shows the true amount of saving for an individual. When a full year passes, and a person does not use a substantial amount of the income made in this year, this amount is subjected to *zakah*. Just as the fasting is supposed to make you think of the hungry in a personal way, *zakah* is supposed to make you think of the poor, in a practical and social way.

Pilgrimage is associated with three stories. First is the story of the building of the Ka'ba by Abraham/Ibrahim and his son. Second is Abraham's "alternative sacrifice animal" which saved the life of his son (Isma'il in the Islamic tradition, if we ignore exceptional voices such as Tabari (d. 310/923)). Third is the story of the search by Hajar, Ismail's mother and Abraham's concubine (the Bible calls her simply *isha,* or woman of Abraham), for water for her son, Ismail, which pilgrims commemorate by a movement back and forth between two little hills. Pilgrimage is performed on the days eight to thirteen in the twelfth month of the year. In circumstances not allowing the pilgrim to spend all six days in pilgrimage, a short visit of two to three days is allowed, if additional animal sacrifice is offered and certain conditions are met. Let us say a couple more things about devotion overall, then about fasting and diet.

3.1 Law v. devotion

There is a whole class of literature on devotion, in which the mystics excelled, that accuses legal discussions of the rituals as impoverished. Well, how can any reasonable person dispute that they have a point? However, since prayers, vows, etc., are human acts, they had to be regulated by the shari'a. The essence of *devotion*, though, is certainly not captured by this treatment. It is one of many limits of the religious law.

The religio-legal view of the prayers looks at ablution, its prerequisite, and the pillars (acts) of the prayer, ie, standing, kneeling, prostrating, and being seated. What makes a single prayer "valid" has more to do with the appropriateness of the movements, silence, focus, and so forth. You can find videos of the performance of the prayers easily.

The Prophet Muhammad is the model followed by Muslim worshipers the world over. His example, however, may not be fully emulated. The Prophet was reported to exert himself in prayers and fasting. Sufi practitioners appeal to these high standards in fulfilling what is agreed to be supererogatory or non-required activities. All agree that generalizing this model to every believer is untenable.

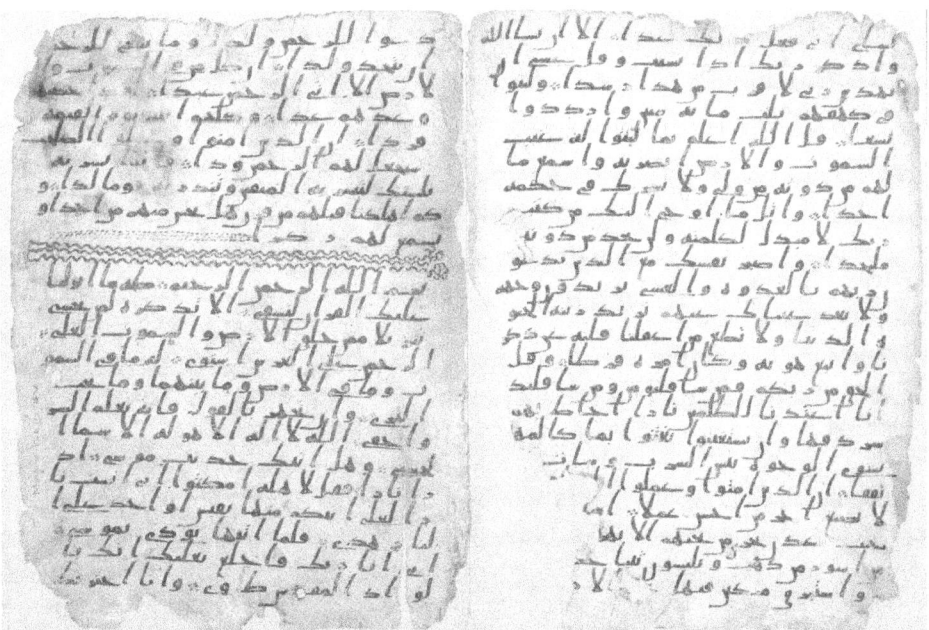

Figure 5.2 Seventh-century CE Quran manuscript held by the University of Birmingham. Image accessed via Wikimedia.

3.2 Fasting

The month of Ramadan is the ninth month of the lunar annual cycle. This is the month where Muslims fast from dawn to dusk, which in most places lasts from about an hour or so before sunrise and into sunset. Fasting means abstention from food, drinks, and sexual intercourse. Jurists, of course, got to work quickly, discussing what "food" means. Does the inhaling of non-nourishing materials by mouth or the taking of nourishing materials via a path other than the mouth break the fasting? Sexual intercourse is easier to determine, as you learned from the criminal law discussion on fornication and adultery. When preachers and Sufi teachers are allowed to enter the conversation, they keep this discussion "real" in a way, by insisting on the meaning of the fasting, its potential to draw Muslims closer to their spiritual goals, and focusing on the fasting of the heart from distractions.

The modern world's rapid transportation added new, interesting questions to the mix. A traditional Muslim is expected to spend most of the month of Ramadan in the same city or town. If this person travels during the month, the trips do not move him or her very fast to the end of the planet. But even in this premodern world, a move during the month raises interesting questions. What if a man begins his Ramadan in a land, which started Ramadan, say, on May 1st, traveled to another land that started it on May 2nd, and the land of his arrival ended up with a twenty-nine-day month? (Remember the lunar month can be twenty-nine or thirty days.) Would not this give this worshiper a twenty-eight-day Ramadan?

When you travel, you have the license to not do the fasting and to make up the day or days of traveling later. But a traveler may also elect to fast, especially in these days' luxurious traveling options. In the modern world, airplanes move fast. They appear to "trace the sun," where the day might become too long to endure. For those who reject the license to break their fast when they travel, the length of the day is a separate question. Some of these new questions can be answered easily based on traditional views, because similar questions occurred in the past. Long days have been known to occur where Muslims lived in northern areas in Europe and Russia. Other questions require fresh thinking, based on acceptable principles.

License to replace the fasting with feeding a hungry/destitute person is available by the Qur'anic text (Sura 2, Verse 184). The Qur'anic text here includes an anomaly, because its apparent language states that "*those who endure the fasting*" may feed a destitute individual. The exegetical and legal traditions, however, assume an implicit negation here, reading that "*those who cannot endure the fasting*" must feed a destitute individual. Supporting this is the view that the license to feed instead of fasting was abrogated as a general license and remains a license only in the narrow cases of very old people (who do not expect to become capable of fasting again) as well as women who go through cycles of pregnancy and breastfeeding and hence accumulate very long make-up periods of fasting. The same verse also offers "making up missed days" as a compensation for those who are "sick or traveling." **The Islamic legal tradition takes this combination to apply two different sets of compensations for missed days.** Those capable will be expected to make up their fasting days, as opposed to feeding a needy person.

Who gets to break his/her fasting during Ramadan days and make up the missed days? The categories deserving the license explicitly mentioned in the verse are the travelers and the sick, as noted, but the legal tradition expounds on this further. A dominant view limits "traveling" that opens the license to a long journey, to a distance between fifty and fifty-four miles, an approximate equivalent of a medieval distance appropriate for using the license. Until the Industrial Revolution, to the best of my memory of the sources, Muslim jurists did not contemplate a broad license not to fast because of regular, daily work. But the question of what to do in the case of excessive day length is old. Muslims in Bulgaria and similar areas in the north raised questions about prayers and fasting, given that the Islamic tradition assumes that: Days and nights are of regular length, stretching or shortening within limits according to the seasons; and days and nights are distinguishable with natural signs, such as the rise of "dawn light" amidst dark skies, redness in the sky before sunset, gradual diminishing of sunlight upon sunset, moon sighting, and the like. There were several views about how to address the absence of these signs and/or excessive lengths of daytime. One strict juristic opinion demands abiding by the fasting and prayers requirement even if the night was a period long enough to allow a normal meal and the night prayers. Three options offered to Muslims in these areas as license were:

1. fast according to a Meccan day (as if you were living in Mecca);
2. fast half the day (12 hours only);
3. fast with Muslims living in a land close to them where the day is of a normal length.

After increases in Muslim populations in areas where the day can be as long as twenty or twenty-three hours, however, this discussion was revived. The most recent debates show the dominance of two views among contemporary Muslim religious authorities (fatwa councils). The first is a license to not fast and make up the missed days during days of normal length. This goes back to the 1950s, when Mahmud Shaltut, the Grand Shaykh of al-Azhar, argued that fasting twenty-three hours out of a twenty-four-hour day went against the wisdom of the ritual. The second option, and one that is becoming an increasingly more powerful view, comes from the Jurists Council of Mecca (Saudi Arabia). This view distinguishes Muslims living in countries lying south of the 45° north line (above the Equator), Muslim living north of the 66° line, and those in between. Those living north of 66° north are allowed to shorten the day and do their fasting as if they lived in the closest town where the signs of the day and night and the progression from day and night and vice versa are discernable. Those south of 45° must fast, unless fasting, on a case by case basis, is considered impossible.

3.3 Diet

For a medieval Muslim jurist, the prohibition of pork and pig fat, on the one hand, and the prohibition of animals not well-fed (*jallala*) or not properly slaughtered (*mayta*) are in the same category. Pig meat and fat are prohibited categorically, as if the animal itself were constitutionally dirty. A goat that suffocates, having fallen from a peak, or from strife with another animal falls into the same category, as does a chicken fed on garbage for so long that its flesh itself becomes inherently dirty. Animals must be treated well, whether they are raised for work or for food, but prohibiting the consumption of animals is a position of a Sufi nature and does not comport very well with standard Islamic legal reasoning. If it seems to be anomalous to say that one must take care of animals and refrain from consuming animals that are not well fed, it is because there was no strong sense that human consumption of animal flesh was in itself an anomaly.

To be asked to abstain from a certain kind of food or drink based on anything other than (normally temporary) reasoned restriction from age or medical condition is seen as unnecessarily restrictive today. From one "law and economics" standpoint, Chicago economist Jim Leitzel made indisputably strong arguments that even the regulation of drugs, such as marijuana, has done nothing but exacerbate a problem that would, in any case, affect only a small portion of any population. He looks back at the alcohol prohibition years in the US (1920–1933) to prophesy a similar process leading to what he calls the re-legalization of drugs (since prohibiting them was the new thing, really). He also cites John Rockefeller, Jr., who abstained from alcohol personally but still thought regulating it was a disaster.

A medieval Muslim jurist is confident that drinking intoxicants is bad. One area that gave much fuel to (Islamic) analogical reasoning was the rationale of wine prohibition. Muslim jurists ask why exactly it is prohibited, and to what extent this prohibition should extend to similar substances. These jurists would certainly have a good day when the debate shifts to how substance abuse leads to date-rape and other appalling incidents. In this context, I must note that the strongest argument Muslim jurists deploy has to do with *the personal well-being* of the individual, rather than calculating the social cost of the consumption of intoxicants. Hanafi jurists assign punishments for "drinking" that does not lead to intoxication (*shrub*) and "being intoxicated" (*sukr*). These jurists think it is a divine blessing to be in sound mind and capable of reasoning. Mu'tazili jurists believe that reason is "sovereign" when they contemplate lawmaking, and you may have noticed (in Unit 2) that Shi'i jurists are keen on reason's capacity to distinguish "good" from "bad." Sunni Ash'ari jurists believe that "humanity" essentially equals "reason": You are fully human when you are fully capable of reasoning. These jurists disagree about invalidating contracts and other commitments made under the influence of intoxicants, many leaning toward punishing the intoxicated by making him or her commit to what they agreed to do while under the influence.

3.4 Vows

The standard medieval expiation for a failure to fulfill a vow is to free a slave (which is often a high cost), feeding or clothing ten destitute individuals, or failing that, fasting for three days. If the vow is seen by a jurist as frustrating to the capacity of the vow-taker, expiation is advised. Vows tend to offer some unusual cases of inequality among possible commitments. As I said earlier, they are part of the category of God's rights, which will not be ignored, but will take a back seat when in conflict with immediate concerns.

4 Science and medicine

Historians teach us that, when Islam came into and then spread out of Arabia in the seventh century CE, Mediterranean science was dominated by Aristotelian natural philosophy, Ptolemaic astronomy (or science of the heavens), and a Hippocratic/Galenic view of the human body. Educated people could believe in "perfect, circular movements" that operate in an exquisitely orderly cosmos and see health and disease as corresponding to balance and harmony (or lack thereof) among the elements (fire, air, water, and earth, manifested in the human yellow bile, blood, phlegm, and black bile)—without much worrying about cells or germs. Muslim scientists continued to contribute to developing and solving the problems of the sciences based on these ideas—until Muslim science screeched to a halt some time—with much disagreement among historians—around the seventeenth century. After that point, Euro-American science went through waves of evolution, moving into a mechanistic view of the world, and later into a sensibility-bound and romantic view of it before adopting an evolutionary approach to all and everything, while Muslim scholarship stood by the side watching, imitating the new, always a few beats behind, and less capable of comprehending what is going on outside of their narrow world.

The point we are supposed to draw from this history is twofold. When the world was seen via a premodern lens, many Muslim jurists contributed to their science of law based on assumptions *that pertained to their time*. You will see jurists who believe in atomism, for example—those who think that the world consists of indivisible atoms—explain matters such as the ritual purity of water when mixed with other, impure, substances with this theory in mind. They will also explain the breaching of one's ablution based on the theory of the elements, pointing to the structure of phlegm or vomit as they discuss whether this or that "excretion" should lead one to redo one's ablution for prayer. The second point is that, once the old sciences were replaced by the new but jurisprudence-based approach, these jurists' assumptions seemed to assume a farther distance from current assumptions about the world, and they lost their ability to make sense of it or teach it.

I do not think that all Muslim jurists took interest in the natural sciences; nor do I think that each aspect of medieval Islamic law was bound to connect to one of these areas of knowledge inquiry. In the modern context, traditionally trained Muslim jurists have resorted to general principles, principles of moral and social nature, to avoid having to work with the modern scientific world and its discoveries, its corrections and counter-corrections. Lay Muslim scholars who came to the scene in the past two centuries crowded juristic and moral reasoning with their view of the modern scientific approach. The resulting range is even broader than the older ones, and this goes beyond the strict borders of natural science. Even further away, the hybrid nature of Islamic finance is due to a reconsideration of the nature of money, in the face of, for example, the disappearance of the gold and silver standards that jurists employed as a reference point in their explanation of the prohibition of usury.

Let's conclude this unit with some cases of Islamic legal reasoning in which medical and scientific inquiries are involved.

4.1 Microscopic knowledge and the extent to which we ought to modify nature

Modern law outside of the Muslim world faces some of the same problems that Islamic law must also address in areas where the rise of modern "microscopic" data, or other forms of scientific knowledge, provides information that would have been unavailable in medieval society. For example, inherited laws assume that children of an existing marriage are attributable to the husband and wife only, and even an affair between the wife and a stranger can always be dismissed as an uncertain indicator of the fatherhood of the stranger. Modern science, however, might provide evidence of paternity that contradicts the presumption that a child of the marriage is attributable to husband and wife.

In medieval Hanafi law, if a husband accepts the paternity of his wife's children, even if husband and wife live apart, the children are attributed to him, and he owes them support. Today, innovations such as DNA analysis add a layer of complexity unknown in premodern times. Before DNA tests existed, the strong suspicion that a child of this marriage was not the husband's was the only indication one might have that paternity could be disputed. Today, however, the child can now be attributed to a specific individual. Modern Hanafi jurists may, however, still elect to insist that DNA evidence does not take away the right of a husband to claim his wife's children as his own, as if the evidence did not exist.

In the beginning of the twentieth century CE, early signs indicated that legal discussions would only heat up, as opposed to calm down, due to the rise of microscopic knowledge. In an inheritance case, a fetus deserves a share of his father's inheritance, when the father dies between the fetus' conception and birth. If the fetus is born six months after the father's death, the fatherhood of the deceased may be contested. It is not contested if the fetus is born *within* six months of the father's death. What happens if an ultrasound or X-ray image detects a fetus at a very early stage of development, and that child is subsequently born six months after the father's death? Ahmad al-Zarqa, a major authority from Aleppo, Syria (d. 1938), says it is not decisive in establishing the fatherhood of the deceased husband of the mother in the case, not because he doubts what the *Roentgen* image (he says) indicates, but because the image does not preclude the possibility that the fetus in the image ended in miscarriage and a new one was generated afterwards that was not an issue of the deceased (fathered by someone else, in other words). (Revising views such as these based on better understanding of what modern knowledge makes available certainly happens, but the point is that jurists do not simply relegate these matters to scientists. They bring up considerations and possibilities scientists do not normally think of.)

In Hanafi law, one may offer a gift or assign a share in one's will or an endowment in the name of an unborn child. Scenarios similar to this inheritance question are thus addressed. The question will not arise if the attribution of the child to his father is immaterial for the purposes of the gift. But if the gift, will, or endowment is contingent on this relationship, the fetus must be born within six months to earn its share (Ahmad al-Zarqa, *Sharh al-Qawaid al-Fiqhiyya* (Damascus: Dar al-Qalam, 1993), p. 81).

An impulse toward modifying nature by medical treatment should serve as a modification of the all-powerful notion of "*nature*" we considered in Unit 4. Questions of medical treatment are governed by two considerations that must be reconciled. The first is that seeking medical treatment, correcting the failure of the human body, is called for. The second is that "modifying" nature for no purpose other than cosmetic or personal preference remains undesirable. Removing a sixth finger differs from many new scientific endeavors in the biochemical sphere.

4.2 Organ transplants, surrogacy, cloning

From a simpler viewpoint, the overriding quality in juristic debates on biological and medical matters is a clash of a practical legal view against a theological one. The argument against organ transplants, made by a popular Egyptian scholar, M. M. Sha'rawi (d. 1998), is based on two elements. First, God is the only giver of life as well as the only one who can deprive someone of life. Second, the human being does not truly own her or his body and hence cannot either give as a gift or in sale parts of it. For those who accepted organ transplants, such as M. S. Tantawi (d. 2010), a rector until his death of the Al-Azhar University in Cairo, the question is simply a question of fairness to both donor and receiver. An organ donor can only donate an organ as long as he or she is not harmed, and an organ receiver may also receive a transplant if this is done in fairness to others who are similarly situated and in need of transplants. Those who accept organ transplants still disagree about financial compensation, its acceptability and its nature.

One of the most interesting bioethical inquiries that are addressed from the viewpoint of Islamic law is the question of surrogacy. Can a woman who is incapable of bearing a child ask another woman to host her fetus and deliver the baby to her? The view more common among Muslim legal scholars is that this is prohibited. The most religiously offensive aspect of this process is the fact that the surrogate mother hosts not only the egg of another woman, but also the semen of a male stranger. The mixing of lineages, or the misattribution of children to parents, is of particular concern in medieval Islamic law. Adoption that includes what modern vernacular calls termination of parental rights (TPR) is problematic for similar reasons. Even the Prophet Muhammad himself was reprimanded for adopting Zayd Ibn Haritha (of the Kalb Tribe) after his father's absence (Q 33/40), and the adoption was revoked.

More lenient views are adopted in the area of abortion, which is believed to be needed in the interest of the mother's life. When there is real danger to the mother's life, there is no disagreement that abortion is in order. In fact, the mother is not allowed to expose an existing life (her own) in the interest of an probable life (the newcomer's). Less unanimous are Muslim jurists on abortion when it is a matter of saving the pregnant mother from threats to her well-being. On the most extreme end of leniency is a view of Abu Hamid al-Ghazali (d. 1111) that, especially in the early stages of a pregnancy, undesirable conditions, much milder than illness, many be sufficient reason for abortion.

Underlying the distinction between "early" and "late" pregnancy is a religious belief that the fetus is *ensouled*—that is infused with a soul—after four months of the pregnancy. The Prophet is said to have described the fetus' early evolution (in the first four months) into three stages, each lasting forty days: first as a combination of semen and egg; second, as a small clot of blood sticking to the womb's wall; and third as a cluster or a lump the size that fits within the mouth (as if a piece of flesh one may chew on). Then, the Prophet is reported to have said that an unidentified angel infuses it with a soul and states its destiny in four matters: Its livelihood/gains; its lifespan; all its actions and deeds; and its fortune and misfortune.

Cloning, even for those who see it as religiously repulsive, is not looked at unfavorably for its capacity to make human beings compete with God in "creating" any living beings. A 1997 gathering of Muslim jurists in Casablanca, Morocco, condoned cloning in the case of animals. A major contemporary scholar, Y. Qaradawi, later condoned it if it applies to organs or parts of the human body, but not to the whole body.

In these and other fast-moving areas, jurists function under a degree of stress. Some of them categorically oppose what they see as the monopoly on human knowledge (including moral and legal knowledge) by scientific (ie, inductive, observation-based interpretations and generalizations of natural, human functions, leading to correctives of old assumptions about human nature). Some attempt to reconcile new knowledge with the old. The latter stance is responsible for some of the most creative hybrids in contemporary Islamic legal reasoning.

5 Conclusion

The personal aspects of the shari'a are harder to study than the social aspects. "Licenses" that allow the mitigation of the obligations of religious law may be used by some individuals in certain circumstances and refused in others. For example, an individual Muslim may elect to skip fasting in a Ramadan day or shorten his or her prayers and combine them while traveling, but he or she may also elect not to take the same licenses while traveling. The personal side of the shari'a, as studied in this unit, allows us to see that:

1. Daily prayers and dietary laws are areas of the law where "explanation" runs thin. Revelation, rather than reason, provides the strongest foundation for the laws in these areas.

2. Applications of the religious law in areas affecting the integrity of the human body, and the concept of the human soul, stand up against requirements to attend to the need for health and to provide medical treatment to those in need of it.

3. An individual Muslim within a non-Muslim majority has a lower expectation of personal autonomy and the capacity to abide by Islamic law.

Review V in questions

- What is wrong with selling a kidney?
- Laws follow geography. Does this mean that Muslims in Europe should not fast in Ramadan?

Notes

- Hanafi and Shafi'i jurists agree that social customs must be accommodated to a degree, but Shafi'is were less accommodative of "incorrect" or deviant social norms.
- The standard of obeying nature's laws appears in many of the personal shari'a's provisions. Moderation in seeking pleasure, respect for the human body, and lack of attachment to unnatural beauty are examples of ideals behind the laws. In some religious literature, what appeared to be moderation for old societies is closer to austerity or asceticism to moderns.

Materials for reflection

- If someone (Muslim or not) confesses to a Muslim that he committed an offense, does the one who heard the confession get to recuse himself from testifying in a court of law about it?
- When wine is transformed into vinegar, it is consumable. This is because the substance of wine has been removed, for juristic purposes, and the liquid could not be said to be prohibited. Jurists also argued that there are cases where a pig's body can be overwhelmed by other elements and transformed in a giant salt-maker, whereby it is said to have become salt and hence consumable. Could the inherent qualities in pigs, for those who believe the prohibition of its consumption is explicable, change such that its prohibition ceases to apply?

Primary source material II (Ibadi Legal Compendium)

Source: Jamil ibn Khamis al-Sa'di (nineteenth century), *Qamus al-Shari'a al-Hawi li-Turuqiha al-Wasi'a* (lit. *A Dictionary of Islamic Law, combining its Multiple Paths*) (Muscat: Oman Ministry of Endowments, 1983), Vol. 2, pp. 7–14. This is a ninety-volume sourcebook by an Ibadi author-collector, with multiple voices arranged by subject, with a degree of overlap among its subjects and some repetition.

Is God's truth one or multiple?

[Author's Title:] On Practical Legal Matters and Reasoning Leading to Answers to its Questions (*Ijtihad*)

Some Hanafi jurists said: Each qualified scholar of the law who aims to answer practical legal matters cannot be said to be incorrect in his effort and his answer to the questions he answers, and will receives a reward [from God]. Malik's view was a matter of contention.

The correct view is that exerting effort in the research for God's law (*ijtihad*) is a requirement, and a reward for those who do it is assigned when they get the result "right"—the reward is assigned to them for getting it right, conveying the correct ruling, and passing a court decision [when the scholar is a judge] according to it. But if the scholar gets things wrong, he receives reward for his effort, except that there can be no reward for extracting a mistaken view. [The reward is for the effort; there is no reward for the wrong conclusion.] This is supported by the saying of the Prophet: "When a judge (ruler; *hakim*) rules correctly, he receives two rewards, and if he judges wrongly, he receives only one reward." [End of Prophet's statement.] Don't you see that he made the scholar deserving of a reward for his "hitting" the correct view and a reward for his effort, and he made the judge deserving of a reward if he gets the conclusion wrong but forgave him for his mistake?

Shafi'i was also reported to have articulated this view, which is the best of all views on the matter. Note, however, that some reported him to have given a different opinion, but the report we forwarded is more authentic. Those who rejected reasoning from analogical reasoning [ie, Zahiris and Mu'tazilis] argued that the correct view can only be one—that is true in any matter in which there is disagreement. Those who arrived at the correct view [in any legal question], which is hinted at by God, is correct, and those who deviated or went in another direction are wrong but forgivable. This is the view of Ibn Abi 'Abla* (d. 152/769), al-Asamm (d. 279/892), Bishr al-Marisi (d. 218/833), and Ibn al-Hasan (d. 143/762).

[The author now turns to the best arguments of his opponents]

Some scholars say: The correct view *consists in* all these [reasonable] efforts. No sin is assigned unless one withholds the results of his research and effort or gave an opinion that is not what he holds to be true. This is because God made it an obligation for all those capable of doing the research to make an effort. When each one does his or her best, he or she may have observed a consideration that is different from those considerations that others took into account. This is the duty God gave each one [the effort, that is], and if he or she were to hide

---

* Text reads "Ibn 'Abla."

the conclusion [or alter it], he would have fallen into sin. This is true even if the consideration one takes as a basis for his view leads to what is in God's eyes an incorrect conclusion. Since the scholar falls into sin only if he hides his view, abandons the research, conveys a view he does not hold, then it is true that God could not hold the scholar to be sinful; God could not consider the scholar sinful, if the latter propagated what he believed to be true. Rather, God rewards him for it—no matter what. If God rewards the scholar for what he did, the scholar's conclusion is then "the correct view" [for this scholar]. Does not God see him as sinful, were the scholar to hide what he concluded? He must then reward him for publishing what he concluded. Is it possible for someone to be in sin for abandoning a duty but not receive a reward for doing it? Is it possible to be sinful to publish something and not be rewarded for abstaining from publishing it? [This is a rhetorical question; the presumed correct answer is in the negative.] God will not ask someone to do something, then when the person does it, deprive him of the reward [assigned to the act]. This is the argument used by those who held that all views are correct, and all are rewarded whether they get it *correctly* or getting it *wrong*; sin is incurred only when they don't do their duty.

Another argument [for them] is that God made expiatory acts (*kaffarat*) one among many options [eg, in the case of failing to fulfill an oath, one may feed the needy or free a slave; other expiatory measures include fasting]. When the person makes a choice among the options, this is God's choice for him. This is true in cases where one may delay or hasten an act of expiation; whether one chooses to feed or refrain from food, or free a slave. Scholars of the law are similar in their position to individuals who owe an act of expiation. *What these scholars, after putting in their due diligence, arrive at is God's correct law.* God says (Q: 2/203) [regarding pilgrims]: "Those who stay two days [in Mecca, after the day of the feast] don't incur sin; nor will those who stay longer." Hastening to depart and staying longer are opposites; yet, they are both "correct" in God's holding. God also says (Q: 5/89) [regarding oath expiation]: [let him who breaches an oath] "*feed* ten of the destitute, taken out of the mean of their own family's food, *or clothe* them, or free an unfree soul." This necessities that all are correct in the eyes of God. God could not require his servants to do what is wrong, and approve of it afterwards, and make it a law for them. The only view that does entail an absurdity is that all legal scholars arrive at a correct conclusion, in the eyes of God. [This last sentence hints at the distinction the opponents make between saying that God's law is *what the scholar decides for himself/herself and their followers* (on the one hand) and saying that God's law is *different in God's eyes* (on the other.)]

[The author then comes back with responses]

We say, with God's help: God, with His benevolence and mercy, did give humans the ability to take matters into their hand. He delegated to them and asked them to decide matters for themselves, and to make up their mind and act on their own views. He made it their duty to put an "effort." For those who made an effort and did not arrive at the correct conclusion, or did not make an effort at all, or did not publish their views, or published views but did not act on them—all have done something wrong and may be punished. *The correctness of the correct, however, is a different matter. There cannot be two correct views for God.*

Disagreement among jurists happens, and they do not accuse one another of being sinful.* Each one may say to the other: You are wrong. If a view is correct, why would it be

---

* Publication sets this sentence at the end of the previous paragraph.

acceptable to call it wrong? On your view [now the author is addressing his opponents], one of these competing views must be wrong [ie, incompatible with your view]. You endorse calling the view that does not conform with yours "wrong." Yet, you hold that all conflicting views are "correct" in the eyes of God! You further say they are allowed to see one another as "wrong" and mistaken. We are also bound to call views we disagree with "wrong." [The author intimates that he is more consistent.] Among the companions of the Prophet himself arose disagreement; some getting it right and others wrong. Otherwise there would be no search for law (*ijtihad*.) 'Ali ibn Abi Talib's was asked by 'Umar [ibn al-Khattab] for his opinion about a woman who had a miscarriage when she received Umar's emissary [as she was startled]. The companions of the Prophet seemed to agree 'Umar was not liable [for compensation], because he was a person of legitimate authority who acted within his authority [as leader of the community]. Ali dissented, saying that, if those who held this view did their best to solve the question, they were wrong, and if they did not reflect enough, they have not fulfilled their duty. Umar, [Ali said], You owe the woman the requisite blood money [to compensate for the aborted fetus], a payment to be borne by your family's male agnates. Ibn Abbas, who disagreed also with the majority of the Prophet's companions, invited his opponents to a prayer invoking God's curse over whoever is wrong. This was in the matter of whether *zihar* applies to concubines. [*Zihar* is an oath not to touch one's wife, which triggers an ultimatum by a judge to either go ahead with a divorce or resume normal marital relations; Ibn Abbas believed it also applied to concubines, not only wives.] The invocation of God's curse is surely greater than considering someone simply wrong.

. . . . .

Primary source material III

Source: Jamil ibn Khamis al-Sa'di (nineteenth century), *Qamus al-Shari'a al-Hawi li-Turuqiha al-Wasi'a* (lit. *A Dictionary of Islamic Law, combining its Multiple Paths*; a ninety-volume sourcebook, Ibadi author) (Muscat: Oman Ministry of Endowments, 1983), Vol. 2, pp. 93–5.

The truth, the laity, and the scholars

On Practical Legal Reasoning (*Ijtihad*), Choosing an Opinion among Many, If Conflicting Views are Equal, Which one to Pick? & *Fatwas* with and without Qualifications/Conditions

PP. 93–4: Abu Said [al-Kadmi] (d. 361/972) said: I hold the view that all [lay and scholars] must exert themselves and seek the correct path to worship God. In each matter where one requires an opinion, one must put an effort to attain it. If those opinions on offer seem equal to him or her, he or she then is at liberty to pick one. This is true even when distinguishing the two competing views is hard. If one finds a way to discern the superiority of one of the opinions out there, he or she must follow it, because it is what is correct [for this person.] What is correct is what should be followed, because it is what is religiously correct for him or her to do, and this correctness is not altered by the availability of another view. *There is only one correct view in reality, and one must aim at it.* Opinions are aimed at via reasoning. The correct religious practice is aimed at by aiming at that which is true. I hold that those incapable of systematic reasoning must aim at the truth, even if this is not realistically possible.

[End of Abu Said's quote.]

. . . . . .

PP. 94–5: Inquiry: It was said that no one should give a general answer in a specific context, nor offer a qualified answer in a context of generality. Similarly, one must not offer a multivalent answer in a context of clarity and concision, and recommend neither a view based on a subsequent revelation in a context where the prior revelation applied, nor a view based on a superseded revelation where the superseding revelation fits. Muslim scholars say that [in the language of the revelation] *concise and clear* rules over the *equivocal*, and one may not apply the equivocal where the concise is available. If one were to be confused by some that it is permitted to take into account disagreement among Muslims in practical matters, this does not apply where one must decide whether the case is one where the broad or the concise is at work. God knows best.

Inquiry: Shaykh Nasir ibn Abi Nabhan al-Kharusi (d. 1263/1847) was asked: Is it possible to prevaricate in answering a question, such as when one is being asked whether one may put to use the hair of a pig or its skin, and the person then answers *that there is a disagreement*, going off to further suggest that *one may use* the hair of a pig after washing it and the skin after tanning it. We see many *rulings* such as these without clear qualifications or conditions. What would it mean then for Muslims to say that an answer should not be offered in general language, when conditions are appropriate and applicable, nor is an answer in ambiguous or unspecified language proper where concise and unequivocal language is required? Please clarify this for us, God's reward awaiting you. [End of question.]

The answer: Religious scholars are distinguished from one another by exactly this quality [the generalizations and specifications they offer]. Most scholars give answers in certain practical questions, and their language would be general in certain respects, with some difference among them, but the answer in some cases fails to be sufficiently general or sufficiently specific. My father [ibn Abi Nabhan's] used to say: The strength of a scholar is known from the many conditions and exceptions he offers in his answer. These [qualifications and generalizations] show that this scholar has applied sufficient reflection and considered aspects that may not enter into [or be a subcategory within] a certain word he uses. Ibn Ja'far sometimes applies a generalized language, and then Abu Sa'id [a commentator] comes up with qualifications to resize the language to fit exactly what the law is. Then the commentator moves on to clarify and detail some of the conditions. Any answer in equivocal language that *encompasses what the answer should not encompass* is an incorrect answer. An example of what is concisely addressed in the law is pig's skin, which is allowed only in certain conditions; an answer is not accepted if it makes the permission in too general a language.

If you enjoy these theoretical discussions, search in your library for Bernard Weiss' *The Search for God's Law*. It is an "exposition" or loose translation of a book by the same Amidi you heard about in Unit 3 in our discussion on consensus and weighing contradictory arguments. Bernard Weiss, Wael Hallaq, and Aron Zysow are the three most important names you want to remember if and when you develop some serious interest in (Islamic) legal epistemology. Or, just check out their work now.

6 The National Shari'as

The influence of the shari'a in modern national laws in Muslim nations is sometimes superficial (even when it is pronounced and overemphasized), sometimes deep (even when it is denied or not well-articulated). If you learn this and can make sense of it, that is enough for me. But to make sense of it, we will need to go on a long journey. Let's start with George Orwell.

Medieval to modern

In his 1945 essay "Notes on Nationalism," George Orwell says that every nationalist is haunted by the belief that the past can be altered. Nationalists tend to rearrange their history to make it fit the narrative they choose for their nation. Every nation, with or without a Muslim majority, has been subjected to altered narratives of its past, whereby customary laws, religious laws, and even the origins of its population, have been reconsidered. This is one danger that besets any reliance on national narratives in order to understand the way contemporary law in these nations has been assembled from diverse elements. For our purpose, we will identify where Islamic law is found to be one of the cornerstones of law in Muslim nations, but, heeding Orwell's statement, we will limit ourselves to a minimalist narrative of how nations understand their religious traditions. We will also limit ourselves to a handful of examples.

Each modern Muslim nation, in addition, stands on a narrative that incorporates *both* Islam and modernity into its foundation and collective identity. Even this can be a matter of disagreement to an extent, but there is usually an agreed-upon outline for the character of the nation in relation to its politics and legal system. You can be sure that outside interpretations, sympathetic ones included, will be disputed. Within the legal profession, there is a more discernable (and reasonably describable) set of ideas and characteristics governing legal and moral activities within the state, which lawyers and judges may, again, dispute to a limited extent but about whose broad strokes they agree. One thing they will all agree on: Their country is not comparable to any other.

Before modern nations with sizable Muslim populations took it as their task to re-interpret and appropriate aspects of the medieval Islamic legal tradition, Islamic law has grown, as we observed in Unit 2, from its "academic" beginnings when it was practiced by a few clusters of private jurists in different Muslim cities. Those credited with being the early founders of Zaydi, Ja'fari, and Hanafi law adopted several techniques to generate questions and answer them. The rest of the Sunni schools engaged the questions of the early jurists and, in turn, adopted different methods of legal research to answer them. Maliki jurists relied heavily on living practice and social custom, and Shafi'i jurists attempted to enrich their legal inquiries

Figure 6.1 Frontal view of the Citadel of Aleppo, Syria. Author: Memorino. Image accessed via Wikimedia.

with theoretical tools derived from the study of language and logic in addition to "reports" of the practice of the early community. The centuries went by, and with them were added new populations, changing conditions, and expansion and recession of Islam's universal domain.

The obsession with Prophetic reports became more intense as the centuries went by. The turn to "reports" of the Prophet's saying as the main source of law and as a standard against which to judge the correctness of legal doctrine is a *subsequent* development in "*madhhab*" law that was *grafted onto* early legal "reason"-based conclusions and method of research. This development gained momentum in the thirteenth century at the hands of Nawawi in Shafi'i law, whose influence continued in the works of the two Subkis in the fourteenth century, Ibn Hajar al-Haytami in the fifteenth, and culminated with the start of comparative law that is anchored in commentary on the Prophet's reports in the work of Ibn Hajar al-'Asqalani (if you've forgotten who he is, revisit Subsection 2.2.2, Unit 2). By the time 'Asqalani wrote his long commentary on Bukhari's (d. 256/870) 4,000+ reports, including (in his commentary) much material in jurists' disagreement and reasoning around this limited number of reports, Sunni Islamic law had completed the tools for a shift in orientation, linking law to reports, as opposed to the free reasoning from principles which Muhammad ibn al-Hasan al-Shaybani had introduced in the eighth century. A beautiful irony is that any good scholar (steep in the Islamic tradition) wanting to comment afresh on statements in the Qur'an or by the Prophet for the purposes of law does either directly borrow from *madhhab* reasoning or reflect an invisible influence from these *madhhabs*, having being schooled in the old ways of reasoning. (Those with modern legal education who interrogate the Qur'an and *Sunna* to address legal queries end up borrowing from ideas foreign to both the Islamic revelations and the long Islamic legal tradition.) Be that as it may, there was a move toward bringing up reports of the Prophet's life as a new foundation for the law. The Hanafi tradition was slow to catch up with this "law-from-reports" trend. A sub-continent "*hadith*" movement started in the seventeenth–eighteenth centuries to do this work. Sunni encounters with European powers in the following centuries brought to the fore something of an internal debate among Sunni jurists themselves, centered on whether the essence of law is Prophetic instructions or legal and moral principles.

In areas such as Egypt and Turkey, an adoption of modern paths to law was ardently pronounced. As these and subsequently other Muslim lands were controlled by new military and legal elites, Muslim populations bore witness to a hybridization of life from local and foreign standards, where law led the way, and social standards sometimes cooperated and sometimes resisted. In due course, the new legal elites acquired their own jargon, derived (in the case of Egypt and Turkey) from Swiss and French ways of speaking about law. A leap toward modernization was taken. Time, however, was on the side of readjustment, and attempts at adapting habits and traditions from premodern times to new realities became the essence of the science of law in much of the Sunni Muslim world.

What shari'a meant certainly differed based on the education of the judge, and there is no way around acknowledging that some ironies in the application of shari'a in Muslim India can be identified. In Pakistan, under the British India regime, judges were cautious in their interpretation of Islamic law; they avoided commenting on what may be called "sensitive" areas of law. With certain exceptions, the Anglo-Indian judges adhered as strongly as they could to Hanafi doctrines. After independence in 1947, Pakistani judges considered themselves free to interpret Islamic law the way they saw fit. In some cases, they explicitly said that they considered themselves authorities in interpreting the system (scholars of the law with an authority tantamount to *muftis* and judges in the olden days). After the Federal Shariat Court (FSC) was established in 1980, the judges took after that trend (which we said started to arise in the late medieval and early modern centuries) of direct interpretation of the textual sources of the law (Qur'an, *Sunna*).*

Shi'i law had grown denser and more detailed at about the same time Sunni law took a turn toward Prophetic tradition. Al-'Allama al-Hilli of Iraq's (d. 1325) acquaintance with the works of the Hanbali Ibn Qudama and the Shafi'i Nawawi, who lived a century before him, allowed him to produce new, long commentaries, which supplemented a much thinner earlier Shi'i tradition. Industrious authorities from Iraq and Lebanon added to the Ja'fari system, from mostly novel interpretations of the old traditions of *tahsin* and *taqbih,* training the human reason to *discern* the inherent qualities that make an act good or bad in the eyes of the law. As modern Iran acquired its unique status as a Persian-speaking Shi'i land at the heart of the Muslim world, building on Safavid (1501–1724) and Qajar (1724–1907) history, it was ready to offer a new model for Islamic law in the modern world, only a few steps removed from, and in constant conversing with, its Sunni surrounds.

Once again and to recap: Today societies with a sizable Muslim population, whether of a Sunni or Shi'i legacy, reconcile *two* traditions, *one* long and deep but increasingly distant (which is the religious tradition), and *one* recent and immediate though short and conflicted (which is the modern tradition). Of course, the more you know about both types, you will see within each one numerous branches, multiple trends, and various streaks, bands, and stripes. Moreover, it would be inaccurate to generalize and insist that all Muslim societies stand at about the same distance from these two sets of traditions. But it is not unfair to say that societies that went too far in the modernization direction had to take a step backward

---

* Professor Muhammad Munir of the Islamic University in Islamabad must be credited with the content of this paragraph. His work (*Precedent in Pakistani Law*) is on your shortlist of "Further Reading," but he also generously gave me feedback on a draft of this unit and Unit 8, including explicit statements that I include here.

and reintegrate (a reinterpreted form of) tradition, and that those who were sluggish in modernization had to make some leaps of punctuated equilibrium in modernity's direction. Laws and morals exist in uneven forms in any society, and so does the application of laws; the streamlining and reconciling of the latter does not occur in a neat and even way. In theory, Supreme Courts and courts of cassation do, when necessary, come up with ways to reconcile the conflicting elements. But in many law cases, just as in ordinary social and ethical life, the conflict survives, and with it unevenness, unreconciled communities, and different assessments of social, moral, and legal life.

1 Colonial and post-colonial transformations

It has been argued that the shari'a had simply become incompatible with life in a world of modern nation states. In this world, we live as citizens of certain *nations*, which demand *loyalty* and (theoretically at least) guarantee *equality* among their citizens regardless of their religion. Citizenship and religious affiliation are easily placed to clash: One must prevail over the other. In a certain way, nationalist affiliations can be seen as comparable to the pre-Islamic tribal affiliations that Islam came to challenge. This, in essence, is why a modern shari'a is taken to be a false shari'a, a shari'a of resurrected ideals in conflict with Islamic ideals. The latter, therefore, are detached from reality.

The difficulty this notion faces, upon reflection, is that *the modern state did, even when led by secular individuals, function as an added authority that enforced aspects of the Islamic shari'a*. And this did not come from copying ideas from medieval texts necessarily. Take the way modern Egyptian law adopts the so-called modern theory in identifying effective "causes" for contracts. Article 136 in Egypt's (1949) civil code states that the "purpose" or "cause" for contract which is not in conformity with public mores and manners makes the contract not enforceable. One simple application is a contract involving compensation for "prostitution." There are discussions of how a theory of "causes" of contract evolved in French and German jurisprudence, as well as comparisons with Islamic law (Sanhuri, *Masadir al-Haqq*, Vol. 4, pp. 11–32, esp. 21). In practice, and this may be an interesting fact to contemplate, is that adopting the newest version of the theory (of causes and contracts) in French jurisprudence and applying it in modern Egyptian law leads to *enforcing Muslim manners* (which are dominant in Egyptian society), rather than French mores.

In addition, the influence of nation state arrangements on individuals has been overestimated and the power of nation states much hyped. In their exaggerated impact, states and their ideologies appear powerful enough to falsify or modify the physical and life sciences. (You may have heard that Presidents Kennedy and Reagan believed a superior American "science" somehow supported the claims of the superiority of the liberal or capitalist systems; one wonders whether they were trying to compete with Joseph Stalin's belief that there was such a thing as socialist science.) Exaggerations aside, national arrangements and political power can only be two among many factors in the social and personal lives of all populations. Of course, inherited social and moral standards can simply be abandoned and wither away, but this is a function of complex developments over time, rather than a short-term (in the big scheme of things, abrupt) development.

In the past, Medieval Muslim jurists had to deal with governments whose laws they opposed. These jurists went so far as to theorize the condition of laws based on "broad" reasoning from public interest, or *siyasa, and you will find references to siyasa-based laws everywhere you look.* To be clear, these are laws the jurists did not make—they were made by the political and administrative authorities instead—but for the most part jurists accommodated and embraced them. When jurists discussed homosexual coition, which they considered unlawful, they considered punishments arising either from the definite religious law (*hadd*), judicial discretion (*ta'zir*), or simply laws of the city or country (*siyasa*), which may have been issued by a ruler with no knowledge of the religious law. They subsequently went further and took the *siyasa* principle as decisive in matters where traditional jurisprudence showed some flexibility. The late Ottoman Syrian jurist Ibn Abidin (d. 1252/1836), for example, indicated that when a judge of the Hanafi school was appointed in his time, this judge had no choice but to decide based on the dominant view in Hanafi law and could neither employ a weak view (within Hanafi law) or borrow from another school (*Hashiya* (Riyadh: 'Alam a-Kuub, 2003), Vol. 5, p. 93). Had this judge been identified as a free or independent jurist in an earlier century, he might have had these options.

Interestingly, an argument has also been made that modernity forced the "*madhhab*" jurists to abandon their schools, so that they could pick and choose from other ones in order for their religio-legal product to survive. You might have noted that Muslim jurists following imperatives other than those of their *madhhab* is nothing novel (Unit 4, section 2.4). Not only did premodern forces such as governments and markets influence how Muslim jurists solved practical legal questions, and not only did extra-legal and extra-juristic commands and authoritative actions (by security forces, armies, and local authorities of different types) infuse Muslim societies with added layers of order jurists came to accommodate, but *Muslim jurists also took their hints from social customs*. Social customs are a force more potent than both tradition and any instance of a democratic choice at a given time, which may change fairly rapidly. We already gave one example of how these social customs affected juristic reasoning (Unit 4, section 3, Intro). In early law, the dowry paid by a man to a prospective wife was regarded as a simple gift, (and as a compensation, it would be) parallel to the advantage the husband draws from the marriage, but gradually it became an offset of the value of any furniture supplied by the wife's family to the couple's future house.

You will see in this unit that *Muslim customs* and *colonial cultures* convoked the new spirit of the contemporary Muslim national societies and determined the contribution of the medieval shari'a in them. National shari'as are still a form of the shari'a as applied by current Muslim governments. They are different from Western laws, and emphasizing the degree to which they are borrowed (now or centuries ago) is arguably not the best way to study them.

1.1 Muslim individuals and their nations

One understanding of the shari'a is that it is a system of law and morality in which government is "smaller" and hence the person is "larger." Even though individuals are not able to make laws or devise moral standards, they participate in both giving these laws social form and enforcing them. Judges in a shari'a society do not deliver surprising judgments that individuals (before they were called citizens) do not understand; rather they do, in some cases, simply remind the population of its own religious and moral commitments. There are, to be sure, intricate points of law to navigate that only a shari'a judge and other specialists truly understand, but these are compatible with and understandable in reference to dominant practices. Law in shari'a society is no equivalent, some argue, to the sometimes brutal, impersonal entity that is the modern state (even when it calls itself democratic), which could eliminate individuals and confiscate property for national interest or "reasons of state."

Continuing this line of thinking, one notes that the "larger" individual of the medieval shari'a society was given, in some areas of criminal law, freedoms that are considered unacceptable in all Muslim societies today. For example, the son of a slain man may prosecute the case against his father's killer. In early Hanafi law, this son was able to *delegate* seeking the evidence against the culprit but not the implementation of the retaliation; that he must do in person (Shaybani (ed. M. Boino-Kalin), *al-Asal* (Beirut: Dar Ibn Hazm, 2013), Vol. 7, p. 5). In the twenty-first century, by contrast, Muslims who have not already turned against the death penalty may at the very least have a problem with a family member taking it upon himself to implement retaliation laws.

This is a more defensible line of thought than the argument that shari'a laws are dead and deserve a funerary service. There is indeed a strange kind of difficulty in comparing (or indeed *contrasting*) one's affiliation with a religious community and with a national state. Individuals may reject their Muslim community by apostatizing and further provoking the community by expressing their rejection of its beliefs. This crime of apostasy, which consists in leveling an affront to one's Muslim community in a manner that may undermine its faith and hence undermine the community itself, would, according to a modern view of the matter, simply be an instance of free-thinking. (In its original form as exemplified by the rebellion against Abu Bakr, Muhammad's first successor, it was an action by a group, rather than an individual, and it was punished by war rather than execution.) When a citizen works against the security of his or her (modern) nation state, this is called treason. If analogizing "apostasy" and "treason" succeeds, it must be possible to easily think of analogies between treason and free-thinking or the defense of freedom (Edward Snowden?).

Religious and national loyalties often clash, and to this extent there is merit in the argument that shari'a cannot live in a world of national states that demand loyalty. The loyalties in question, however, are hard to understand in reference to one another; both comparing and contrasting them promises surprising analytical turns.

The view that the shari'a must mean something else in the modern world is taken for granted in this book. The historical background that led us to where we are is long, contentious, and ultimately beyond the scope of this work, but we do need to be aware of a few things. For example, European colonialism was a case of increasing competition among European nations for hegemony and resources. The colonial experience lasted for centuries, during which time European societies changed significantly. Muslim societies also changed over time. They grew in terms of population. They became aware of how to use their resources in modern ways. They became more "secular," if we assign this problematic word a basic sense hinging on the idea that religious life was crowded with new institutions, new habits, and new ways to earn and dispense of one's property.

In any case, this unit looks at how Islamic law finds some space in modern national laws, which gives us an opportunity to speak of the national shari'as. Once again, we will not cover all 50+ Muslim countries. Remember even in those countries with a majority-Muslim population, Islamic law does not always dominate. Also remember that with more than 180 million Muslims, India may be said to be the third largest Muslim country (after Indonesia and Pakistan and ahead of Bangladesh and Egypt), despite the fact that it has a non-Muslim majority.

Note also that religious laws in the Muslim world are not limited to Islamic law. There are aspects of national law in Muslim countries where ecclesiastical courts exercise power over Christian populations, and where other religious-legal institutions enjoy jurisdiction over the non-Muslim population.

As you learned in Unit 3, legal doctrines and arguments may conflict and hence require mechanisms of reconciliation or support for one view over the rest. Now, religion in a national law may simply provide one argument among many, leaving other arguments that are foundational to national legal doctrines to come from social standards or a local interpretation of natural laws or the principles of equity. The father of modern civil law in Egypt, Abd al-Razzaq al-Sanhuri (1895–1971), famously enumerated four sources of modern (civil) Egyptian law, in this specific order: legislation; custom and tradition; the Islamic Shari'a; natural law and the principles of equity. This is stated in the language of Article 1/2 (= article one, paragraph two) in Egypt's 1949 civil code. How then does Islamic law find room for application in this and other national Muslim laws?

1.2 Competing for space

In modern Egyptian jurisprudence, legislation by the people's representatives (in The People's Assembly or House of Representatives) is called a foundational source of law of general reach (*masdar asli 'am*). Religion, in the narrow sense of Islam, has been historically considered a foundational source of law within a restricted reach, more potent in family and probate matters than in purely civil law matters. Religion, now broadly incorporating both Islamic law and other Egyptian religious laws, has been (and remains) the main source of the laws governing family and charitable endowments. But with the advent of the 1949 civil code, it is also acknowledged as a *complementary* source of the law applying in all civil matters. By the same code, social customs and standards are counted as another complementary source of the law—filling in gaps created by the absence of direct legal rules governing a case. The sources' theoretically determined reach does not preclude the potential of being equal-cum-conflicting in certain matters. We must now note that the fourth of four sources of the law enumerated above, namely natural law and the principles of equity, is seen as a source of interpretation for legal codes, and it provides a reference to the objectives of the law or its basic rationale or essence, rather than being a separate source for it. Conflicting arguments of equal power will simply arise from friction among the three sources of the law: legislation; religion; and custom.

One quick example of how the different legal conceptions at work may diverge. Article 917 of Egypt's civil code states that, "were a person to transfer his/her property to one of his/her inheritors but keep physical control of the property and draw benefits from it for the remainder of his/her life, the property transfer is presumed to fall under the laws of the will—as long as no evidence militates against this presumption." Medieval Sunni Islamic law would consider this a case of undelivered gift, which, if administered while the owner is in full possession of his or her health and mental faculties, is valid and will hence exclude the purported property from the inheritance. Article 917 makes the transfer essentially invalid.

Conflicting legal imperatives involve medieval Islamic law's role in modern laws in Egypt in an array of issues. The marital contract, for example, while part of the category of contract, is governed by special principles of Islamic legal provenance. Challenges to these principles come in different forms and measures. Repudiating the marriage of a Muslim female to a male, whose belonging to the Islamic faith is in question, led to well-publicized controversy in the 1990s (known mistakenly as an apostasy case, where apostasy is not an offence Egyptian criminal law considers). In these matters, the secular commitments of the Egyptian judiciary are tested once and again.

The idea of an appellate system changes aspects of this discussion again. In medieval Islamic law, conflicting arguments would be reconciled based on standards that were developed over time. Whether it is reconciling Shafi'is' two doctrines, conflicting legal codes that compete for geographic or temporal jurisdiction, or even conflicting sources of the same national law (religious, customary, and legislative), there are standards by which all conflicting elements of legal argument can be forced into harmony. But what happens when judges disagree, not about how to interpret a legal principle or reconcile conflicting ones, but about how to apply relevant principles to one and the same case? In the discussion on equal and conflicting arguments from Unit 3, we learned that a Muslim judge should not judge one case twice, effectively acting as if he were two judges. In this discussion, we do not hear about two judges having authority over one and the same case. Although the modern appellate system was not in place, this condition was addressed in medieval Islamic jurisprudence, but it was addressed as an exception to the rule, an example of judicial failure leading to judicial correction. In the modern context, where judicial correction is normalized, a new argument is needed for considering a Supreme Court's decision juristically and legally superior to a district court's decision.

The appellate system is a test of how conflicting arguments of equal strength are treated in modern judicial practice. A hierarchy of courts, ascending from local to appellate to yet higher Courts of Cassation and Supreme Courts, while political and arbitrary from a legal and epistemological standpoint, provides the modern solution to the problem of conflicting arguments and ways of reasoning. That is, because a final word will be rendered and made obligatory for all lower courts when a Supreme or High Court decides a matter about which the low courts disagreed, the disagreement is resolved once and for all. But is this all there is? If yes, law (and all legal science) is ultimately a wrinkle of political science, unable to provide its own defense for its behavior.

1.3 Shari'a and nations

If Islamic law can find its way to an American court, it has a stronger jurisdiction in a court in the Province of Aceh (pronounced Atcheh), Indonesia, which since 1999 has been able to employ a wide spectrum of Islamic legal doctrines and practices. And Indonesia is not a lone exception. The presence of the shari'a in modern national laws in Muslim countries is hardly an aberration, although it is found in different degrees and it means different things in different national settings. Also keep in mind that shari'a courts are not the only courts that enforce Islamic law. There have been no shari'a courts in Egypt since 1955, for example, but many aspects of modern Egyptian law reflect Islamic legal doctrines.

Also keep in mind that all contemporary forms of the Islamic shari'a are influenced by *modern* ideas. In some cases, they are influenced even by *ancient* ideas that were not taken seriously by *medieval* Muslim scholars in centuries past but which have come to the fore in their modern form. For example, medieval Muslim political theorists and jurists knew about Plato's *Republic*, and Ibn Rushd (d. 596/1198) wrote a summary/commentary of it, and agreed (as we will see in Unit 8) with Plato, for example, on the difficulties facing democratic rule. Plato, however, is nowhere near influential in medieval Islamic political theories that emanate from mainstream legal scholars. But Khomeni (1902–1989), the man who inspired and rode the unstoppable waves of Iran's 1979 revolution and shaped its modern Islamic Republic, re-read Plato's *Republic* with a modern view of the philosopher king, in the sense of an enlightened, benevolent dictator. As you will note later in this Unit, the philosopher king here became fused with the capability of a religious jurist of the Shi'i tradition Khomeni espoused.

This is because legal doctrines have continued and still continue to evolve, with new questions and new answers to old questions. For the purpose of this unit Muslim countries are those countries whose laws allow a judge to draw on Islamic legal reasoning, not those with either a Muslim majority or a significant Muslim minority. In these Muslim countries, the judiciary played (and still plays) a major role in determining the extent to which a new doctrine of national law is developed and incorporated. As you will see, this was by design at least in Pakistan, Egypt, and Saudi Arabia. It was not that these countries took the same paths to where their legal systems are today, as you will see in some detail.

Egypt, for example, abandoned Islamic law in the criminal arena almost at once,* and by the end of the nineteenth century, established a sovereign, foreign judiciary within its borders that handled cases involving foreign interests and foreign citizens based on European and American legal doctrines. When it was time to draft a civil code after the 1937 Montreux Convention, which gave Egypt a degree of economic and legal freedom, the main source of inspiration for that new code was how Egyptian judges (via the national courts that had been established in 1883) interpreted even foreign legal doctrines, moved these a step closer to local social standards and expectations in order to address cases that involved Egypt's population. Since 1971 Egypt's constitution has stated that the Islamic shari'a was a principal source of law (interpreted by modern Egyptian jurists to be a "supplementary source of general reach," as will be explained). By then, it was a mix of judicial habits, reconciliation of legal imperatives via comparative Egyptian jurisprudence, and new political reality that determined the direction cases could go and the role Islamic law plays in deciding them.

Need is one legitimate ancestor of inventions. It did take both a "need" and a "degree of creativity" by judges to incorporate Islamic law into modern national laws, at least in places such as Egypt and Pakistan. To an extent this is analogous to how, in American law, whether the Supreme Court intervenes in a legislation and discovers a constitutional right that limits the legislators, depends on a lawsuit, with well-articulated arguments, and judges who are sympathetic to an interpretation of the constitution that supports the claim. This is all contingent, needless to say, on the possibility of turning the new doctrine consistent with old doctrines, to the extent possible.

---

* This followed extensive deliberation between government officials and religious law scholars about how to modernize old notions of crime and adjust punishment practices to match nineteenth-century realities in urban and rural areas. These efforts ended in frustration and suspicion between scholars and government. What seems to be an abrupt development, in fact, hid in its background much discussion, effected by a mutual misunderstanding between government and scholars.

Many differences distinguish the presence of Islamic law in national laws from the case of constitutional rights that are made to fit inside the American legislative and executive world. Court jurisdictions remain flexible in places such as Pakistan, which makes Western observers jump to words like "chaos" to characterize Pakistani legal and political life. The appetite for comparative law that incorporates shari'a reasoning in places like Egypt seems to Western observers to be overly political and ideological. It certainly does not look anything like that to those invested in these legal systems in Muslim countries. Modernizing Islamic law in the Middle East and Muslim India is seen by Muslim lawyers as a much-needed contribution to global law and legal institutions. Back in 1952, Sanhuri (d. 1971) maintained that Egypt's modern laws needed to reflect Egypt's particular nature and long cultural and historical experience, which included Islamic law, but also had to make a further step to be part of a conversation about global, comparative law ('Abd al-Razzaq al-Sanhuri, *al-Wasit fi al-Qanun al-Madani*, vol. 2: Nazariyyat al-Iltizam, page "h"—general intro). Sanhuri's counterparts outside of Egypt, as well as his successors in the Muslim world, continue to debate their role in similar terms, albeit with differing degrees of optimism.

What remains, to complete this Unit, are examples from *five national settings* of where national Muslim laws are found. Three cases (Iran, Egypt, and Saudi Arabia) are closer to a centralized system in their legal and political structure, while the other two, Indonesia and Pakistan, are closer to a federation, with Indonesia the most decentralized of all.

2 Islamic law and modern nations

2.1 Iran

The Islamic revolution that led to the founding of Iran's Islamic Republic was more a moment of innovation than a return to its roots or traditional practice.

The ingenious solution to the absence of a religious leader (*imam*) who descends from the Prophet's lineage and possesses a claim to being his successor was to assume that jurists (religious, legal scholars) would take care of the Prophet's community until the appearance of this *imam*—whose awaiting is ultimately a folkloric/religious equivalent of the Second Coming of Christ. The doctrine of the jurist's work on behalf of the *imam* is translated as the leadership or guardianship of the jurist. It won't hurt to memorize this one term (Arabic/Persian) when you are in a good mood: *wilayat al-faqih/vilayat-e faqih*.

Iran gives us one of the best-integrated forms of Islamic law within a national legal system in the world today—next only to the Saudi system. The basis of this system is not that all secular laws adopted by Iranians, with the possible exception of the penal code and a handful of civil statues, had to be abolished or reviewed one by one via a council of jurists. A council of twelve scholars—six of them appointed by the religious leaders and six by the legislatures—exists to look into national law's compliance with the principles of Islamic legal reasoning. Not all pre-revolutionary laws, however, were reviewed or could be reviewed.

The jurist's all-encompassing jurisdiction here simply means that, on orders of priority, laws will be made and modified with the spirit of complying with Islamic legal principles and the idea that a living jurist must approve new solutions to new legal questions.

The dramatic language given in Iran's 1979 constitution about courts being able to ignore all laws that do not comply with Islamic law has to be understood in this light. Judges cannot simply make a new law; they must apply the principles most compatible with other existing laws. Since 1979 the task of a modern Iranian judge has been to act as *a participant* in pinpointing areas where laws must be augmented and improved, rather than as a dictator with overreaching jurisdiction.

The power of the Council of Guardians over legislation that does not comply with Islamic law is also not absolute. In custody laws, a disagreement lingered as to divorced mothers' right to be the presumptive custodian parent of their sons after they reach age seven. In old Ja'fari doctrines, the mother was the presumptive custodian for a daughter until age seven and a son until age two. The new (proposed) laws made no distinction between boys and girls and named the mother the default custodian for both until age seven and the father the default custodian for both thereafter, in such instances where the father and mother are equally capable of taking care of the children.

After some back and forth, the Council of Guardians acquiesced to the suggested change and since 2002 the law has put boys and girls on an equal footing in this regard. The Council argued that traditional Ja'fari law explained the difference between boys and girls in a way that made the innovation unsupportable. The new view triumphed, however, with a new explanation: That boys and girls are equally in need of their mother's supervision in normal circumstances, until the same age as the girls.

> With a view to safeguard the Islamic ordinances and the Constitution, in order to examine the compatibility of the legislation passed by the Islamic Consultative Assembly with Islam, a council to be known as the Guardian Council is to be constituted with the following composition:
>
> - Six "adil fuqaha" [ie, jurists of good character] conscious of the present needs and the issues of the day, to be selected by the Leader, and
> - Six jurists, specializing in different areas of law, to be elected by the Islamic Consultative Assembly from among the Muslim jurists nominated by the Head of the Judicial Power.
>
> Article 91 (Iran's Constitution)

The law now allows even a working mother and a mother who uses a live-in babysitter to be the presumptive custodian for her son until age seven.

If you still remember the MMK case from Unit 1, you will remember that unbecoming behavior endangers a parent's right to custody. This is also true in the Iranian system. In some cases, Iranian courts have given custody to third parties when both parents were deemed incapable of it. It is usually grandparents (grandfather then grandmother), followed by someone whom the court appoints as both capable and trustworthy.

The Council, albeit reluctantly, also allowed banks to charge interest on loans, despite the prohibition of usury. The bank can give you a loan and ask you to return it within a short period of time, where inflation is insignificant. After that period, it may ask you to compensate for failing to pay your debt. This issue will be revisited in Unit 7, when we look at Islamic finance in the modern world. For now, one must note a few facts:

1. Shi'i jurists have not accepted the Sunni idea that usury can apply even when an undelayed (immediate) exchange takes place. Sunnis think that an immediate exchange of two unequal quantities of the same commodity is prohibited, because it is unfair.
2. Both Sunni and Shi'i jurists agree that interest on loans is not allowed.
3. Shi'i jurists also realize that in the modern world, money moves faster and loses value faster, and large gains are made faster. This is one of the reasons for the Council's decision.

2.2 Indonesia

In 1989, the Islamic Judicature Law extended the scope of Islamic law in Indonesia to matters of public finance. It also ended judicial review over shari'a courts in that country by civil courts. Law 7/1989 regulating the religious courts simply opened the door for more integration of Islamic law into modern Indonesian laws. Law 3/2006 explicitly extended the jurisdiction of Islamic law way beyond family matters into Islamic banking, insurance, pension funds, mutual funds, pawn operations, and business contracts. It also gave a mandate to these courts to develop their own judicial principles, recognizing that a complete code derived from Islamic law is lacking.

The size of the Islamic finance market in Indonesia grew 74 percent annually between 1998 and 2011 (rising from 479 billion rupees in 1998 to 2,712 billion in 2011 according to the Indonesian Central Bank). These are small numbers by US sizes, but the speed of the growth is the crucial factor here. If you read these facts closely, you might get the impression that there is a degree of fluidity and a potential for expansion in the terrain of Islamic law in modern Indonesia—and you would be correct.

To complicate the picture and remind you that modern Islamic law can be a surprising scion of the medieval tradition, however, studies that attempt to look in detail into the extent to which modern Indonesian laws are based on some Islamic element or other reveal that 45 percent of the laws that derive from Islamic law are not "strictly" based on any interpretation of the sources of the religious law (invoking local and national moral standards, more than anything else), and the remaining 55 percent, which reference Islamic law, do not reference classical *fiqh* categories at all (Robert W. Hefner, *Shari'a Politics: Islamic Law and Society in the Modern World* (Bloomington: Indiana University Press, 2011), pp. 281–2).

Like many Muslim countries, Indonesia experienced a colonial rule that allowed the local population a degree of independence in applying their social and economic laws, as long as these laws did not compete with colonial interests. On the one hand, certain matters were not negotiable, and higher courts could revoke a decision by the courts of the natives. On the other hand, many of the natives' affairs were not important enough to come to the attention of the colonial government. Add to this the fact that Dutch rule in Indonesia did not extend over all its territories until the twentieth century. It is true that a "commercial" colonial presence goes back to the beginning of the seventeenth century, and it is also true that colonial powers were oppressive and obsessive about resources, yet the native population's ability to reclaim the right to make their own laws led to reconsiderations of both premodern and modern legal institutions and practices.

The end of this highly irregular colonial rule was another irregularity. Japan defeated the Dutch armies in Indonesia and ruled it between 1942 and 1945. Japan's surrender (August 15, 1945) left us with four contested years between 1945–9, when the Netherlands officially acknowledged Indonesia's independence, but Indonesians cite 1945 as their independence date.

At the time of its independence in 1945, Indonesia was said to stand on Pancasila (or Pantchasila), that is, five principles or foundations: religion; national unity; human/international values; democracy; and social justice. The sense of each one of these and how to reconcile them are contested. Between May and August of 1945, and after some deliberations, the order in which the five pillars were enumerated was changed by the country's founders, where it moved religion, or more accurately *monotheism*, from number 5 to number 1. The initial language of the article concerning religion, while broad and encompassing indigenous and grass-root religions in Indonesia, stipulated that Muslims are expected to conduct their lives according to Islamic law. This part was later omitted, but it seems to be present *in practice* since 1989, despite its official absence.

> The State recognizes and respects units of regional authorities that are special and distinct, which shall be regulated by law.
>
> The State recognizes and respects traditional communities along with their traditional customary rights as long as these remain in existence and are in accordance with the societal development and the principles of the Unitary State of the Republic of Indonesia, and shall be regulated by law.
>
> Article 18-B of Indonesia's Constitution

Islamic law in Indonesia has always lived in conjunction with local customary laws, some of which were in conformity with it and some not. When Islam was new to the islands, a compromise was struck between the new (Islamic) rules and local rules. When colonial powers took away the people's power to make their laws, they still allowed for an area that became known as *adatrecht* (the Dutch/German word for law (*recht*) stuck at the tail of the Arabic word that meant customs (*adat*)), which by then stood for agrarian, family, and inheritance laws that had become familiar to the population since Islam was introduced to the islands and became laws even for Indonesian non-Muslims who embraced prevailing customs.

Adat-law (customary law) is not always in conformity with Islamic law. For example, a widow does not inherit from her husband but gains access to half of what is called "communal" property—basically where she lived with her husband—as long as she does not remarry. In the Sunni Islamic law known in Indonesia (Shafi'i law), she would receive a quarter of the inheritance if there the deceased had no children or an eighth if he did. In *adat*-law, in essence, what she shared with her husband, such as house, furniture, chattels, and the like, is now divided and she gets the share she had when her husband was alive (half), while his share is considered the share of his inheritors. In fact, if the widow continues to run the house after her husband's death, she would not be an inheritor, strictly speaking, and no division of the property of the deceased takes place at all. This means that she does not really inherit a share in his property. If her husband had separate property, this would go to his children.

The Supreme Court in Indonesia allowed itself to decide *similar* cases from different regions *differently*, depending on which customary standard applies. Daniel S. Lev has traced the Supreme Court's behavior in deciding matters involving customary, local laws. He thinks that the (normally Javanese and cosmopolitan) Supreme Court judges employed the mechanism of change in custom (or *adat*) to change the law gradually in different areas. For example, a female's share in inheritance of her husband was strengthened by change in the cultures, including the rise of the appreciation for women's role in society (which reached their highest point in achieving independence from the Dutch), the emphasis on the nuclear family, and the spread of the habits of the large island of Java into the rest of the country. There is an interesting picture from Lev's study of 1962, at the edge of this shift. In *The Supreme Court and Adat Inheritance Law in Indonesia*, (pp. 219–20), #11 on the Further Reading list, he states:

> In 1955 the Supreme Court considered a case from Bali, in which a customary court had ordered the eviction of a widow from the house of her deceased husband. An uncle of her son by the deceased had sued to take the house as his inheritance, on grounds that she had committed adultery and therefore must be denied the rights of a widow. The Supreme Court reversed the decision and ruled that only the son of a deceased father (in patrilineal Bali) can claim his inheritance, and in this case the son had specifically stated he did not want to claim against his mother. Also in 1955, in a case from the Balinese area of West Lombok, the Supreme Court held that the heir of a childless deceased is his sister. But the widow must receive one third of the inheritance, since she is responsible for her husband's cremation and other affairs. A 1956 decision held, by implication, that a Sasak (Islamic Lombok) widow is not an heir of her husband but is entitled to one third of community property plus one eighth of the remainder for taking care of the inheritance. The Court ruled in 1957 that in Bali a gift of land to a daughter can be claimed by the heirs of her deceased father if she commits an *adat* crime that results in loss of her caste.

Gradually, the Supreme Court started to develop its own modern jurisprudence in inheritance cases, whereby certain aspects of old customary law became an indispensable part of the national law and other *adat* or customary laws were incompatible with the broad legal edifice. Lev, at the end of his piece on inheritance law states:

> The Supreme Court has taken a long step indeed towards making law for the entire country. There is still one qualification of the widow's inheritance rights, and it is based on an *adat* law concept. Her right to inherit is certain, but remarriage may entail loss of the separately owned property of her former husband. Until then, she may do with the property as her interests demand.

2.3 Egypt

Modern Egyptian jurists (such as M. H. Kira, *Usul al-Qanun* (Cairo: Dar al-Maarif, 1958/2nd ed.), pp. 318, 321, 364) speak of "religion" (*al-din*) as a source of law in two different ways. First, religious laws of the Islamic shari'a are a special, original source (*masdar asli khas*) of law in the realm of personal status laws. The concept of personal status laws includes all laws that respond to the status of the person, whether male or female, legally dependent, minor, or an independent adult who is free of interdiction, married or unmarried. This concept was enlarged by a decision from the civil circuit in Egypt's Court of Cassation on June 21, 1934, to include matters of property law, such as gifts and inheritance, which were considered part of personal status law by extension, because, as the Court explained, they are handled by individuals as matters where one's behavior is governed by one's religion. The laws of endowment were also included in this area where Islamic law was considered a special and original source of law. In these same areas of the law, religious laws of the non-Islamic (Jewish and Christian) shari'a of those sects that enjoyed long presence in Egypt applies to these populations (most notably in their family law affairs), as long as they share their sectarian religious affiliation in the case in which the laws apply. For example, when an Armenian Orthodox couple experience a disagreement that requires legal intervention, their church's laws apply in the case, but if one of the couple is an Orthodox Christian and the other a Roman Catholic, Islamic law retains its general jurisdiction in these matters.

Second, Islamic law is a general source of complementary role (*masdar ihtiyati 'am*) in all civil matters by virtue of Article 1 in the Civil Code of 1949. This article enumerates the sources of the law a judge may use in the case of the absence of relevant legislation (hence complementary sources) as social standards (*'urf*) and Islamic law (*al-shari'a al-islamiyya*). While this is a broader jurisdiction for Islamic law, encompassing all matters of contract and property laws, civil torts and compensation, legal personality and responsibility, the status of Islamic law limits deriving laws from its sources to cases where the judge could find neither a legislation nor a social standard or custom that aids him or her in making a proper legal determination. Note that the mentioning of social standards before the Islamic shari'a is seen as a way to prioritize Egyptian customs and standards over foreign (non-Egyptian) shari'a principles and practices that may be found in sources of medieval Islamic jurisprudence.

The spotty presence of medieval doctrines in modern Egyptian law follows the pattern we have observed in other Islamic national laws. The national shari'as are hence an extension of Islamic law, but *not only* of Islamic law. In the aforementioned Article 1 in Egypt's civil code, drafted in 1938 and codified into law in 1949, the sources of the law, once again, are enumerated as official *legislation, custom and tradition, Islamic sharia,* and *natural law and the principles of equity*—corresponding to the national, religious, and human or international aspects of the Egyptian nation. Democracy and social justice made their appearance in other documents. It seems to be the same story, broadly speaking.

The dramatic language of Article 2 in Egypt's constitution (see textbox), for example, seems to embrace the full extent of Islamic law, public and private, but indicates something much narrower in scope to the practicing Egyptian lawyer. This language does not by itself guarantee a broad jurisdiction for Islamic law, but it has its applications in many areas of the law.

This sentence means to convey that the general themes and principles of the shari'a are one of the main foundations of the law in Egypt. Any ambiguity is left to an institution called the Supreme Constitutional Court

> Islam is the religion of the state and Arabic is its language; and the principles of the Islamic Sharia are the principal source of its laws.
>
> Article 2 in Egypt's Constitution
>
> (First appeared in this form in 1980; in 1971 it would read Islamic legal principles *a* principal source, rather than *the* principal source of the laws.)

(SCC) to dispel. Below this court, lower courts of different types provide explanations of civil, criminal, and family law that attempt to reconcile these principles of Islamic law with the rest of the legislation, judicial tradition, and authoritative jurisprudence.

On November 4, 1978, Dr. Sufi Abu Talib (the Speaker of the Egyptian House of Representatives) stated that the Shariʻa Clause of Article 2 must become the foundation, not only of new laws' compatibility with shariʻa principles, but the foundation of an active effort to streamline existing laws with well-established shariʻa principles. This set in motion a forty-month effort (December 1978 through July 1982) by eight different legislative and technical committees (from criminal and civil law to commercial and maritime, and from social laws to the laws of financial and economic practices). In the middle of this period (May 22nd, 1980), an indefinite article in the Shariʻa Clause was replaced with a definite article, where *the Shariʻa* became *the* principal as opposed to *a* principal source of the laws. No scholar of Egyptian law takes this as indicative that all laws in Egypt are shariʻa compatible.

Sanhuri (d. 1971) is considered responsible for both introducing the language of shariʻa in the law (in Article 1, Section 2 of his civil code of 1949) and the hybrid method in instituting modern laws that are shariʻa compatible. The first draft of his civil code underwent much discussion among high-court judges, lawmakers, notable lawyers, and executives. It seems that a cycle of limited interest in the shariʻa (as in the one between 1949 and 1978) started to take place as of the early 1980s. A brief interest in shariʻa language after 2011 also stalled.

The by-now familiar view that all modern rearticulating of medieval shariʻa doctrines, even by the greats, are instances of misunderstanding, twisting, and appropriation can apply to many of the novel ways of reading medieval Islamic legal doctrines by Sanhuri and his successors. Again, this may well be very much correct from a certain standpoint. There is something wrong about being obsessed about how the interpretation of inherited legal views only in the modern world are wrong and all premodern twists and turns of doctrine are authentic and justified. (In any case, I do not claim the expertise of practice, even in Egyptian law, which I spent some time studying. There will always be lawyers and judges who are uncomfortable with considering their modern legal traditions to be based on Islamic law. And, you know, one of those who disagree may be wrong, and that may well be me.)

Modern Egyptian law remains a depository of basic principles and practices of Islamic law. In **criminal** jurisprudence, severe punishments are assigned to crimes that spread narcotics and prey on weak individuals (or "agents"). The medieval idea of *hiraba*, or large-scale corruption, (though not the specific punishment) finds its way into anti-drug trafficking and human trafficking laws. In **civil** law, especially in contract theory, protection of the weak agent, which has been interpreted by many scholars as a manifestation of a socialist tendency, also bears the language of medieval Islamic jurisprudence. Terms such as "trickery" and "duress" and their applications invoke the old terms *tadlis* and *gharar*. In **family** law, the old idea that marriage is a contract with rights and responsibilities for *both* parties (husband *and* wife) and protection for future offspring dominates the reasoning in this area in family court cases.

Egyptian public law is influenced by many aspects of Islamic law. Public conduct is regulated by a notion that both modern French law and Islamic law support: the notion of public manners. This is a good example where Egyptian lawmakers and judges find no distance between the objectives of modern European law and those of Islamic law as understood and practiced in the Egyptian legal tradition.

Lawyers who become judges in Egypt have not all invested hours of study in Islamic law; many of them found it enough to attend to a required subject in law school, called Islamic shari'a. It simply depends on how much dedication the judge gave to studying medieval jurisprudence and the long history of modern Egyptian law that drew on shari'a principles. And at the end of the day, if a judge goes too far in deferring to these old ideas and ignores the way modern practice may have modified or even superseded them, his or her decisions will be subject to reconsideration.

In many cases of actual practice, the shari'a is invoked, and its invocation passes muster. Again, it depends on the case and how much the relevant legislation and judicial practice allows room for employing old juristic ideas (in addition to the judge's effort and interest, as stated). Shari'a is invoked in administrative cases, for example, because administrative law goes back to basic principles more frequently than civil law. Shari'a is also omnipresent in family law, as even the legislation in this area is directly influenced by medieval ideas and practices.

The financial sector in Egypt is also hybridized. Islamic finance institutions and globalized investment entities are both active. (Ultimately, you will learn in Unit 7, the financial markets are not dominated by Islamic moral or legal standards.) Finally, urban environments in Egypt, especially of the upper middle class, are heavily influenced by the standards of modern life. They increasingly show a tendency toward the weakening of the families and an emphasis on careers and work ethics.

2.4 Saudi Arabia

While lacking a document called a "constitution," Saudi Arabia has a "Basic Law" consisting of eighty-three articles. Initially it considers the Qur'an and *Sunna* to be the country's constitution but moves on to describe the monarchy. Articles 7 and 8 then repeat what is now to us a familiar pattern of considering Islamic law a foundational source of its laws. But note the nuances, even in the English translation.

In our discussion of the asylum of MMK in Unit 1, we discussed Saudi legal doctrines on adultery and suspicion of it, lewd behavior, child custody, and guardianship. One distinctive quality in modern Saudi law, compared to many of the national versions of the shari'a, is its ability to draw modern opinions and court decisions from medieval juristic commentary directly, without the intermediary (often transformative) of modern legal codes.

In a thirty-volume publication, the Saudi Ministry of Justice put out summaries of hundreds of cases that were decided during the judicial year 1434 (of the Hijri Calendar). Now that you all are adept at using your converter, you will know that we are talking about the time between November 2012 and November 2013. (Also, review Unit 1, sections 1.2–1.5, and references to it.) In the beginning of these volumes, the Minister of Justice, who is also the Chief of the Supreme Judicial Council, wrote an introduction, spelling out some of the characteristics of the modern Saudi school of law and adjudication and how they contrast with Latin, Anglo-Saxon, and federal American law and adjudication.

The broad regional influence of modern Egyptian law, with its hybrid sources, is not noticeable here. The crux of the discussion in the Minister's introduction is that both judicial principles (from Saudi practice) and judicial precedents are binding on judges when they handle similar cases. This is when the principle or precedent is established by a high court (eg, the Mecca Appellate Court or the Riyadh Supreme Court). But every new case may have elements that require new

> **Article 7:**
> Government in the Kingdom of Saudi Arabia derives its authority from the Book of God and the *Sunna* of the Prophet (PBUH), which are the ultimate sources of reference for this Law and the other laws of the State.
>
> **Article 8:**
> Governance in the Kingdom of Saudi Arabia is based on justice, shura (consultation) and equality according to Islamic Sharia.
>
> Basic Law of Saudi Arabia

reflection and new jurisprudence. As long as these elements are convincingly stated, the judge has a degree of freedom. But without that, a new case should be decided in a manner that confirms to the established judicial principles and practices.

The Chief of the Supreme Judicial Council then discusses an old, medieval principle that states that "one, valid juristic argument does not revoke another." This principle, while ostensibly puzzling, does not really say more than "one case cannot be decided twice, unless it is (clearly) wrongly decided." Because judges (and *muftis*) have the freedom to decide "gray area" matters, and they will decide that inevitably differently, and there is no "neutral" arbiter among them, once a case is decided correctly by one judge, it should not be decided again. What an appellate court does is identify mistakes, and if there are none, it confirms the first court's decision.

What makes the system predictable and uniform is the *agreement* among judges and jurists *about the standards of correctness*. No legal or judicial system will withstand wide-ranging freedom in deciding cases. This is why, at some point, aberrations will be brought to conform to these standards, via the higher courts.

This system has many similarities with all the legal and judicial systems discussed in this Unit. It has an unusual confidence, however, that it can arrive at practical solutions to all modern questions of law, from a fairly *limited number* of juristic ideas that have been spread around in medieval legal literature and another finite number of modern legal and judicial principles and practices.

Let us now take one simple case to learn about examples of these principles and practices. This is a case where the law of gifts and the laws of inheritance overlap. A man who deceased in 2010 leaving two wives, each with six children, gave a four-story apartment building as a gift to one of his wives and her children only five months before he died. The plaintiff in the case, one of the six siblings who did not receive the gift, argued that the gift was given in a circumstance that made it void. (If you give a gift in the illness that leads to your death, the will is rendered invalid.) The plaintiff was given the right to represent three of his siblings; the other two seemed uninterested in the case. The father's illness, this plaintiff argued, left him 60 percent paralyzed in the right side, according to a hospital report. He made the gift under the influence of this paralysis.

The hospital report, however, showed that the father had improved significantly after the paralysis, and regained a stable and fairly normal state. This made the (lower) Mecca court decide in favor of the defendants. After all, individuals' legal actions must be presumed valid, unless otherwise is demonstrated to the court's satisfaction. Since it was not demonstrated that the deceased was under undue pressure, stress, or duress, his actions were presumptively valid. The burden of proof clearly lay with the plaintiff. The son of the deceased should not only have shown that his late father was sick, but he also had to demonstrate that the illness *caused him to act* in a manner that made his actions void.

The Sixth Circuit in the Mecca Appellate Court delivered a final decision in early 2013. This appellate decision was in agreement with the lower court, confirming that it was decided based on a correct understanding of the legal priorities affecting the case (Vol. 9, pp. 252–9).

The decision appealed to basic notions in medieval Sunni law such as the autonomy and freedom of the individual to act as he wishes in his property, placing the burden of proof for an individual's failure of judgment on those who claim it, and the principle that duress, stress, and similar impediments of judgment must be demonstrated in obvious terms that are recognizable to all—whether they are or are not medical doctors. However, the court also employed medical expertise to an extent. The language of the decision, once again, expresses interest in the marriage of old and new forms of knowledge.

2.5 Pakistan

There is enough literature that attacks both Egypt and Pakistan for their extensive but inefficient state legal and judicial apparatus, which had led to regular violations of human rights. Pakistan is even further criticized for a much weaker rule of law, where stronger *tribal and social forms of law* and order can be identified. Pointing to an element that derives from Islamic law as part of the mix is usually sufficient to identify the culprit in violations of human rights. As noted, I continue to think that the mix is what needs to be observed and explained.

In strong contrast with Egypt, in any case, Pakistan bears a heavy colonial heritage of an Indian-British shari'a (the Indian version is *Hindu* and *Islamic*, hence Anglo-Indian and Anglo-Muhammadan). When it applies today, the British side of modern Pakistani law turns the clock backward to the common law tradition with its long (about 800-year) legacy. The

Figure 6.2 Supreme Court of Pakistan. Author: Usman. Image accessed via Wikimedia.

hallmark of English law is its judicial quality, its emphasis on dispensing justice through court activities and administrative edicts.

Consistency in the common law is achieved via following precedent. That is to say, a judge has to follow the decision of an equal or higher judge when he or she decides a similar case. This goes back in origin to the so-called Royal Commissioners (in the time of Henry II (r. 1154–89 CE)), who traveled around England to decide cases and chose to bind themselves to follow old decisions. The term (*stari decisis*) is loosely translated as "let the decision stand or let us stand by the decision." Like Pakistan, India and Bangladesh have also followed the common law tradition since the eighteenth–nineteenth centuries (the Mughal Muslim rule ended officially in 1857). Islamic law has also been part of the mix that is now modern Pakistani law and continues to militate against an idealized perfect consistency—just as it did under British rule.

In Pakistan, the Federal Shariat Court (FSC) has jurisdiction to review lower court decisions for conformity with traditional Islamic law. The only judicial authority higher than these courts is the Pakistan Supreme Court itself. Equal to the FSC are five high courts, one for the capital (Islamabad) and four for the four provinces that make up the mainland (Peshawar, Baluchistan, Sindh, and Punjab—the latter known as the Lahore Court). Below these are regular courts. Tribal areas have a degree of legal autonomy, and disputed areas in *Azad Jammu Kashmir* and *Gilgit-Baltisatn* in the north-east (at the fault line between India and Pakistan) have their own system.

An example that shows the degree to which modern Pakistani judges felt entitled to interpret their legal tradition and modify it is the role they assign the courts in deciding divorce cases. Divorce, traditionally, was a private matter, and the husband, who bore the financial burden throughout the marriage and immediately after divorce, enjoyed a higher degree of control over it. If a woman wanted to initiate a divorce—and given that we are still in a traditional setting—she had to forfeit her financial benefits (dowry and gifts, in principle), while the children of the marriage were protected to the fullest possible extent and would receive financial support from their father even if they were young and in the custody of their mother. This divorce at the wife's initiative was called *khul'*. It was not traditionally an act of judicial divorce, with the judge overseeing the process and assigning rights and responsibilities. (In Hanafi law and in Maliki law, the supposed inspiration of this new law in Pakistan, a judge was not even required; Khalil (d. 768/1365), *al-Mukhtasar* (Beirut: Dar al-Fikr, 1981), p. 134). Traditionally, this "divorce at the wife's initiative" was something in the order of a repudiation of a private contract.

Changes in the modern family made many husbands and wives equal in the degree to which they bear financial responsibility, however. Courts thus needed to adjudicate in divorces (initiated by husband or wife), and divorce itself ceased to be a private matter. Following the Family Court Act 1964 (as emended in 2002), Pakistani courts started to supervise divorce at the wife's initiative. These courts have thus innovatively interpreted traditional standards in a manner that allowed the courts to play a larger role in administering what was traditionally the *work* of the husband, the wife, and their families.

Pakistani jurists have complained that their system is not easy for outsiders to understand, partly because it keeps evolving, and updates are noted only sparingly. Furthermore, what catches the interest of foreign legal reporters is not necessarily what is representative; in most cases, it is what is, in the large scheme of the legal system, *odd or unusual* not only in comparison with the different legal systems from which the legal reporter comes, but also odd by the standards of the system that is the subject of reporting itself. Legal reporters are also unable to tell the full story; their interest seems to wither away when things are less exciting or eye-catching. The US media made numerous references to something called the Hudud Ordinances (1979), passed under General Zia-ul-Haqq's leadership of the country, because it brought up corporeal punishment, including the death penalty, for adulterous women. But since 2006, when the Protection of Women Act was passed, after which no adultery case was brought to court for a decade, interest has waned rather.

Other cases that get attention are criminal law cases where corporeal punishment, punishment for honor crimes, or punishment for apostasy form part of the case's substance. Some scholars accuse Pakistani judges of tolerating cruel tribal laws and underestimating the value of the freedom of religion. Others accuse the judges of privatizing state criminal law as they allow family members of murder victims to forgive the killers of their relatives, which is a principle that is derived from medieval Islamic law. One such case is *Mohammad Riaz v. The Federal Government, Etc.* (1980). In this case, the principle that applying the death penalty is contingent on the approval of the family members of the deceased is established (Tahir Wasti, *The Application of Islamic Criminal Law in Pakistan* (Leiden: Brill, 2009), pp. 76–81). We will return to this issue in Unit 8.

In another case, *Dr. Pir Muhammad Khan v. Khuda Bukhsh* (CA No. 503, 2006), the Supreme Court of Pakistan considered a matter of pre-emptive sale (Arabic: *shufʻa*). Traditional pre-emption laws require a seller to offer his neighbor and partner the "option" to buy his neighboring property or share before executing the sale to a third party, at a price matching what is offered by a third party, according to their market's supply and demand conditions. If an individual fails to comply with pre-emption laws, the sale may be revoked and the offer of pre-emption at the offered price is then given to those who deserve it. In this case, a pre-emption claim was dismissed at an earlier stage in the lawsuit, because the sale was incomplete at the time. In another attempt, the decision in the case was challenged by the fact that statutory laws that regulate pre-emption laws were lacking. The Supreme Court, however, stated that the absence of statutory instructions does not turn the claim void, because pre-emption was to be regulated based on Islamic law (the Court used the term Muhammadan (spelled Mohammedan) law). It finally dismissed the claim of pre-emption for its failure to provide crucial information including the date, time, place, and the names of witnesses, which are required to establish or debate the claim of sale against the laws of pre-emption in Islamic law (Supreme Court Annual Report 2014–15, pp. 138–9).

In financial matters, where Islamic institutions seem to grow stronger in Pakistan, more innovation is found. Yet many laws hark back to times when India and Pakistan were one and the same country. (The Criminal Procedure Code of 1898 remains relevant, for example; and in the rules of Pakistan's Supreme Court (1980), the word "Code," by default, refers to the Civil Procedure Code of 1908—both preceding the formation of Pakistan.) Leftover banking practices in Pakistan are therefore not different from those pre-dating Iran's Shah system after 1979, such as the presumption that a reasonable interest may be charged on loans.

2.6 Modern Islamic law

The relevance of shariʻa arguments in modern national laws is enhanced in cases of vacuum or indeterminacy in national laws, especially in areas where the shariʻa has functioned in its broad scope in the past. Its use depends on creative arguments by scholars, both of the national and the religious laws.

We already mentioned Article 917 of Egypt's civil code, which states that, "were a person to transfer his/her property to one of his/her inheritors but keep physical control of the property and draw benefits from it for the remainder of his/her life, the property transfer is presumed to fall under the laws of the will—as long as no evidence militates against this presumption." One clash of legal imperatives relevant to Article 917 concerns its retroactive application. It is not in disagreement that the law of gifts was extracted from personal status laws and made a normal part of civil law proper. Conflicting legal imperatives, however, persisted. Does Article 917 retroactively apply to inheritance that occurred before October 15, 1949, the date the code became enforceable? This hinges on whether the article establishes a substantive law or a rule of circumstantial evidentiary presumption. If the former, it does *not* apply retroactively at all. If the latter, it tells the judge that when ambiguity befalls a certain property that is part of an inheritance, where the property was given in sale or as a gift to one of the inheritors but not delivered before the death of its owner, the judge must take the incomplete delivery as a presumption that the property was intended by the deceased to be part of the inheritance. Its retroactive application remains a matter of juristic disagreement.

In his *Remedies for Breach of Contract in Islamic and Iranian Law*, S. H. Amin points to an argument by Shaykh Murteza Ansari (1781–1864) on the conditions that allow "rescission" of a contract. One condition is when the fulfillment of the contract is so much of an undue burden that it creates a mandate for rescission. In this case, two conflicting considerations of equal power, the initial commitment created by the contract and the consideration of avoiding undue burden, clashed. As a result, the jurists decided to consider them to be "null and void"—appealing, that is, to the idea of conflicting and equal considerations canceling out each other.

Modern Iranian jurists took the crisis of conflicting legal imperatives and turned it into an opportunity. They applied the clash of legal imperatives in a creative manner to solve the problem of the prohibition of usury that which they inherited from medieval Islamic law, and which seemed to be unimplementable in modern financial contexts.

Here we witness a broad application of the idea that conflicting considerations cancel out one another. The result is a restatement of the legal obligations of those who are parties to a contract leading to a financial obligation. Rescission of a contract and a contractual obligation is caused by the presence of "undue burden," effectively overpowering the initial contractual commitment. Beyond this rescission, a modern Iranian lawyer, jurist, and judge all aim at a fairer or more just formula for contracts involving monetary obligations that are affected by money's constant loss of value.

Modern Iranian lawyers have tried to understand why dealing in usury appeared to be so unfair in medieval markets, while prohibiting usury in modern financial markets also appears to be unfair. The point here is the conflict between two considerations, which on the face of it seem to be of equal power. The first consideration is that, in a medieval loan or inadvertent debt emanating from medieval market dealings, the lender is guaranteed a profit, while the borrower is not. In modern market dealings, money simply loses value over time and unless it is invested, its value decreases. Keeping the value of a debt at the same level as its initial amount (at the time of its transfer from lender to borrower) is, in effect, committing a degree of injustice toward the lender. Modern Iranian lawyers thought that the discretion given to a judge to implement "judicial remedies" to correct an imbalance in a contract allows for a normalization of reasonable interest on loans. They thus state that a contract establishing an unfair return of the same monetary value creates a legal imperative in competition with the legal imperative of avoiding unjust commitments and undue burdens in contractual obligations.

The idea of taking the "undue burden" standard as a "ground" for revoking a commitment or rescinding a contractual obligation also appears in medieval Islamic law and other modern national laws. Let us give an example from medieval Islamic law and one from modern Egyptian law to make this case. In medieval Sunni law, *iqala* (or rescinding contractual commitments) was recommended to party A in a contract in which party B has what we now call "buyer's remorse." Medieval Sunni jurists have also considered the extent to which *iqala* may involve unacceptable modifications to the initial contract. For example, a standard permissible loan or sale may be modified into a usurious transaction, once a rescission is conducted improperly (Ibn Rushd (d. 596/1198), *Bidayat al-Mujtahid wa Nihayat al-Muqtasid (The Jurist's Primer)* (Beirut: Dar al-Ma'arif, 1982; 6th ed.), Vol. 2, p. 141).

Article 147/2 in Egypt' Civil Code states that:

> should exceptional, unforeseeable conditions of a general character arise, and should their rise lead to a condition where the implementation of a contractual obligation be, while not impossible, so burdensome for the party carrying a debt, leading to an inevitably and unusually large loss, the judge, taking the circumstances of the case and the interests of both parties in the case into account, may resize or restate the obligation to a reasonable threshold. . . .and all disagreements against this estimate become null and void.

3 Conclusion

How many times did we mention the year **1980**? In 1980, the Federal Sharia Courts of Pakistan were founded, Article #2 in Egypt's constitution considered Islamic legal principles *the* principal source of its laws, and it was on October 24, 1979 (a few weeks before 1980 started) that Iranians ratified their constitution with a referendum. This leaves Indonesia and Saudi Arabia. The Saudi Basic Law of Governance, which stipulates that Islamic law is the law of the land came in **1992**, and Indonesia's Constitution, the oldest of all these, having come out of its independence in **1945** (on August 17th, two days after Japan's unconditional surrender, and ten and eight days respectively after the famous nuclear attacks). The year **1980** is vital in three out of the five countries you learned about here.

In each one of the five countries we mentioned here, there are basically two legal systems, sometimes working in tandem, sometimes clashing, and most of the time coexisting. The first is a national legal system that is not necessarily in full compliance or cacophony with shari'a principles. To decide this compliance with shari'a principles, a case has to come up in order to force the judges and lawyers to hit the books and do some research. The second consists of laws that are derived from shari'a principles, according to the legal authorities in each country. When a review of court decisions or even legislation considers the conformity of national laws with shari'a, some reshuffling and readjustment occur.

How is it possible? How is it done? To an extent, like most laws, change is a work in progress. This was the way the medieval shari'a itself operated. The yardstick against which

Review and reflect VI

Do you remember that?

- Muslim nations reconcile their version of Islamic law with international and moral principles they have adopted in the modern context.
- Some premodern customs of non-Islamic provenance are reconciled with medieval Islamic legal reasoning and modern notions of morality and justice.
- Muslim nations with quasi-federal arrangements allow a large degree of legal and moral pluralism.

Five nations

- In Egypt, since 1949, the civil law includes many elements of Islamic law. As of 1971, constitutional support for employing medieval Islamic law was added, although in practice this has not led to the modernizing of old institutions on a large scale.
- In Iran, since the revolution, laws must be reviewed for conformity with the Ja'fari legal tradition.
- In Saudi Arabia, judges enjoy a degree of freedom in relying on the medieval tradition in family, civil, and criminal matters.
- In Pakistan, the Federal Shariat Court occasionally intervenes to streamline modern legal practice with Islamic law.
- In Indonesia, a complex of old customs, some Islamic and some not, is reconciled with modern notions of justice.

the process is measured is local customs and the established recent ways of doing things—unless, of course, the government decides to do some blunt social engineering with the laws.

Arguments that contemporary lawyers lack the training to participate in the making of Islamic law will always exist, but they will also not deter current legal and political authorities in the Muslim world from continuing this pattern of lawmaking and examination. The jurisdiction of Federal Sharia Courts in Pakistan, for example, and the Appellate Shari'a Bench of its Supreme Court are supposed to not intervene in civil procedure or constitutional matters. Islamic law's jurisdiction is seen when these high courts are asked to examine a law's compliance with Islamic legal principles. But the argument is not infinite. The buck stops with the Appellate Shari'a Bench of Pakistan's Supreme Court, just as Egypt's Supreme Constitutional Court ends all disputes about the meaning of the shari'a clause in Egypt's constitution.

Primary Source Material IV (Hanafi Legal Maxims)

Source: Ahmad Muhammad al-Zarqa (d. 1938), *Sharh al-Qawa'id al-Fiqhiyya* (A Commentary on Legal Maxims) (Damascus: Dar al-Qalam, 1993), pp. 311–14. This one-volume commentary explicates the ninety-nine maxims that appear as Articles 2–100 in the 1876 Ottoman codifications of civil laws, known as *Majallat al-Ahkam al-'Adliyya*.

Authority of a narrow jurisdiction trumps a general authority

EXPLANATION

Particular (or area-specific) authority trumps general authority, because any element that is less general has a higher force, a stronger impact, and a farther bearing. The Arabic word, *walaya* means "support" in its lexical usage, and the word *wilaya* [from the same root with different vowels] denotes authority and control. The second word is used in the religio-legal vernacular to indicate legal power over others, whether they accept or refuse this authority. And authority can either be general or of a particular jurisdiction.

General authority may extend over religious and worldly affairs, and may apply to persons or property. This is the general authority of the community's overall leader (*imam*) or his delegates. By this authority, the leader has (general) jurisdiction over preparing the armies, defending the soft bellies of the state and its borders, collecting financial dues, within the limits of what is lawful, and as long as he allocates and dispenses of them properly. He also has an overall authority to appoint judges and local rulers, preside over the organization of pilgrimage and the congregational prayers, apply criminal punishments, thwart the seditious and the transgressors, and protect the land and the religion. He is also responsible for resolving conflicts and ending tussles, appointing overseers [for endowments and the property of minors and those under interdiction] and holding them to account, and marrying off those with no supervision by family members—among other matters [that affect the totality of the community].

Specific or limited authority also applies in: first, matters pertaining to both persons and property; and second in matters of pertinence to property only. The first kind covers four areas, where the authority has: a strong force in both [person and property]; a force weak in both; or a force strong in one and weak in the other.

An example of the first area [where authority is **strong over both** person and property] is the authority of a father (or grandfather) to marry off his children, supply them with basic domestic-medical treatment and the like, and administer their property on their behalf, as is known in marriage and probate laws (with all the conditions discussed in these laws, including that the supervisor be a free person, able to shoulder legal responsibility, and be of the same religion as those he supervises—whether both are or are not Muslim).

An example of authority that is **weak over both** [person and property] is that of a custodian who is a stranger or a relative caring for a minor, when a closer relative can be identified. The custodian has jurisdiction over the minor's person and property, but this jurisdiction is weak. The custodian [within these limits] may instruct or even punish the minor, prepare him for a profession, buy for him what he needs, accept gifts and charity on his behalf, and protect his money.

An example of authority that **is strong over the person and weak over the property** is a non-father (and non-grandfather) relative-supervisor of minors, whether he be from the father's or mother's side. These supervisors have powers similar to the father/grandfather with the same conditions, when the father/grandfather is absent, but are audited if they marry off their supervised one to a non-peer (an inappropriate spouse) or on an inappropriate dowry. These supervisors have power of attorney and can buy in the name of the supervised one, accept gifts or charity in their behalf, and protect their property, but cannot freely handle this property (even if this property was a gift the supervisor himself gave them). An exception [to the rule of auditing on selecting a marital partner and dowry] is the case of a son who marries off a parent, since the son's authority over her/his parents is tantamount to that of a parent over the children. It remains true that the son's authority over property is limited.

As for authority that is **weak over the property, strong over the person**, it is the authority of financial supervisors [appointed by father, grandfather, or judge]. The supervisor has power over the supervisee's property but none over their persons and behavior, not unlike a stranger with some limited supervision over minors.

An example of the second type, **authority that is absolutely limited to property**, is that of an endowment overseer, and those with power of attorney over the property of those absent (traveling or missing). These people can sell the movables and estates to repay a debt or a will *only* if the estates would have been sold by the owner if present, and if the debt or will could only be satisfied with the sale of estates.

APPLICATION

A judge has no authority over an endowment where an overseer is appointed, even if the judge himself appointed that overseer. [Their authority may not operate simultaneously and one must be presumptively over the other.] Were the judge to apply a rental agreement of an asset, receive payments normally receivable by the overseer, or an exchange of currency on its behalf—all such acts are non-executable (auditable, conditionally executable).*

Similarly, a judge may not handle the property of a minor, while the custodian (appointed by a father, grandfather, or the judge) is available. As for the case of a custodian appointed by the mother of a minor, or a relative with a weak jurisdiction over the minor's property, the judge's authority prevails.

EXCEPTIONS

Some jurists argue that an exception to this maxim is as follows. They say that a custodian could not demand retaliation (for murder) from the killer of a person who would be inherited by a minor under his custody. We know that a judge may demand this execution in behalf of the minor. This shows that the judge's authority here [the general] prevails over the custodian's [the particular].

In fact [the author now expresses his view]: There is no exception there [ie, these scholars got the law right but explained it wrong]. The power to demand retaliation in murder cases for a minor is a case of jurisdiction over the person (not the property). The custodian has no jurisdiction over the *person of the minor* [eg, he does not get to force him to receive a certain kind of education or profession] in his custody. [His jurisdiction is financial.] If there is any

---

* Hanafi jurists make fine distinctions among actions that are "invalid," "corrigible," and "conditionally executable." The first applies to incorrigible transactions, and the second to ones that are corrigible but require added actions for correction. Non-executables require a review and confirmation (in this case, they will be given to the one who possesses the authority to vet and execute).

amount of power over the minor's person, it is a weak type and does not exceed the authority of a stranger who happens to raise the minor in his house [eg, if married to his mother].

A proper exception from the maxim is that an endowment overseer could not hire and fire employees for the endowment, unless the terms of the endowment explicitly allow him to do that. A judge, by contrast, has this authority.

A judge may also lend the money of a minor, while the minor's father* or custodian could not.

A judge may also borrow for the endowment, exchange its assets for others (within the parameters and conditions of the endowment), and even rent its assets for a long time without having to refurbish them, but an overseer may not perform any of these actions.

NOTE

What we said regarding the judge's disqualification from handling a matter under the jurisdiction of an overseer or custodian, even when the latter is appointed by the judge, is specific to *cases where the conflict of jurisdiction does not undo the basic responsibility assigned by the judge to* the overseer. [The ship can't have two captains, in other words.] Hence the judge oversees the work of custodians, supervisors, and overseers and can fire those found guilty of embezzlement or of any other instance of dereliction of duties. All these "apparent" exceptions are based on the fact of the generality of the jurisdiction for those who have general jurisdiction. By the same token, a judge may rent an asset of an endowment to the *endowment overseer himself* or a relative of the overseer (whose testimony for the overseer is not taken in court given the relationship—a very close relative, in other words).

Exercise

- The basic idea of this text is simple: The specific trumps the general when they clash in jurisdiction. When the teacher assigns a leader for a discussion group, the teacher does not keep overruling the discussion leader, and the discussion leader does not keep asking the teacher what to do. But are there surprising elements in the discussion. For example, would you think that an endowment overseer should have more power than a judge in interpreting the terms of the endowment? Zarqa has it the other way around, based on the exceptions he mentioned.

---

* Think of a judge appointed to preserve the minor's inheritance from his deceased mother.

7 The Transnational Shari'a

You have now heard, at least twice, that Hanafi jurists developed the doctrine that laws follow geography (Unit 4). They also thought that non-Muslim communities living in Muslim-governed towns should develop their own laws, as long as these did not contradict public laws. At first, non-Muslim communities living in Muslim cities were subjects Muslim judges were encouraged to protect, even in an area *modern* jurisprudence blocks off as *personal status* law (eg, marriage, alimony). In this scheme, non-Muslim communities inside Muslim lands developed a degree of autonomy; they were seen as free, for example, to develop their own family law and financial laws within the family as they pleased. Later, non-Muslim communities would be able to resolve their own legal disputes without the assistance of a Muslim judge.

An interesting shift in this area in legal reasoning took place as Islamic law evolved in its early stages. Abu Hanifa (d. 150/767) is reported to have allowed a Hanafi judge to apply Hanafi legal doctrines to adjudicate a claim of financial support by a mother against her son, who is also her former husband, because Zoroastrian laws allowed this incestuous marriage. This "mixed court" procedure (mixing the Zoroastrian marriage and claims of financial support under Islamic law) was rejected one generation later; Abu Hanifa's student, Muhammad ibn al-Hasan al-Shaybani (d. 189/805), disagreed with the master, and Shaybani's view carried on for the subsequent millennium as the standard Hanafi doctrine. Such a speedy rejection of a doctrine is explained (according to later Hanafi authorities) by a shift in the conditions and customs of the times. Many Zoroastrians, who lived in Kufa and sought judicial protection, could not be ignored by Muslim judges active at that time; later, this became a false (ie, non-existent) problem not in need of a solution. The old view clearly complicated a useful doctrine Hanafis were on the verge of developing, and one you are now very familiar with: Laws follow geography, and religious minorities must develop their own laws within a Muslim town or city, as long as these do not clash with public laws.

The theory of the "abode of Islam" (Unit 4, section 1.1) developed, and with it the notion of legal death (*mawt hukmi*), which stipulated that the financial assets of person A living in a Muslim abode disappears (ie, his property must be distributed among his inheritors or creditors) when he permanently departs to a foreign abode. This is barring an agreement between the leaders of the two abodes (or nations) covering an exchange of property across the borders.

Shaybani was indeed the true founder of both the "two-abode theory" of the law and the "legal death" theory. These state that a person who emigrates from an abode of Islam to an abode of unbelief or vice versa loses his legal "personality" (hence, his marriages dissolve, his property is distributed among inheritors, among other applications). Al-Asl's discussion of the marriages of those of the *unbelief abode* (where even if some Muslims live permanently, they live among a non-Muslim majority) shows an inclination to consider cases involving non-Muslims to be outside of the scope of Islamic adjudication. For example, a conversion to Zoroastrianism of a Jew or Christian who is married to a Jew is not contestable in a Muslim court, since marriages between Jews and Zoroastrians do occur (*Asl*, 4/463). This last explanation seems similar to what the teacher Abu Hanifa taught in that Muslim courts accept and leave in peace other religious communities and practices. His other conclusion, that a Hanafi judge could still hear disputes arising from non-Muslim communities, was becoming a piece of legal history. This stance, which became the final norm for the coming generations, was that divergence between Islamic and non-Islamic family laws means that non-Muslim communities must take care of their marital conflicts outside of Muslim courts, as otherwise the latter would need to develop legal and judicial practices *outside of* Islamic law.

According to a view of the world that admits of sometimes cooperative, sometimes conflicting political entities (which we call "nations" to simplify things), transnational law is an exception to the norm where laws are developed and enforced within nations. But does it really exist, and if so, in what form? If any such transnational law exists besides occasional agreements among nations, a religious law ought to be the last possible candidate for a law that transcends nations. In fact, the presence of a transnational shari'a would be seen as an anomaly from the viewpoint of early or traditional modernity. The Islamic shari'a is supposed to be a religious law, functioning in the personal life and, after the rise of Muslim nations, within the national borders that are governed by national laws. On a supranational scale today, only "modern international law" should be operative. The presence of Islamic law on any scale transcending traditional communities, no matter how small, does require an explanation.

Mixing things up

It is precisely because the Islamic shari'a, when compared to modern laws, is a different kind of law in many respects that we see it functioning even as the nation state's reach is limited or non-existent (where individuals are free to direct their money to this or that investment, marry or refrain from marrying individuals who share or do not share the individual's religion, enter into agreements with others that do not explicitly violate existing laws). It is undeniable that the presence of Islamic law on a transnational scale has developed in recent times for a variety of reasons. Modern national and international institutions, which have in some cases shown a strong preference for (if not a total adherence to) modern Western ideas have also shown no strong commitments or adherence to these values when the cost–benefit analysis led to that end. Late modern and postmodern economics, for example, has few ideological commitments. These systems are thus able to accommodate Islamic financial institutions of different types as long as they accept the framework of what qualifies as *profit* and what is taken for granted as *value*.

Power relations are often more complex than academic categories allow, and much is in a state of conflict, with power of any kind ebbing and flowing. As early as 1966 Paul Bohannan said that the Western frontiers have finally closed, and Western people were becoming "doubly aware of boundaries and frontiers. They themselves [are] the people who are in the way" (*Beyond the Frontier*, edited by Paul Bohannan and Fred Plog, (Garden City,

NY: 1967), p. xi). The post-colonial decades afforded the Euro-American populations no choice but to accommodate non-Euro-American populations and their customs—albeit reluctantly.

In the Introduction we discussed a vision of a (twenty-first-century) fully-fledged globalization looking forward to a reconciliation of the world's legal systems. This reconciliation cannot start until there is a broad recognition that it *must* start, however. For now, and in many parts of the Muslim world, as we showed in Unit 6 there is a mix of *modern institutions*, understood in their Muslim environments fairly differently from their environments of origin, and *older institutions* from the medieval traditions. These new mixes are what need to be reconciled with foreign laws. In this unit, the impact of the nation on the laws will look relatively weak. Broad (transnational) instances of the borrowing of ideas from different origins will dominate.

In this context, many organizations of transnational character experimented with ideas that ostensibly did not have a sufficiently modern character but which have nonetheless survived. This movement is slow, which is why, as this Unit will show, one must study the presence of non-modernized or non-Western traditions and the new borrowing from the past into the modern world in tandem with reactions from and resistance by modern institutions. Conventional (modern, that is) Western finance still exerts a strong degree of control over Islamic financial organizations, and the same can be said about other transnational endeavors that derive inspiration from medieval Islamic legal traditions.

1 Islamic financial jurisprudence

Islamic finance is one of the shari'a's areas of transnational presence. There is a good amount of caricaturing (not all undeserved) of Islamic finance in various types of literature. Islamic finance seems to be nothing more than validating or *islamizing* an existing transaction or scheme (in a mutual fund, for example) after renaming it. Home mortgages, which are sales with payments in installments, are called "diminishing partnerships" (*musharakah mutanaqisa*) In the sense that the bank and the buyer are "partners" in buying the house, with the bank's share diminishing over time, reaching zero at the end, so that the buyer becomes the full owner of the house. Complex descriptions of the same familiar capitalist process become the essence of Islamic finance. In these representations, the prohibitions on usury and contractual ambiguity, a balanced approach to contracts and promises in financial dealings, and a balanced view of setting prices and regulating markets in Islamic financial jurisprudence are depicted merely as one useless strawman after another. Why would we study Islamic finance, if it were at best a complicated way of saying the same thing one may learn in a straightforward manner and at worst a dusty, unintelligible system?

Islamic financial jurisprudence rests on some simple principles. When value is generated, it can be allotted. Investment, via partnerships of different kinds, needs to happen, and growth needs to take place in order for this value to be distributed among the partners. If that presumed or hoped-for growth does not materialize and losses are incurred, these are shared by both sides. In other words, no party in a partnership should emerge unaffected by any losses arising from it. Contractual ambiguity should be eliminated, as it helps to create unequal positions and hence injustice. Many argue that Islamic financial jurisprudence is constructed from the two "ingredients" of the prohibitions on ambiguity and usury you briefly learned about in Unit 2 (sections 2.1.1 and 2.1.2). There is today enough secondary literature based on the understanding that Islamic finance, in essence, is about the *fair* distribution of risk. One could also argue it all comes down to eliminating the element of "unfair compensation." This last category is broader than unfair distribution of *risk*. (Is it obvious why?) Make a point of reading this and the next two sections with these assumptions in mind. Try to test them to see which one works better to tie up the following elements of this "system."

One anomaly in modern Islamic finance is that (in practice) it allowed the traditionally weaker schools of law (eg, Hanbali law) a stronger presence. Traditionally dominant Sunni schools, such as the Hanafi traditions, became less dominant, compared with their Hanbali counterparts in areas not addressed in medieval legal literature. Hanbali law provided significant service to modern Islamic finance, given its reliance on "fuzzier" notions such as *maslaha* (legitimate utility), which results in an inclination toward allowing innovative forms of partnership, whether these involve property or simply the potential for new ideas of partnership and investment. The category of *sharikat al-abdan*, which are agreements to enter into partnerships based on potential gain from one's efforts or creative schemes, was looked at suspiciously by the so-called *ashab al-ra'y*—legal scholars who relied mostly on reason in their judgment of market laws. The highest representation among the four Sunni schools of these (*ashab al-ra'y*) jurists was in Hanafi law. These scholars regulated partnerships that involved property provided by one side of the partnership and potential work or activities by other sides as deals that involve salaried work, while Hanbali jurists acknowledged that these arrangements may take into account possibilities uncontemplated by these jurists (there are multiple cases in Ibn Qudama, *al-Mughni*, Vol. 7, pp. 111–28, for example). In simple terms, a partnership based on potential is allowed in Hanbali law. This philosophical difference has an impact in allowing unchartered territories of investments that involve credit and future derivatives.

Furthermore, Hanbali reliance on the flexible notion of *maslaha*, or legitimate utility, allowed them to go on and build up legal generalizations (maxims) that came in handy when modern Islamic institutions were looking for guidance from the medieval laws to establish their organizations on solid foundation. The flexibility of legitimate utility opens doors for new schemes for investment as well. Islamic law's paradigms of justice and fair investment, however, remain uncomfortable, to put it mildly, with compounded derivatives and the presumption of future money being part of the contemporary market.

All Islamic financial institutions gain their legitimacy from a critique of conventional Western finance but in practice want to be part of the (corrupt) system they reject. Money is like government; you may not like its ways, but to rebel against it, difficult calculations must be made. We should now explain the meta-view of current finance and its contrast with principled Islamic finance and later explain how the hybridity of actual Islamic financial practices makes it ultimately comport with the presumptions of potential growth leading to presumptions of real growth, and the legitimacy of constant debt and derivatives that are superimposed on debts, among other basic flaws in current capitalist practices.

1.1 What is wrong with conventional modern finance?

The two basic criticisms leveled against conventional, modern financial markets by Islamic financial principles are as follows: First; the lifetime of transactions and debt, uninterrupted by review, is too long; second, there is a relaxed acceptance of considering "future money" as part of *present* markets. These two points are related, but for clarity's sake we will take each separately. We will then talk briefly about bubbles and scandals and their role in revealing those weak points in the conventional (capitalist) economic system that arise from what Islamic financial jurisprudence rejects.

1.1.1 THE ADDICTION TO DEBT

Participants in financial markets are always moving their money and seeking to gain a return on it. Moments of accountability—stopping to take stock of where one's activities have led one, or making sure we know who owns what or how much we actually own—tend to be all too brief and ineffectual. In fact, they are non-existent by the standards of Islamic financial jurisprudence.

The fast movement of money in a conventional system is supposed to be an advantage. It fulfills the promise of the happy marriage between the industrial revolution and capitalism by permitting us to do more with money (and materials for investment) than our ancestors were ever able to. Of course, it is true that the world has witnessed unprecedented financial turbulence in recent times, and it is also true that fake investments have increased. These fake investments are possible because true accountability is rare, movement is fast, and there is something of a new science or art of scamming that takes advantage of what, in late twentieth- and early twenty-first-century markets, some economists have termed "super-capitalism."

Take Ponzi schemes and ask yourself why they are possible. I can take a good amount of money from you and promise to invest it, telling you it will generate a very competitive X percent profit. I then put some of the money back into returns, creating the appearance of a solid investment and then, having spent the remaining money myself, plot how to perhaps move to another location that would not force my extradition to where I would have to pay back what I took away. If I can get many people like you to give me even more money to invest, I can buy more time and think of more sophisticated schemes to recycle the group's money around the investors. None of these scenarios is fanciful. They all happened and have been recorded. And, yes, many of their perpetrators have been caught, but often at a great cost of time and capital.

In traditional, premodern finance, three qualities would make these schemes somewhere between hard and impossible. First, credit was rare and short-term. Second, large-scale operations also were rare and identifiable in relation to *real assets*. Third, the average person did not normally participate in these sizable operations. Add to all that one more thing: If you or a government were to invest a large sum, the investment would be reviewed constantly, and you would need to show me the real assets—land, houses, cattle, or crops, for example—that proliferated from, were improved by, or were generated by the investment. No one would be able to simply take a huge chunk of other people's money and attempt to move out of the country.

Keep in mind that credit does not, and should not, simply be presumed to generate interest, when there are no real economic activities to generate that interest. If there is a genuine partnership that leads to creating profit, partners make profit. A loan by itself does not guarantee a profit, though. Also keep in mind that ambiguity in a contractual agreement may lead to conflict and injustice for one of the parties—normally the "weaker" one. In

Islamic finance, the prohibition on usury and the fear of ambiguity, deliberate or not but which typically ends up by benefiting the party that created the agreement in the first place, creates a world antithetical to these forms of fraud.

1.1.2 FUTURE MONEY

When people invest money today, they assume that their investment will generate some type of profit. (And they want the largest profit possible.) They end up anticipating this profit (which is "future" money) so much that they begin to assume it exists. Or, they are led to believe it does exist. This encourages them to count the notional profit as part of their current wealth, which means that it is part of the existing market.

In 2008 a housing market crash catalyzed a recession in the US and beyond. The practices of the lending banks were blamed for it, and banks undoubtedly awarded loans to buyers who could not afford the houses they signed up to buy. A million-dollar house requires, in some cases, a monthly payment of about $7,000 (assuming a modest 10 percent down payment) for thirty years, which (realistically) requires a monthly income twice that and which needs to be capable of growing over the years. When buyers are not vetted, you end up with many people who default on the payment. The future money that has been *assumed to exist* is clearly not there.

There is a more fundamental problem. If I sold my house for $800,000 in 2005, and the new owner sold it on for $825,000 a year later, and each subsequent buyer sold it for a profit a short while later (depending on the kind of market of which the house was part), it is easy to see how the house could eventually earn a million-dollar price tag without really being worth a million dollars. Laws and good market practices are supposed to impede, rather than encourage, these conditions. It gets worse, the more frequent and rapid the sale of the same property. The central point is this: There is a demand that has created "fake" value. At some point, the bubble will pop, at which point we will all discover that the presumed value of the house is not there. Some poor guy will have bought the million-dollar house only to find that in reality it is worth much less than that, and end up losing money, rather than making money, on it.

Shari'a scholars considered high interest rates to be an indication of exploitation by lenders who charged them. They were told there was a new phenomenon in the world to be loosely called "rapid" growth—which made such rates not only fair, but also an essential element of preserving financial fairness. When constant growth started to look unlikely and, simultaneously, interest rates fell, the banks' addiction to lending based on so-called derivatives (again, imaginary value) caused the old critique to become valid again. When there is an increase in the return on the value of any loan, this return must correspond to some value people understand. When this value is only presumed or half-imagined, something is wrong. Looking at bubbles and scandals complicates and clarifies this a little more.

1.2 Bubbles

In the US, the Securities and Exchange Commission (SEC) was established as a federal entity charged with preventing fraudulent exchanges and protecting first-time investors. It was created after World War I, when many people hoped to move from rags to riches, as it were, if they invested in the right business. The SEC website relates the following sad turn of events, however. During the 1920s, approximately 20 million large and small shareholders took advantage of post-war prosperity and set out to make their fortunes in the stock market. It is estimated that of the $50 billion in new securities offered during this period, half became worthless.

Worthless market shares, as exemplifying fake economic value or "hope" for future economic value, did not stop there. The market getting ahead of itself became a stable feature, as exemplified by its "moments of truth," such as the so-called great inflation of the 1970s. Fast forward to the Great Recession of 2008, and you will find examples of houses whose value was *below the price paid for them* (how did that happen?). Bubbles and readjustments, no one now doubts, are a structural feature of modern markets and will occur frequently as long as value continues to be haphazardly assigned in the financial world. The modern SEC is, of course, not really against usury. The SEC is against *fraud*. The line between usury (where risk is borne only by one side) and fraud, as it is regarded in traditional Muslim jurisprudence, would not be as easy to draw, though.

Usury is unfair because it includes an element of exploitation, Muslim jurists believe. In a usurious interaction one party always has the upper hand and is in control. Further, this party will not be burdened by the future impact on the value he or she is exchanging for a guaranteed return. In a traditional market, I may loan you one pound of dates or raisins and guarantee a return of a pound and a half. You may well generate a value of two pounds in the meantime and earn a half-pound. But you may also fail and owe more than you can return.

When you make a bad investment—let's say you buy stocks that lose value over time—you are subjected to a different kind of exploitation if this entity you have invested with simply vanishes or is bailed out by the higher (and not so hidden) hand of a central bank. Muslim jurists have been trained to think of the essence of usury as this kind of unjust exchange, see these actions as essentially one and the same. Even if you are informed about the stock, and even if good financial theory tells you to buy and take the risk, making a loss ultimately renders you a victim of the same usury dynamic—bidding on future activities to generate value, while you owe part of this value immediately upon entering into the contract.

Former chief of the US Federal Reserve Bank Alan Greenspan has been quoted as saying that one can never be sure whether a bubbles exist or not when we are in the middle of it; one can only be sure there *has been a bubble after it bursts*. Joseph Stiglitz, Nobel Laureate for economics, has said there is a good argument for that. In an important sense, one can never really be sure that (even in a capitalist, growth-obsessed context) presumed value matches the capacity of the markets to operate in order to generate that value. It is only when the market acknowledges that it could not essentially "lie to itself" any longer and confesses activities were lagging far behind presumed economic value that one can be sure a bubble existed. The result, whether we accept this rhetoric or not, is the same. Capitalist markets do get ahead of themselves and presume to work with value that is imaginary. Islamic finance does not, in theory, assume that only verifiable value exists (look ahead to see how "endowments" in Ottoman times were, to a limited extent, the precursors of modern European banks). But the degree of review of economic activities to prevent the suffering of those in debt is more considerable in Islamic financial jurisprudence. This, in a modern interpretation, is the essence of the prohibition of usury and contractual ambiguity.

Like it nor not, bubbles are a characteristic of the way people do business now. Islamic financial justice frowns upon an emphasis on growth that allows these bubbles to exist in the first place, and in particular sees their "bursting" as an instance of clear injustice, the effects of which are most often borne by those with the least access to good advice and legal backing. The Islamic financial remedies, if applied as they appear in the traditional printed sources, would be seen as monstrous, backward withdrawals of the tremendous gains of modern finance (a view shared even by modern Islamic financial organizations, as well seen presently). But being part of the modern capitalist reality is also a call to action for jurists, rather than washing one's hands of the whole thing. This is why modern Islamic finance takes the weak points for granted and attempts to build on the shaky foundation. The resulting system is ultimately a hybrid of elements of Islamic financial justice and reasoning derived from necessity. Does it work? We will see that when we address Islamic finance as a melting pot of medieval Islamic financial laws and the modern system Islamic moral and legal schemes would be just as happy to attack and indict.

1.3 Scandals

One easy way to attack modern, US-style, finance is to point to a scandal such as that of Enron, which caused such a stink in late 2001. The elements of this scandal have been identified in detail, and include fraudulent accounting (euphemistically called "enhancing the company's financial statements"—hiding losses and exaggerating gains, basically) and incompetent leadership (Milhaupt 2008, pp. 48–51; #12 on the Further Reading list). Some argue that these violations have little to do with capitalism per se, but there is an argument that capitalism's promise of high returns tempts people to engage in illegal behavior, and its high speed weakens review processes. More importantly, the issue at hand is how reasonable these increases in value that people expect today are.

The purchase by the British telecommunications company Vodafone of the German Mannesmann corporation clarifies this point further. In February 2000, Vodafone acquired Mannesmann (which started in the coal and steel business but later added telecommunications to its portfolio). This "merger" benefited both businesses' shareholders (win–win) such that Vodafone was willing to pay Klaus Esser, the departing chair of Mannesmann's management board, and a lawyer himself, a retirement package of 15 million euros. Esser refused the money as a gift from Vodafone and wanted the money to be paid by Mannesmann, the company he served. Mannesmann's supervisory board agreed to pay him, and a criminal lawsuit proceeded, where German prosecutors before the Dusseldorf District Court and the Federal Supreme Court accused them of breach of trust. Ultimately these suits went nowhere. The American commentary (from a *Fortune* magazine headline) was that only in Germany is high pay a crime (Milhaupt 2008, pp. 70–4).

From a traditional American standpoint, everything looks good: everyone made money, so who is the curmudgeon and what is her or her problem? From a German nationalist perspective, a German economic asset has become British—hence "bad." The question for an Islamic jurist would be where the presumed value (that is compensated immediately at this very high price) came from—the value that allows someone to be paid millions as a departing gift (more millions were also pledged to managers junior to Esser—all in portions smaller than 15 million). Is the promised value to compensate for what is called a departing "gift" so certain? Is it really around the corner? Is it possibly exaggerated? (If it is a compensation, then what for? If it is not a compensation, what is it?)

1.4 The problem is not credit itself

So we now understand that in an ideal situation as far as Islamic jurisprudence goes, presumed value generation must be real in the sense of "present" to be taken as real. It should not be taken to mean that credit itself is either immoral or that it leads to exploitation. Muslim jurists, past and present, have accepted the practice of credit and building commitments based on debt, in general, and direct or clear loans, in particular.

Credit, in an Islamic financial scheme, must be a temporary intervention followed by real investment, however. If not, it is exactly what a usurer does to those whom he lends money at an interest, regardless of whether they drew any benefit from their investment or used the loan for consumption. Time does potentially allow money to increase, but it does not *guarantee* that increase.

Hanbali jurists have a simple formula that explains how time may affect money or property of value, which can be observed in how they resolve contests of how to evaluate what is owed in cases of misappropriated property. If a commodity has a tendency to increase in either a natural manner or via normal market activities, this increase is to be applied to cases of misappropriation of money. If I steal an animal of yours, what the animal produces that is either another commodity (such as milk) or its progeny (a cow begets a calf) or both must be returned with the animal (that is, the "addition," milk and calf), not only the original stolen object. Similarly, if I steal an apartment of yours and keep it empty or use it for nine months, I owe nine months' rent on top of the value of the apartment. If a stolen object is destroyed, its value at the time of its destruction is owed.

If a stolen object loses value while under unlawful possession, the clock goes backward. I will have to return your animal that lost weight in my possession with an added compensation equal to the value removed by its losing the weight. An amusing question Hanbali jurists ask is this: What if an amount of grape juice belonging to a Muslim (which is lawful and hence possesses a value) turns into wine in wrongful possession? The answer is the value of the original juice must be returned, because alcoholic drinks are as good as nothing. (If you are a non-Muslim, you get to keep the wine.) If the juice becomes vinegar, hence losing value, jurists disagree. Some say the thief must return an equivalent juice or its value; others say a compensation should be added to the vinegar and the vinegar returned.

Note that Hanbalis are still realists and do not presume the existence of future value until it is generated, or in the case of misappropriated value, until the time passes within which the increase has been or could have been generated. They are not as strict about "increases" having to be generated from trade. They think it is simply generated by investment added during the passage of time, but that value is accrued only when the defined time actually elapses. (The Hanbali view of turning "remedy" into a basis for compensation, some of you may note, is similar to the post-revolutionary Iranian (Ja'fari) solution to the problem of interest we mentioned in Unit 6, section 2.6.)

Let us take another shot at how the two ideals of a just and fair Islamic finance and the more productive and risk-friendly modern finance are different. This time we will do it from a point of describing the ideals within Islamic financial jurisprudence, as opposed to criticizing modern finance from the latter's standpoint. We will later move to explaining their supposed "marriage" in the hybridized modern Islamic finance.

2 Markets, banking, and mortgages

2.1 Historical markets

Markets are places (virtual or real) where objects of value are exchanged. In an agricultural society, land, crops, animals, and animal products are objects of value. People may exchange these and other objects of value directly in a barter contract (grapes for apples; milk for honey) or via a price, made mainly of gold, or silver (and increasingly of copper as so-called *fulus* or currency for small amounts in medieval and early modern markets) or something else. But an agricultural society does not only eat and cultivate food: Its population uses clothes, for example, and hence values materials such as woven cotton and wool. When they have a chance to acquire these items, they will pay or barter to do so.

Value is assigned to all that is needed in society. A society slightly more complex than that described above will assign value to "trade" that brings forth materials hitherto not available to it, even if these are not essential. Think of musical instruments. Our little village may thus exchange these traded goods for things they produce. Another kind of value is generated here when merchandise is moved from one place to another. You may be a merchant who makes money simply by moving things around.

But what happens if the village, which is now growing to enjoy access to the products of other societies that produce things its inhabitants like, has a member who invents, through trial and error, a little machine that makes their agricultural activities better or more efficient? This invention will also have value, an estimated price. The machine may be exchanged for crops, or working hours, or some other services, or a standard price, such as one gold coin.

We now have a sense of how societies become ever more complicated and assign value to things they did not value earlier. The population can generalize the sense of "value" in a society this way. When medicine improves, it acquires value. Teaching acquires value. Its tools acquire value. When entertainment evolves and becomes sophisticated, it is also matched with a price, because it possesses value.

In the early history of Baghdad (in the eighth century, specifically), house prices were very high. Properties were nevertheless purchased by famous musicians and culinary artists, such as Mawsili (d. 850) and Ziryab (d. 857). In this particular society, the value of entertainment and luxury items was obviously paramount. Think of all this when you try to imagine the environments in which early Islamic financial jurisprudence operated.

The early rise of a large city like Baghdad should give us pause when we assume that the modern, nineteenth-century cities were a challenge for Islamic jurisprudence because old Islamic law was assumed to function in small towns only. The freedom associated with large cities—and the assumed weaker bond between family members, not to mention wider mixes of ethnicity, language, and similar elements—led to a relaxation of moral standards, reportedly frowned upon by religious scholars. Ahmad ibn Hanbal was reported to have either sadly or sardonically said that one may not be certain that one's prayers were "valid" inside Baghdad's city borders because it was like a large bathroom, and all knew that prayers were invalid if performed inside a bathroom. You will note, however, that many of the laws regarding protecting the weak in a contract (invalidating contracts that include an element of duress or intimidation) have an added importance when they are used to solve problems that occur in large city societies.

When jurists devise rules for contracts, they try to attend to the contracts that are likely to be most useful in their society. Medieval Muslim jurisprudence grew in environments where simple agriculture and simple trade flourished but also where one could find complex trade in overseas and cross-continental routes. This generated complex activities demanding a system of contracts of leases, partnerships, and rules to regulate inflation adjustments.

But even in the fastest-changing and most complex Muslim societies of the past, Muslim jurists never believed in the value of "future money"—value that has yet to be generated—in the loose manner modern economies accept. This is one quality that distinguishes Islamic financial jurisprudence from any modern, credit-based regulations of the market. This quality will come back to create much controversy among Muslim jurists of modernity.

2.2 Consent, take two

Why should a desire for growth and trust in one's capacity to generate future economic value—both basic engines of the modern economy—be suspicious to a tradition-bound Muslim jurist? Because he or she believes that a natural interaction in the market is equitable, but that it also requires the *protection of the weaker party*. This is why deals may be judicially revoked in cases of duress, deception, or contractual ambiguity.

The most straightforward and equitable kind of transaction is that of a sale whereby two parties exchange two equal commodities (one is called a price), and express their desire to complete the exchange in clear terms. In a sale, each one of the two parties is allowed to negotiate a price or an equivalent to what he or she is offering. If I am selling you a watch for $100, I am demanding that price for that item. You could say no. If you are able to say no but negotiate for what you see as a better price, the transaction is equitable and fair. If your freedom to negotiate is impeded by any factor, or any kind of undue pressure, the sale is not valid. The first activity of the jurist is to ensure that each party is truly "content" with his or her dealings. And the operating presumption is that a free individual whose judgment is not impeded by fear or any other factor (alcohol, for example) is able to decide in her or his best interest. When this presumption is shown to be mistaken, the two questions of first, revoking deals, and second, compensation, arise.

One of these cases would arise if an individual believes that they do not have the right to inspect and gain sufficient information about what they are buying. Muslim jurists emphasize the right to return or revoke a deal. This is guaranteed when the negotiation is incomplete, within a stipulated period for further inspection, or when a defect is identified in a merchandise. If the condition of a merchandise changes in the possession of the buyer or if the buyer acts in a manner that he or she is considered to have made "usage" of it, this right to revoke is superseded. In other words, there are standard ways to revoke a deal (*khiyar*) if the revoking is done within a certain time limit, or after an identification of a deficiency in the product, or if the return was stipulated after reviewing the deal. (The *khiyar* or right of return does not apply in the case of currency exchange, for the obvious reason that currency is *standard*.)

The idea that transactions which lack meaningful (informed) consent may be revoked is at odds with the presumption of the freedom of the parties. In an ultra-capitalist system, there should be no to minimal protection of this kind. This is not to say that claims to duress or deception would meet a low bar of scrutiny in Islamic law: In Hanafi law in particular, there is a good deal of scrutiny of these claims, and they fail quite significantly.

2.3 Prices and regulations

Discomfort with the control of prices requires reflection; it sounds, by the way, like a conservative, de-regulatory position only ostensibly. The Prophet Muhammad is reported to have admonished against "fixing prices. . .let God give people their designated share (*rizq*) one from the other." This is an invitation to allow the invisible hand of God (as opposed to Adam Smith's invisible hand of the *market*) to work things out for the benefit of all. In Abbasid and Ottoman history, this idea was suspect, and there were instances where prices had to be set to prevent monopoly, but calls to go back to it came periodically. There was always a sense that if this divine invisible hand was not at work, some "hidden" (as Robert Nozick would have called it) rather than "invisible" hand, of a ruling class or a government was attempting to manipulate the markets.

When there is no strong hidden hand—or indeed any other kind of hidden hand—an Islamic market stands on the ideal of shared profits and losses. This is the essence of the *mudaraba* agreement, a partnership where both money and expertise are exposed to the same degree of risk. In a *mudaraba* contract, one party provides money and the other work, and the profit is shared according to how the growth of these two elements are estimated at the start of the contract. Should any losses be incurred, these are also distributed proportionately. This traditional model of finance "likes" the surprises of investment, and such a position strengthens any aversion to regulating prices or any other market-related matters.

In modern Islamic finance, to anticipate the next section, a larger controversy centers on the extent to which "regulations" should govern actual transactions and whether standardized forms for contracts should be available to Islamic banks. It is not that medieval transactions did not have their formal side or that medieval laws did not enforce norms for all merchants. It is that modern standards are different. Allowing commercial partners to wait for their business operations to decide the degree to which the profit is distributed seems to be a fair practice from the viewpoint of old markets, but they might appear to be an open door to manipulation and unfairness in their modern form. Islamic banks usually have to strike a hybrid path: Their reference point is that of a modern market, accepting of a degree of (modern) risk and uncertainty and rewarding those who take the risk to make a larger margin of return. Aside from areas where the small, old models are sustained and separated from the modern markets, Islamic finance remains a wrinkle within modern finance.

2.4 Unjust enrichment and contractual ambiguity

If the elements of "unfair increase" and "contractual ambiguity" should be avoided, what exactly is an unfair enrichment and what is an ambiguous commitment today?

Unjust enrichment is a technical term indicating an ownership that has not been deserved. If an amount of money is accidentally deposited into my bank account, for example, there is no wrongdoing on my part, but any interest accrued on that erroneous deposit over, say, a year would enrich me unjustly, even if I return the principal. Contrary to a strong tendency in Roman law, Anglo-American jurisprudence does not like to solve such problems conceptually and seems to go into a casuistic, case-by-case reasoning, while some legal philosophers argue that this particular example is an obvious ramification of property law (Charlie Webb, *Reason and Restitution: A Theory of Unjust Enrichment* (Oxford: Oxford University Press, 2016)). In the 1950s Sanhuri (*Masadir al-Haqq*, (Beirut: Dar Ihya al-Turath, n.d.), Vol. 1, pp. 45–6) stated that Islamic law, while allowing applications of mistaken enrichment and discussions of actions by non-owners that benefit owners (*fadala*), is closer to English law in this regard.

The perfect example of unfair enrichment in an Islamic financial system remains a usurious transaction (I loan you $10 and you owe $12 in X years' time, for example) as in a partnership where there are multiple dealings and the partner with an outstanding debt pays interest on top of the debt. Unfair enrichment *in the broad sense* exists in these cases. The modern concept of unjust enrichment takes for granted that enrichment via increases in debt does not constitute unjust enrichment. This is because existing laws allow usurious transactions in this broad sense. In Islamic financial jurisprudence, any increase that does not correspond to a creation of new value or where loss is borne unequally by trade partners is usury.

As discussed, in Islamic financial jurisprudence, there is also a strong aversion to ambiguity (*gharar*) that may lead to conflict. Ambiguous commitments come from ambiguous expressions, which may arise from built-in uncertainty when referring to future conditions. For example: I will sell you my car for $X after I fix it. A Muslim jurist will say: Fix it first then sell it. Ambiguity in agreements might lead to quarrels. This is not to say that quarrels may not happen after ambiguities are resolved to the satisfaction of the parties *at the time of the agreement*. The point here is that *predictable* disagreements should be avoided.

In Hanbali legal manuals, a salient discussion shows that excessive fear of contractual ambiguity or surprises can debilitate market possibilities and must hence be rejected. Hanbali jurists realized that this fear can be taken to an extreme. For example, the Mutazili Abd al-Rahman Ibn al-Asamm (d. 279/892) is reported to have rejected the lawfulness of hire and rent contracts (*ijara*), because the utility that is exchanged is in question—was non-existent, in fact—at the time of the contract. This is true whether it is a workman's effort or the utility of an apartment. Hanbalis argue that this utility can be exchanged only in a gradual manner that leaves the positions of landlord and tenant unequal and hence the contract could not be seen as problematic. This allows countries that employ Hanbali law to have a greater degree of flexibility as they adjudicate modern dealings that include elements of ambiguity.

Muslim jurists knew that eliminating *all* possible ambiguity at the time of an agreement was unfeasible. As you read in Unit 2, Hanafi jurists considered *lawful* some contracts that *did not lack ambiguity* if the custom of the population showed tolerance for this ambiguity. This was based on reasoning from a combination of subtle reflection on the conditions of trade—*istihsan*. The same can be said about Maliki, Zaydi, and Ja'fari jurists who put a premium on social and market standards in their *fatwas*.

Modern Islamic finance moved Islamic law away from this position. Islamic finance, thus, became an arm of capitalism, if anything, while hoping that the slot now preserved by Islamic financial institutions would be occupied by better Islamic financial institutions in the future. It also connected contractual ambiguity with types of unjust enrichment in a novel manner.

The prohibition of both an increase unmatched by the generation of value and ambiguous contracts remain foundational principles of Islamically acceptable or so-called shari'a-compliant transactions. However, in contemporary finance the factoring of future value and the expectation of speedy transacting makes it impossible for Islamic financial institutions to avoid a measure of unfair enrichment and contractual ambiguity. Banks borrow and lend at a high volume, and the idea of even tracing the money of one transaction in separation from all others is fanciful. This has led to a new standard, which modern Islamic financial institutions accept. The new standard can be explained in simple terms as follows. The value that seems to acquire consensus and avoids traditionally impermissible activities (gambling, intoxicants, narcotics) is an acceptable starting point. Islamic financial institutions still disagree about how to apply this standard, with some being more lenient than others.

2.5 Endowments and investment

One tool used to expand the potential of Islamic finance into new areas and link it to its historical roots is to draw on a doctrine that the Hanafi school developed by expanding the activities of endowments (which Abu Hanifa himself, interestingly, was reluctant to accept as an institution separate from executing wills after death, but the Hanafi *madhhab* came to recognize and even develop, in the Ottoman centuries, to a great extent). Endowments were historically establishments, such as schools and hospitals, that were founded by someone for a purpose other than profit. A rich person might have dedicated a house and a farm for the purpose of building a school with its dorms, say, and have assigned the endowment director or overseer the task of running the farm for the purpose of covering the faculty's salary and student expenses. Or, the properties could have been dedicated as a hospital, where doctors were hired, and the hospital's expenses covered by the revenue of the farm.

These non-profit entities, however, were built with specific "conditions" or standards for the way they are supposed to be run. The endowment founder was allowed to come up with these. Some schools of law were stringent in their interpretation of the founder's conditions: For example, they would not allow the director to "replace" the site of the endowment with another that brought about a greater revenue. Although in principle (as we saw in Primary Source Material IV) judges have a much more extensive power to interpret the conditions of an endowment than the endowment overseer, Hanafi jurists were lenient about this, as long as the director could show that she or he acted in the endowment's best long-term interest. Another way these endowments become important players in the market was when they engaged in investments. Historically, common investments included share-cropping and partnership, of an agricultural, industrial, or commercial nature. In the modern world, lending-based investments have been added to the purview of endowments. This makes endowments act in many respects as "limited banks" that offer low interest loans for specific purposes.

2.6 Liability rules old and new

Historical liability rules were based on considerations of the nature of markets at the time, rather than religious principles of equity. For example, a medieval jurist thought that a tailor was liable to pay the price of a piece of cloth provided by his customer, if the latter were not satisfied with the product; had the tailor provided the material, he would not have been liable. There is a common sense reasoning operating here. When the conditions of the markets change, jurists were willing to restate the rules of liability to allow them to go with new conditions.

If the new jurisprudence were to be loyal to the principles Muslim jurists accepted over the centuries, one standard has to remain the same: Weak parties must be afforded some degree of protection. The presumption of consent on the part of one party (eg, partner, buyer) with a less than good understanding of his or her duties should not be made. Modern Islamic finance (being a hybrid of capitalist principles and principles taken from traditional Islamic law) is not consistent on this. As you will see in one case below, "pay what you owe" will be the motto of use when appeals are made to old principles in new markets.

3 Modern Islamic finance: The hybrid

We noted in Unit 6 (section 2.1) that post-revolutionary Iranian law, which prohibits usury, allowed instating an interest ratio on a loan as if this was a stipulation by a bank. (It was a legislative assumption on behalf of the banks, a stratagem to reconcile the prohibition on usury and the new nature of money.) This is because the bank can decide to ask for the loan to be paid back, say, within two weeks, and any delay after that is compensated by interest. In the case of the sale of property (such as a home, whose price will normally be paid over a period of twenty to thirty years), stipulating the interest upfront makes sense.

Appendix V shows a standard investment contract according to Islamic finance. On page 2 of the form, the two paths to a partnership between the bank and buyers or investors are explained as follows.

1 Commodity *murabahah* (cost plus profit). This is a buy and sell contract between the bank and customer of which a specific shari'a'h-compliant commodity will be identified and used as the underlying asset for the sale and purchase transaction between the customer and the bank for the purpose of availing the funds for the financing.

2 *Musharakah mutanaqisah* (diminishing partnership). This is an Islamic property financing option based on a combination of shari'a'h contracts of *musharakah* (partnership) and *ijarah* (leasing). It is a form of diminishing partnership contract whereby the customer and the bank jointly acquire and own a property. Once the bank leases the property to the customer, the installment payments gradually transfer the bank's ownership to the customer.

The two ways of buying a property via a loan are *murabaha* (cost plus profit) and *musharakah mutanaqisah* (diminishing partnership). In the former, the investment is between a party that contributes money and another who uses it while paying its price on installments. In the latter, a party buys a property (say, a house) and the other party pays its share over time (as in a mortgage). This model is also modified to apply to partnerships for commercial activities, not only consumption. The reason these two models were adopted is that they were flexible. We will see in *Bimb v. Lim Kok Hoe* (decided by the Putrajaya Appellate Court, Malaysia, 2009) that a confusion about the goal of home mortgages can lead to dire consequences.

Let us, then, state two of the most important elements of modern finance that Islamic finance has to abide by. First, there is no such a thing as a promise, only fully enforceable

Figure 7.1 Housing Bank & Islamic Jordanian Bank's Branches in central Amman. Author: Freedom's Falcon at Arabic Wikipedia. Image accessed via Wikimedia.

contracts and agreements. The modern market only takes into account concluded agreements in the form of contracts. Second, loans must be compensated with an addition when time passes. Money does not grow on trees, but it does grow like children, over the years.

3.1 Contracts *v.* promises

We said that sale was a perfect contract in the mind of Muslim jurists. But this is a standard contract of exchange, not investment. In the latter case, people expect to make a profit, and they have to face some risk in this scenario. If you have money and I have the expertise, we must both be ready to lose (you your money and me my time and effort) and hope we will gain, not lose. But when you have the money already, and I have only the promise of *future* money, could we really work together?

If you are a bank and I am an employee who expects to gain the price of a home over the next thirty years, it is simple: You pay now, and I pay later. But I must pay interest. What I am doing is buying the home now and paying over time. In a medieval financial system, I could not have paid unless I had the money there and then. Today, what I am really doing is *promising to pay*. Can this promise be considered a simple contract?

The emphasis on the clarity and certainty in contracts allowed participants in the old system of Islamic law to make a promise to engage in a transaction without fully committing to it. That is, I could go to a merchant and say that I will purchase such and such from him and for the majority of jurists, this would not be a contract, and the promise is not binding. This made perfect sense then. It was good policy, fair, and a good protection for both parties. Today, this a strange proposal. (It still has limited applications when one is allowed to order a book but is not bound to buy it, given the ability of the merchant to sell it on to another person relatively easily.) Thanks to an aberrant traditional view that treated such a promise as if equivalent to a contract, modern Muslim financial gurus could still cite the old views and get the modern conclusion.

In modern Islamic finance, then, what was regarded as the "weak" view historically is now the norm. Most recently the Shari'ah Advisory Council of Bank Negara Malaysia (the SAC) in its 159th Meeting (May 26, 2015) stipulated that any promise of purchase is a contract, and the promisee is entitled to compensation in the case of failure to fulfill the promise. The category of promise, in other words, is not a category that describes real activities in the market.

3.2 Loans

Let's go back to an Iranian example from earlier in the book. Before the 1979 revolution, as we said, an annual interest of 12 percent was an acceptable ratio (Article 719 of the Civil Code) to be imposed on all breaches of contracts, even if the parties agreed to a higher percentage. Suppose you and I got into a partnership agreement, and I failed to deliver what I owed, and by the time I was able to deliver, the value of the debt increased via currency inflation. Article 4 of Iran's constitution, which allowed the Council of Guardians to review all laws for their compatibility with Islamic law, gave the council the authority to reconsider this practice. The Council did allow a penalty to be imposed, not as interest, but as compensation for breach of responsibilities. Mohsen Norrbakhsh, the Chief of the Central Bank, asked the Council whether the Bank may insert a stipulation of a payment (estimated by an interest) on loans, if their borrowers fail to deliver their payments on time and received a positive answer on 1/14/83 (S. H. Amin, 1984, p. 43). It remains the case that any additional payment (in the form of a percentage on any loan) must be justified either as a price of inflation, a penalty, or some legitimate cost for an activity, as opposed to a simple expectation of interest.

The idea that ambiguity or duress can invalidate a contract was also adopted by Iranian courts after the revolution. There was a case where a man owned a third of a piece of mining land and, unaware of its true value, rented it for .09 of its market value, while the owner of the remaining two-thirds rented it for its true market value. The Court of Cassation (a high court with the power to revoke lower court decisions) ruled that this was a basis for invalidating the rental contract that amounted to unfair treatment for the owner of the one-third (S. H. Amin, 1984, pp. 24–5).

It is clear then that modern Islamic finance cannot live by the standards of the past's slower way of life, or insist that investment be tied to real assets as it was historically. So what is the result like? Some argue it is nothing but an onerous, inefficient way of doing modern, usury-friendly, finance. The following case provides an opportunity for reflection.

3.3 BIMB v. LIM KOK HOE (& others); Putrajaya Court of Appeals (Malaysia), 2009

In this decision, the Putrajaya Appellate Court revoked a decision by a high court in Kuala Lumpur, Malaysia, which aggregated a group of twelve cases and condemned Islamic mortgages commonly practiced by the Bank Islam Malaysia Berhad. The High Court said Islamic law did not endorse these thinly covered loans with interest and asked the Bank to refrain from seeking the payment of interest by those who defaulted on their payments. The Appellate Court said that the Islamic transaction was one of sale, while the usurious transaction (common in conventional, Western, finance) was a loan.

> The comparison between a BBA contract and a conventional loan agreement was not appropriate. The two instruments of financing are not alike and have different characteristics. BBA contract is a sale agreement whereas a conventional loan agreement is a money lending transaction.
> *Cambridge Law Journal*, [2009] 6, p. 23

The Appellate Court refused what it said was a familiar and un-novel criticism of sales with a delayed payment (Ar. *bay' bi-thaman ajil* or BBA) as applied in modern Islamic banking and as authorized by shari'a boards of specialists in these banks.

To illustrate the BBA contract, we will refer to the facts in Civil Appeal No. W-02-918-2008. In that case the customer applied to BIMB for a financing facility to purchase a property known as Unit B10-3 Jenis Excelsa, Taman Universiti Indah, Fasa 111C ("the property"). BIMB purchased the property from the customer pursuant to a Property Purchase Agreement dated October 16, 1996 for a purchase price of RM145,800. On the same date BIMB sold the property to the customer pursuant to a Property Sale Agreement for a sale price of RM450,954. Again on the same date, the customer executed a deed of assignment in favor of the BIMB to secure the payment of the sale price. The sale price was to be paid by the customer by 360 monthly installments of RM1,252.65 per month. The customer had paid the sum of RM105,556.13 before he defaulted in the payment of the sale price. The balance sale price due was the sum of RM370,425.05. That was the sum claimed by BIMB from the customer.

In other words, *you pay what you owe*. If you think it is usurious interest, bear in mind that: you should not have signed up for it; and experts in the shari'a don't share your view, and their opinion matters, while others, at this point, do not.

Modern conventional finance does not prevent financial institutions in the Muslim world from coming up with creative methods to apply the desired restrictions on participants in

Islamic finance contracts, which prohibit exploitation whether originating from deception (as in the *gharar,* that is, the surprise or ambiguity problem we considered in Unit 2) or positions of advantage (as in the usury problem we also considered in Unit 2). In many cases financial institutions came up with many imaginative solutions and new formats for contracting and investments that bring the values of the old system alive. In other cases, the game seems to be conformity with modern standards and twisting inherited ideas to match them. The future of Islamic finance certainly depends on enlarging the former category and limiting the latter.

4 Islamic cyber jurisprudence

Cyber *fatwa* cases have grown into one of the most unpredictable aspects of Islamic law in our time. The number of questions and answers continue to grow exponentially. Questions on everything from the areas of rituals, to marriage, divorce, and their consequences, to all areas of public Islamic law are posed and answered by multiple authorities. It is one of the least safe and least controllable versions of Islamic law. But it is a thriving element, and it does contain some ingenious and thoughtful material.

This *fatwa* case law that was generated in under twenty-five years has also led to the recrudescence of certain discussions of a transnational character. One may, for example, ask and discuss whether "international" Islamic law approves of current war and peace activities under the dominant international regimes. The relative anonymity afforded to an impersonal email account encourages this action. It is also common to engage in speculations about how to answer these questions, where the old Islamic tradition was called upon to answer these modern questions.

It is not only an imagined law of which we speak. Some "practice" has followed from these questions and answers, which have covered issues ranging from forming new armies in the name of the transnational shari'a, to theories of "self-immersion" in war activities (as in a suicide mission) and advancing a war activity that may result in destroying civilian or non-combatants (including Muslims)—which draws on the so-called "shield question."

The traditional formula of the self-immersion question (Arabic: *inghimas*) is when a fighter enters a sparring match with multiple members of the enemy and has only a very small chance of survival. The traditional formula of the "shield question" (Arabic: *tatarrus*) is whether one may attack a shield of Muslim captives, who would be the first to die at the outset of the battle, as the enemy has put them in front of its own soldiers on a battlefield. In other words, the question was whether a Muslim army may attack an enemy, even if it is sure its first victims would be Muslim captives at the front of the enemy's army. This was redirected and restated as a question of one's liability to committing the sinful act of killing a Muslim, if a warrior would have to kill some Muslims in order to accomplish a military goal. A new code (Arabic: *La'iha* or *La'yha*) was produced to regulate new forms of Islamic *jus in bello* (rules of engagement in war), which altered many of the traditional principles of the laws of war. For more on this, see Muhammad Munir, "The *Layha* for the Mujahideen: an analysis of the code of conduct for the Taliban fighters under Islamic law," *International Review of the Red Cross*, Vol. 93 Iss. 881 (2011); Available at: http://works.bepress.com/muhammad_munir/3/.

No one imagined that the issue of slavery would once more be under (lively) discussion today, but cyber jurisprudence took it on, particularly because the question of Islamic slavery has been something of a mysterious dark matter in legal terms. Why did Muslim jurists associate slavery with war? Some of them thought of slavery as a punishment for the defeated army. But the expectation in a war in the broad Near East (for lack of a better label) in which Islam arose, as attested in the Justinian Institutes, is that both sides in a war must accept being subjected to slavery when they lose the war. Slavery arises only after war; chattel slavery (which was practiced in the United States and others across the Atlantic in recent centuries) is another institution that was regulated differently (from both Roman and Islamic slavery). But one puzzle Islamic legal texts introduce for us is that the decision to take slaves seems to be given to the leader of the Muslim community. It is up to this *imam* or leader to take slaves in the first place (Ibn Qudamah, *al-Mughni*, Vol. 13, p. 44). Uniform standards for what to do with those captured on the battlefield are an intentional lacunae. These issues are debated in detail elsewhere. I will not pretend to know enough about this. Perhaps some of you could do the requisite research and get to the bottom of where these discussions are going.

Islamic cyber jurisprudence has also contributed to developing the area of Islamic finance, which we discussed earlier, and has also had a hand in developing many other aspects of the personal and social shari'a we encountered in previous units in this textbook.

Each major scholar has his or her own online source of *fatwas*. We have already referenced *fatwas* by Iran's Supreme Leader (Unit 4) and the Jurists' Council of Mecca (Unit 5). Large entities, such as governments, religio-legal councils, and other independent agencies, also have useful information. See, for example: Fiqh Council of North America (http://www.fiqhcouncil.org); Dubai Government (http://www.iacad.gov.ae/en/Pages/default.aspx); and International Commission of Jurists (Geneva) (http://www.icj.org).

In this text we have moved a fair distance from the extreme taught by historical approaches to the subject, which speaks of the end of the shari'a as an event of the past century, to a world where the shari'a can be found everywhere. But if the shari'a functions as a personal law and a set of social laws, and is found in national laws and transnational dealings, where else would the shari'a operate? Certainly not on a supranational level, since at this time and in this stage of international law that allows for the exertion of power over a single state by aggregates of states, there are no institutions that developed notions of global or regional power based on Islamic legal imperatives. This has been true since at least the waning of Ottoman power in the seventeenth–eighteenth centuries.

But is there an extraterrestrial shari'a, albeit in overlap with the personal shari'a of which we are now familiar? Even if this is a tongue-in-cheek question, it probably deserves a serious answer. And the answer is in the affirmative. An Muslim astronaut who is planning to be away from earth for a few years and who would like to comply by the laws of the daily prayers should pray only five times by earth's daily cycle, could combine prayers as needed, based on the license about which we learned in Unit 1, and should not have to stand, sit, kneel, and prostrate himself if this proves impossible; reciting the words of the prayers would be adequate in most cases. Whether to fast in Ramadan or feed one needy person per day, depends on how able this person is to do it and whether it fits with his task. The same maxims of need and necessity apply to these and other questions and conditions, and legal scholars can get creative in their answers to these questions.

It is obvious this extraterrestrial shari'a is bound to be limited in its social aspect. That is, unless former US representative Newt Gingrich's reported dream of multiple colonies on the moon materializes. In this case, new limits will have to be imposed on social interactions, to obey the new environment. If this were to happen, the voices from the last century that denied men ever having landed on the moon will have been long forgotten. As things stand today, even a transnational Islamic finance and shared religious law in cyberspace does nothing but preserve a slot for potential growth for these institutions in the future.

5 Conclusion

1 The slice of the financial markets impacted by Islamic finance amidst regular financial life (which cannot imagine growth without what would qualify as usury, duress, or another Islamically undesirable element of trade) is only 1–2 percent. The size of the world economy is something like $100 trillion, and Islamic financial institutions have a reach of around $1–2 trillion.

2 The Great Depression (1929–39) and subsequent burst bubbles and scandals that exploit the presumption of constant and rapid economic growth give advocates of Islamic finance an argument against conventional finance.

3 A new kind of *fatwa* case law has been generated and developed rapidly in the cyber age. It has allowed *fatwas* for the first time to not be tied strongly, and in some cases not at all, to a specific local context. The rulings resemble the language of some *fiqh* books, which deliver doctrines with some qualifications, but do not tie the ruling sufficiently to specific conditions.

Review VII

- The transnational shari'a is found in cyber jurisprudence, where new scholars of Islamic law develop argument-based (as opposed to system-based) laws, and Islamic financial institutions, which have shari'a boards that test their practices for compliance with the shari'a.
- Islamic finance is a hybrid of conventional, modern/Western finance and old principles that do not allow the freedom of the free market to perpetuate a concentration of wealth. The wiggle room, within which innovative practices that aim at mitigating the impact of debt on small borrowers operate, varies.

Problem

- Do you still remember the inheritance case (Unit 1, sections 3.1–3.4) that depended on who has the title of owner for a certain property in Iraq, which would affect the share of a client in this property that is taxable in the US? Imagine a scenario where this property is sold to the client in the case (A.J.) by another (as in the BBA format in the BIMB case). Would this person be considered an owner in the view of a Muslim jurist? Would jurists disagree? Why?

8 The Triangle of Society, Law, and Government

In the Introduction to this book, we touched on the connection between law, society, and government, including Iran's revolution and the more recent (unhappy) revolutionary movements in the Arabic-speaking world. We come full circle now, back to a basic question of how **society** and **government** in the Muslim world shape each other and—with **law** being an important "invisible hand" that strongly influences social and political reality in Muslim societies—all form **a triangle of elements** that influence, expand, reduce, and, in a word, *shape* one another. Treatments of this topic have been affected by a modern political science and history approach that sees ideas as coming only from outside of the Muslim world, just as it sees agency as limited to those who live outside it. If I had shared these views I would have saved myself much headache and probably aimed at a recapping of the secondary literature on this topic. I will take another path.

1 The past couple of centuries

Between 1800 and the early years of the twenty-first century CE, five major developments or movements left a strong impact on the world's Muslim populations. In Islamic *history and calendar* terms, these developments took place in the thirteenth, fourteenth, and fifteenth centuries respectively. These were:

1. the anti-Ottoman reform Wahhabi revolution at the beginning of the thirteenth century (nineteenth century CE), which came to be seen as a force of retrogression by the end of the fourteenth century (twentieth century CE);

2. the founding, with popular support, of a large political entity in Muslim India, first (1366/1947) as Pakistan (which was initially in charge of Bangladesh), then after 1971 as two separate countries;

3. Arab nationalism (1370/1950s and 1380s/1960s), with its impact on national laws in the Arab world; political Islamic movements in the Arab world are shaped by Arab nationalism, despite voices within it that speak of a broader Islamic unity;

4. the Iranian revolution at the end of the fourteenth century (twentieth century CE), an event whose impact continues to be assessed; and

5. revolutionary movements that went by the name of "the Arab Spring" at the beginning of the fifteenth century (twenty-first century CE), and which continue to brew.

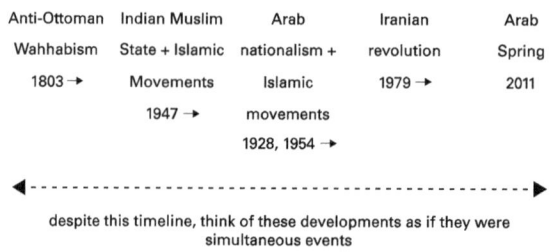

despite this timeline, think of these developments as if they were simultaneous events

Interpreting these and other events is, unfortunately, all in the eye of the beholder. One sure bet is that today's Muslim societies have retained, after their long histories, *residing elements* in their ethical and cultural life, coupled with *modern legal institutions* that are embraced by judges and legal and political elites, both of which keep the old legacies alive, albeit with some new texture. Modern institutions also push for change. When governments force changes on the population, the latter do not always rebel—indeed, sometimes they embrace the changes and even go farther in supporting them—but some pushback is likely. Rapid change is always painful, especially when inexplicable in terms of benefits for the population. This rapid change may come in the direction of swift modernizing, as the case was in Egypt in the nineteenth century and Turkey in the early twentieth, but it may also go in the direction of (what we call for a lack of a better word) Islamizicization, such as Zia-ul-Haqq's reforms in Pakistan and the changes that ensued from Iran's 1979 revolution.

The English language has by now hundreds of thousands, if not millions, of books and websites that regard all changes in the modern Muslim world as external, forced, and, one must add Western, colonial, etc. Foreign forces were important, but the full picture cannot be seen in the fog of these West-centered presentations. Let's confine ourselves to some basic points on how to read the past couple of centuries and their impact on the presence of Islamic law in the world.

One of the mainstays of Middle Eastern studies is a discussion of a 1923 book on government in Islam by Ali Abd al-Raziq (d. 1966), an Egyptian judge and scholar, who argued that the system of succession of the Prophet Muhammad, the caliphate (since its very beginnings in the seventh century CE), was nothing but a bad experiment in Islamic history. Abd al-Raziq's influence is undeniable, but to the extent that he was more or less describing a centuries-old condition, his work has a much longer pedigree. The practice of the caliphate, at least since the Mongol invasion, if not earlier, was an attempt at keeping the name without the object. Over 600 years ago, Ibn Khaldun (d. 808/1406), for example, speaks of Muslim history with the caliphate as one model among many for a Muslim government. Later in this unit (section 2.3), you will note that the end of a single government domain (the caliphate) was studied by jurists from the fifth century (eleventh century CE).

The made-up equation I included in the Introduction made the point that comparing revolutionary movements in the Sunni and Shi'i worlds would not work, but *thinking of these two sides of the mock equation as belonging on one and the same side of the evolution of contemporary Muslim societies is necessary*, not just fruitful. In fact, I want you to do something a little difficult here, especially for those who have a strong historical sensitivity

Figure 8.1 View of Islamic architecture from inside the Al-Aqsa Mosque in Jerusalem.
Author: اغبارية توفيق معتز المصور. Image accessed via Wikimedia.

and who will always want to put the events in order and think of their sequence as the most important factor in interpreting them: Think of these five developments as part of one world, today's world, as if these were all simultaneous events. I also want you to think of events as reaching backward in time in a sense, because they all have attachments and, while they occur (or express themselves) at a certain point, they come to occurrence, carried on currents that preceded them.

Take fourteenth-/twentieth-century revivalists' production of romanticized versions of the shari'a. Some histories show that revival movements accelerated after the failure of nationalism in the Arab world (especially after the Six Day War of 1967) and the Iranian revolution of 1979. This may be true, but it is also true that the Islamic political movements originated in the pre-Arab nationalism world and were considerably shaped by it.

Even more important for us today is the fact that the 1930s witnessed the early forms of government-sponsored movements to reform national laws in order to curtail colonial legacies in Egypt, for example. This legal reform was in the background of Arab nationalist ideas of how modern law incorporates tradition. Political Islamic movements that opposed it came around to champion it later. At the time of the legal reforms of the 1930s and 40s, India's independence (which occurred in 1947) was still in the future. The founding of Pakistan (as an Islamic, Indian nation) at the time of India's independence added fuel to the movement of reassessing the colonial legacy's lasting impact on Muslim societies. This "reassessment" continues to shape today's laws and cultural, religious debates in the broad Muslim world.

The legacy of these five developments, to get to a *take-away*, comes down to five points as follows:

1. A (reform or regressive) movement, such as Wahhabism in Arabia (dating to the early 1800s), played a role in creating the discourse of **modern, romanticized shari'a**, albeit a shari'a that, in some cases, is based in Arabian traditions and "reports" of the Prophet's life. Wahhabi/Saudi Islam never fell into the trap of super-nationalist aspirations and remained a nationalist, Arabian movement.

2. The gradual end of colonialism left Muslim scholars and societies with the task of **hybridizing the long medieval legacy with the more recent and intensely powerful modern, colonial legacy**. Legal systems in new nations needed a long time to stabilize. Egypt officially gained its independence in 1922 and had its first constitution in 1923, but its hybrid civil law came into effect only in 1949. The older, colonial Anglo-Indian mixes of Islamic and modern English laws were part of the background to this effort.

3. The **Islamic movements** in India/Pakistan and the Arab world exchanged influences throughout the fourteen century (twentieth century CE). By the end of this century, the impact of the two opposites, the Wahhabi and the Iranian reforms, had receded to the background.

4. Muslim intellectuals who claim aspects of the Islamic legal tradition as part of their legacy are either *nationalists* or *post-nationalists*. The nationalists, as we learned in Unit 6, consider the national interpretation of the Islamic legal system, with all its eclecticism, to be an authoritative foundation for how Islamic law applies in their land. The post-nationalists are a group that ceased to believe that the modern nation states as carved by colonial calculations and necessity have a leg to stand on and see the Arab Spring as a beginning for new demarcations of polities in the Muslim world. Because terrorist organizations and political actors, such as *al-Qaida*, *Jabhat al-Nusra*, and the so-called *Islamic State* (with its branches in Iraq and Syria, in North and West Africa, and elsewhere), have claimed the mantle of post-national political organizations, all those who will follow in their footsteps will suffer guilt by association.

There are, however, signs that new regimes in softer national "bellies" within the Muslim world will likely be generated and will do the requisite search for a point of cohesion for the society they build, shopping for old ideas on good government from Islamic history and political thought.

5   The idea of the caliphate is often given undue importance in imagining the romanticized shari'a, but it may exercise some impact in the real world in the future. The success of **recent calls for the need for post-nationalist** states in the Muslim world is closer to possible than impossible, but this development awaits the test of time.

When you look at politics in the Muslim world, you will see a huge amount of disagreement about how to read the old history itself and how one should relate to it today. We can also be sure that the five developments listed earlier, and others the walls of the future may be hiding, can go in many different directions. The material from which to draw, however, is hiding in secret. This takes us to the next section, which covers the historical movement of Islamic law, history, and government, including the questions of the caliphate and democracy, among others.

2   Older structures of state and society

You will have realized by now that the ingredients from which medieval Islamic law is made include: texts; history; and principles. In the past century, the modern element of the "nation" was added to the picture. In market matters (Unit 7), customs and practices are paramount. In the modern versions of Islamic law and finance, texts play an important role, especially as these texts are transformed into principles (no usury and no contractual ambiguity or preying on the weak). In family and personal laws (Units 5 and 6), a concept of nature looms large.

Now, keeping these elements in mind, one may consider the element of "government." Note that the study of government in Islamic history was strongly affected by the study of history. It will likely continue on this path. For us to become conversant with discussions on Islamic government, we cannot study it only from political and legal manuals such as Mawardi's *Ordinances of Government*. We will need to look at histories such as Tabari's (d. 310/923) for the early centuries and Ibn Khaldun's (d. 808/1406), for example, for the middle centuries.

Political philosophy also tended to exercise an impact on thinking about government larger than any form of (foreign) moral philosophy was able to influence social life. The vision offered by philosophers such as Farabi (d. 339/950) is that jurists can only be popular explicators of a much higher truth unavailable to both population and lay scholars such as these jurists. True knowledge is philosophical knowledge. In the same vein, Ibn Rushd (who studied both Islamic law and philosophy) stated in his summary of Plato's *Republic* that knowledge of the natural world is the only foundation for any true knowledge. He clearly respected tradition and participated in lawmaking and adjudication but never abandoned the idea that human affairs were run according to what was possible and doable, while accepting universal ideals of justice that made him interested in Greek politics.

While rulers and jurists appeared to be either important allies or important enemies, the philosophical vision assigning jurists a role of popular administration was closer to what many Muslim rulers saw as appropriate in government. Muslim jurists who served as judges and *muftis* were seen by philosophers and many politicians as functionaries and preservers of the faith. Philosophers would add that the jurists were guardians of popular practice of the religion via their reliance on dialectical and rhetorical, as opposed to true philosophical arguments. In a synthesizer such as Ibn Rushd and Nasir al-Din al-Tusi, government and ethics in Islam are seen from a broadly philosophical perspective and not the perspective of the religious individual. You will find critiques of tyranny and of democracy as equally bad ideas to be adequately clear in this writing.

Today, appeals to democracy seem to come with a strong force from Islamist political movements. These movements seem to think that popular support is on their side. The good thing about democracy, then, is that, if it truly allows the Muslim majority's voice to lead their nations, it will also lead to stronger support for the Islamists' political platform. It is true that modern Islamic political reasoning has grown more sympathetic to the notion of democracy, often with some caveats, in the more sophisticated treatments of the topic. Many of the treatments of Islam and democracy appeal to basic principles of equality, and in many ways, reformist Muslims argue backward from conclusions, rather than allow the research to get them to a conclusion.

In political theory or government theory, it makes a difference whether you are a Sunni or a Shi'i. For Shi'is, the Prophet told his community what his government should look like after he passed. In this scheme, texts (the Prophet's testaments) are paramount, because for Shi'is government was regulated by the Prophet, either explicitly or implicitly. Ja'faris think the prophetic dictum here was explicit, and Zaydis think it was by hinting at who the right *imam* is (and the Zaydis also added the condition of seeking political power to identify the *imam*, rather than simply deserving to be an *imam* but sitting quietly at home). For Sunnis, once again, you will see that history plays a large role in theorizing about government (note Mawardi's treatment of the subjects, section 2.1 below), supplemented by certain basic principles regarding the function of government at the bottom line (Juwayni, who is mentioned in section 2.3 below clarifies that government's legitimacy comes from taking care of the population, rather than the personal religiosity of rulers). The Sunni treatments of government are clearly broad in scope, but they boil down to a few points. Below I add unorthodox voices (even from philosophers) to draw something of a full picture for the discussions that addressed the caliphate, rebellion and legitimacy, single *v.* multiple government, and popular rule (the free society).

2.1 Caliphate

Mawardi (d. 450/1058) provided a theoretical treatment of the caliphate that exercised great influence. His book, known in an English translation as *The Ordinances of Governance*, provides a definition of the caliphate, the standards of electing a caliph, rulership *under* or *in tandem with* the caliphate, and the conditions under which a ruler or a caliph may be removed.

The Arabic word *khalifa* (caliph) means successor. The caliph is a successor of the Prophet Muhammad in administering the affairs of the community. Properly speaking, there was only one such successor, and this one was the Prophet's lifetime friend, Abu Bakr, who died just over two years after him (d. 13/634). Abu Bakr's successor was Umar, who would have been a caliph's caliph, but tradition avoided the ridiculous possibility of a list of caliph's caliphs and gave Umar the title of "Commander of the Faithful." It is still customary to speak of Abu Bakr, Umar, and at least their two successors, 'Uthman and 'Ali, as the rightly guided caliphs. After the death of 'Ali in 40/660 and the founding of the first Muslim dynasty (the Umayyads) under the leadership of Mu'awiya (d. 60/679), the rightly guided caliphate ended, but the emotional value of the word caliph persisted.

Al-Walid ibn Abd al-Malik, the Umayyad Caliph who commissioned the Grand Mosque of Bani Umayya in 706, died before the Mosque opened in 715. The great Kurdish leader Salahuddin/Saladin (d. 1193), the liberator of Jerusalem and leader of Muslim armies during Europe's Third Crusade, is buried in its vicinity. Some apocalyptic Muslim views see current wars in Syria as indicative of a new universal Islamic regime to take Syria as its center.

The Umayyad dynasty lasted ninety years, which ended in a revolution and the founding of a new dynasty, the Abbasid (after the name of the Prophet's uncle, Abbas, whose lineage the dynasty claimed). The Abbasid dynasty also called itself a caliphate, but it was nothing more than a coherent federation of states, and it was that only for a century and a half, or two centuries in generous estimates. And this federation was also nothing but an eastern federation, leaving the Islamic west (centered in Spain) with a commander of the Muslims (*Amir al-Muslimin*) who is a contemporary of the eastern commander of the faithful (*Amir al-Mu'minin*). Yes, you guessed it, the Muslims and the faithful should denote the same group. There is no way around acknowledging that, by the third century (ninth century CE), government in the Muslim world had become normalized as the familiar phenomenon of societies and leaders arranged across lines of culture and interest. What distinguishes a Muslim society from others, after all, is its overall character. Again, government is not insignificant, but regulating it via the law had to follow something of a familiar line of negotiations and give-and-take.

By the time Mawardi was born, circa 370/970, the days of strong federal unity were over. The caliphate had its center in Baghdad, but the caliphs themselves were "ruled" by military leaders. First the caliphate was controlled by a Shi'ite leadership (the *Buwayhis* or *Buwayds*), who were contemporaries of Mawardi, and toward the time of his death, a new military leadership was on the rise (the Saljuqs). Mawardi's theorizing of government then had to account for the existence of a succession of dynasties, revolutions, and the presence of "legitimate but ineffectual" rulers (the caliphs) and "practicing rulers" or sultans.

In Mawardi's theory, the caliph is elected by one of three processes, each one of them is accepted as a form of due process. The first is being **elected by the community's leaders** (*ahl al-hall wa-l-'aqd*), for which the precedents are given in the elections of Abu Bakr, 'Uthman, and 'Ali. The leaders (*ahl al-hall wa-l-'aqd*) are the ones who have *the power to bind and loose*, not in the sense of making ecclesiastical laws and deciding other religious matters (such as a pope), but in the sense that they are electors of the person who will hold what is at least in theory a powerful office. The second way of electing a caliph is by **an appointment by a previous caliph**, who was elected by the community's leaders, and who hence holds the same power given to him at the time of his election. The precedent for this was established by the appointment of 'Umar by Abu Bakr and all peaceful transitions from one leader to the next (often in the same family). The third is **simple seizing of power**, which is found in sometimes peaceful and sometimes disputed transitions of power. This is because those expected to lead within a dynasty are sometimes disqualified and their power

> **ON POLL TAX AND LAND TAX:**
>
> Both poll tax and land tax are rights given by God to Muslims, originating from non-Muslims. They are similar in three respects and different in three respects. The rules regulating them are very detailed. The similarities between the two taxes are as follows: first, each one of them is collected from an unbeliever, as a statement of recognition of defeat; second, each can be dispensed in the manner in which non-battle spoils are spent [as in Qur'an 59/7]; and third, they are collected only at the end of a calendar year and cannot be requested in advance. Where they differ is that: first, the poll tax is established by revelation but the land tax by human reasoning; second, that the minimum amount of poll tax is established in law but its ceiling is open to reasoning, while the land tax is calculated by reasoning alone; and third, that the poll tax is imposed on "individual" subjects, and its name implies *equivalence*, because it was either a way to punish them for battling us [he means Muslims] or as in return for our life together peacefully [after war].
>
> Mawardi (d. 450/1085), *Ordinances*, opening of Chapter 13

seized without bloodshed; if there is resistance, though, non-peaceful transitions occur. An example of the latter is the rise to power of Mu'awiya after the first civil war (38–40/654–6), that of Marwan after the second (64–5/680), as well as the rise of the Abbasids after the first revolution in 132/750.

The ability of leaders to command "obedience" is what makes them leaders in the first place. If there is resistance to the authority of a political leader, he or she may or may not survive. When the resistance ends and power is cemented, it is almost tautological, but here legally useful, to say that authority has been established.

What makes Mawardi's theory explicable, aside from its immediate context (which is the rise of Saljuq soldiers and the potential that they become leaders of the community as effective rulers, with the approval of the nominal caliph), is also the way Islamic history evolved until his own time. Mawardi is simply following the directives of the founder of his *madhhab* (Shafi'i (d. 204/820)) when he says that a man of Quraysh (the strong tribe of the Prophet) would simply be a legitimate ruler if three conditions are fulfilled. This person must be:

1 qualified to be a leader (sound reason, experience);
2 must want to be a leader;
3 have conquered all his competitors and hold the reins.

In a situation where a Qurayshi person (from the tribe of Quraysh) of questionable qualifications holds the rein of power, he must be obeyed. In simple language, Shafi'i believed that when a person from Quraysh leads the government, revolution is not required. The condition of being from this tribe lost its meaning in the three centuries inbetween Shafi'i and his distant student Mawardi. But the idea of measuring legitimacy against the question of whether revolution is a requirement remained operative.

By Shafi'i's time (second century/eighth century CE), debates had become heated about what made a government legitimate. The reign of the rightly guided caliphs (10/632–40/660) ended in civil war, and the Umayyad dynasty needed a "correction" (shifting the rule from the descendants of the weakening Sufyan line to the stronger line of Marwan, both scions of Umayya) from within the Umayyad House in 64/682 that ended in the Marwan side taking power from the Sufyan side. Some of those who had studied the Prophet's tradition and had some knowledge of war remained on the sidelines. But revolution was always tempting. For those who studied the Prophet's tradition and had some knowledge of war, defeat seemed inevitable. Zayd (d. 122/740), whose name is given to the Zaydi school of law, was among those who went back and forth on whether to lead a civil war or not. He ended up losing his life around the age of forty-five or forty-six (depending on whether you count by the lunar or the standard solar years) when he threatened the order of the day. Zayd's cousin, Abdullah ibn al-Hasan (quoted in the Ibadi text), did not even participate in the revolts against Abu Ja'far al-Mansur (d. 158/775) but died in jail because his sons *had* taken part.

From experience, not from theory, both Hanafi and Shafi'i jurists arrived at the same conclusion. There are types of pressure to which legal reasoning must adjust, rather than attempt to repeal. In the case of these pressures, jurists must attempt to change incrementally, attend to one condition at a time, and refrain from imposing utopian thinking on real populations. This, by the way, is not limited to government. It includes how jurists address strong social pressure. This is also why Islamic legal reasoning accommodates social and market standards, while attempting, when possible, to modify them.

2.2 Legitimacy, revolution

It is thus clear that the ideal (or theory) of the caliphate overlapped with its history to an extent, but not perfectly. The most important points of overlap are as follows:

1 The election of caliphs always looked at the early model of political practice for emulation and interpretation.

2 Muslim societies' ideal of unity was probably taken for granted by legal and political theorists, despite their awareness that there had been two large Muslim states (the Umayyad in Spain and the Abbasids in Baghdad) since the eighth century.

3 The reality of politics was that regional, smaller-sized states ran the population's business, but they paid tribute and respect to the central Muslim government.

On the side of divergence from theory, Muslim history witnessed many rebellions and other forms of rejection of central power. The premodern conditions of limited communication meant that such conflicts had limited impact, however. Virtual independence, therefore, dominated in many areas of the Muslim world. There were no premodern Muslim nations in the sense in which there are modern Muslim nations and nation states today, but some areas, such as Iran, have kept their premodern geographic form for the most part over the past 500 years.

Muslim jurists theorized revolutionary action as *baghy*, or transgression over the rights of sitting governments. Rebellion receives the benefit of the doubt from some jurists (most notably Shafi'i, Shi'i, and Zahiri scholars) because the government may be an unjust one, and the rebellion may lead to a new, more just, order. Until this happens, however, the assumption is that the sitting government has the right to defend itself and its population, whose legal and social order depends on it. Islamic history has cases where revolutions succeed and cases where they failed. The *baghy* theories were of maximal use to settle and explain both types of revolution.

Hanafi jurists were accused of being the governments' jurists. There may be some reason for that, but the more you know about them and about Islamic history and government, you will find this generalization to be facile. The Hanafi *madhhab* certainly adopts a realistic view of revolution. Rebellions can come from a very good place in the heart, but mostly do not succeed. And they cause much damage. When rebellion succeeds, or when it is about to succeed, what one should do is a different question. (That is, one may join the winners at no moral cost and no obligation to compensate anybody.) When it does not succeed, the jurist has to solve the problem of who pays for the damage, how to settle the disagreement, who is a criminal and who is a legitimate authority that suffered unreasonable resurrection, and so forth.

Shafi'is were realistic, for the most part, but often returned to one basic principle: Government is there to establish justice; why, then, is supporting an unjust government acceptable? Shafi'i jurists prohibit the government from pre-emptively striking down a rebellion. They do not hold the rebels liable for damage, unless it is excessive. Perhaps the most sympathetic view of rebellions lies with Maliki and Hanbali jurists, whose (sometimes lax) *maslaha*-based reasoning (that is, reasoning based on the collective good of the community) pushed them in the direction of prioritizing the hope that justice will dominate over the fear that worse conditions will ensue from rebellions.

While having to live in imperfect societies, Zahiris and Shi'is diverged in their legitimacy theory with the overall Sunni line of reasoning. For them, a moral claim was more important that stability. There would be no difference between a government based on idolatry or atheism and an ostensibly Islamic government that is Islamic only in name. In their discussion of rebellion, they end up taking a position that focuses on the argument of the rebellion (if the argument is legitimate, the rebellion is legitimate), and as much about the cost–benefit analysis of revolution.

The question of how to assess that immense injustice has been inflicted, and hence rebellion is required, was up to each scholar and his time and environment. *Jurists from all schools or* madhhab *affiliation contributed to rebellions.* For more, see: Khalid Abou El Fadl, *Rebellion and Violence in Islamic Law* (Cambridge: Cambridge University Press, 2009).

2.3 The end of single government domain

A little over a century before Ibn Rushd passed on, a Persian Shafi'i jurist known as Juwayni (d. 478/1085), who was a young contemporary and critic of the same Mawardi we encountered earlier, wrote a treatise where he answered the question: What happens when one lives under a bad or no government? Whether this was a simple thought-experiment, something of a description of the author's own context where weak and bifurcated governments dominated, or a prophecy of what may come in the future, this treatise is an important piece of Islamic political reasoning.

The short answer to the question of what happens when government is ineffective is that the populations must take care of themselves. This does not mean what it seems to mean. It ends up coming down to *deference to the authority of community leaders, market leaders, scholars, and other acknowledged authorities*. According to one reading of this theory, power goes back to the same representatives of the people and those who elected the leader (*ahl al-hall wa-l-'aqd*). If legal and political scholars have at least one share in this pie, the theory is self-serving. Self-serving or not, it seems to have been persuasive and would return in the late 1970s as the operative principle of Iran's modern revolution.

Juwayni had anticipated a condition that was on its way to becoming reality, perhaps because the signs were there for those who want to see them. In the seventh century (thirteenth century CE), the Abbasid Caliphate's death certificate would be issued, and the adoption of the title "caliph" would only be for nostalgic purposes thereafter. For example, a Mamluk leader in Egypt and Syria may have imported a descendant of the Abbasids to live in Cairo and be named caliph, while ruling absolutely none of the people's affairs.

After Frederick the Great's death (1250), European princedoms and small city states rose to fill in the gaps created by the end of the Holy Roman Empire. The continent was plagued for centuries by papal power struggles, which the Muslim world did not have. But similarities can still be observed. Albert Rigaudière says the word "status" (for state) was usually followed by an adjective (hence, *status republicae, status regni, status coronae*), but:

> this was not because the state did not exist, endowed as it was with its principal component parts and with a government whose smooth running did not cease to hold the attention of the theorists. Throughout Western Europe in the fourteenth century, except in Italy, the nation state became reality every day and secured its own sovereignty.
> Michael Jones (ed.), *The New Cambridge Medieval History* (Cambridge: Cambridge University Press, 2006), p. 23. Article by Albert Rigaudière.

In the Muslim world, political systems were much more sophisticated than their European counterparts, and there was also much more unity among the political entities that inherited the caliphate ruled in the east and south of the Mediterranean, while grand empires in India and West Africa were formed. Later, one of the world's greatest empires, that of the Ottomans, stretched across three continents. But the new norm of small government and quasi-national polities could be found all over the Muslim world.

Figure 8.2 Cairo Citadel. Author: Sailko. Image accessed via Wikimedia.

2.4 Law, *madhhabs*, and government

Muslim politics, both traditionally and today, connects with economics (see excerpt from Mawardi in the textbox) and the practical organization of society. As we learned in Unit 2, the *madhhabs* started as individual efforts by scholars and became systematized ways of thinking about law and devising laws. If you were a Muslim born in the eighth century, you would not have recognized the four Sunni schools and two schools of Shi'i law (among others) that represented the system of Islamic law. The Sunni *madhhabs* reached their zenith of status and monopoly in the thirteenth–fifteenth centuries CE, despite some voices of reflection and critique. After the Ottoman and colonial centuries, the *madhhabs* reached a low point. They still survive, but in new hybridized forms. And today, another new stage is starting.

Madhhabs and government have a curious relationship. The Abbasids (second–seventh centuries/eighth–thirteenth centuries CE) gave much support to Hanafi law, and so did the Ottomans (ninth–thirteenth centuries/sixteenth–nineteenth centuries CE). Muslim India also showed deference to the same *madhhab*. Pakistan today thinks of itself as having built its law on Hanafi legal models. Arabia was not a Hanbali land until the Saudi state decided to adopt a modified version of Hanbali law after its modern monarchy was founded. Morocco makes a similar claim to the Maliki heritage. Indonesia has some attachment to Shafi'i law, while adopting and developing Ja'fari law has been Iran's points of pride.

Some Muslim nations, such as Indonesia and Iran, seem stable and strong. If they survive the test of time, their national shari'as will form the foundation of future Islamic law in these nations. Less cohesive nations may end up with a different political form and hence new forms of shari'a, whether the surviving entities are larger or smaller than the nations that morphed into the new entities.

Throughout this textbook, you have learned about ways of legal reasoning in pre-democratic environments (societies that preceded modern appropriations of what seems to be an ancient notion and practice, but in reality is a new idea and practice). One thing Muslim jurists prided themselves on is that their legal reasoning had to include explanations. These explanations sustained different degrees of potency across the large Muslim world. The ways of some *madhhabs* looked "obvious" or even self-evident in certain territories but could only be seen as foreign and problematic in other regions. But *legal reasoning always rested on an explanation*, which if the population did not fully understand, at least the jurists understood and debated. In a modern environment, the ways of a democratic law, if it is truly democratic, require no explanation. The law is this way, because the people (via their representatives' deals and compromises) agreed that was the way it has to be. This, which appears to be a virtue in modern laws and societies, would only be seen as a large law in the idea of democracy, even as it was understood in its ancient form. This takes us to the next point.

2.5 Democracy

Before the Dutch seventeenth-century CE philosopher Spinoza, philosophers were suspicious of democracy, and many after Spinoza also critiqued it. Plato famously considered it one of the bad regimes, to be contrasted with the rule of a philosopher, a wise person who has the full picture, of which others see only parts. One of the Muslim jurists who were also widely read in philosophy, was the Maliki jurist and judge Ibn Rushd (d. 596/1198), who was also a celebrated commentator on Aristotle's philosophical and scientific works. Ibn Rushd's brief digest on politics, which is a summary of the themes of Plato's *Republic*, includes a memorable critique of democracy.

Ibn Rushd depicts what he calls "the collective city" or the city ruled by the total population as a place where individuals enjoy—or perhaps "suffer" may be the right word—a good degree of freedom, but also as a place that lacks character altogether. In an aristocratic government (aristocracy being one of Plato's standard regimes or ways of ruling), the values of the aristocracy dominate, and in an oligarchy, the values of the oligarchy dominate. In free, democratic cities, no particular values are identified. The collective city is also a microcosm of cities: It is a mish-mash of aristocratic, oligarchic, tyrannical, and plutocratic systems of values.

Although Ibn Rushd's critique is couched in terms of a summary of the large themes of Plato's *Republic*, his specific examples about the Spanish Muslim dynasties, which he characterizes as examples of "collective cities" or "cities of collective rule," betray his lack of

Figure 8.3 Averroes statue of Ibn Rushd, Córdoba (Spain). Author: Américo Toledano. Image accessed via Wikimedia.

sympathy for government arrangements that are not rooted in "principled reasoning." His limited participation in Maliki jurisprudence, and his more commonly known contribution to comparative jurisprudence, may not allow us to have a full understanding of how the legislative function in government is discharged. The model of jurist-legislator, then, is all we have.

When Nasir al-Din al Tusi (d. 672/1274) aggregated ethics, household economics, and politics in one compendium, he offered a similar critique of democracy. He refers to the "city of the free" (madinat al-ahrar) as a hodge-podge of legal and political life, innocent of true systems and philosophy. His attacks on tyranny and democracy are equally potent, leaving the reader with an assumption that a true philosopher and doctor of both soul and society is to be trusted with the knowledge required for government. His comments about the desirability of steering away from power and the cost one must pay if one were to be "subjected" to having to be present in courts of political power leave us with a sense similar to what Ibn Khaldun one century later creates when he states that "true scholars are not usually concerned with power."

Nasir al-Din al-Tusi was accused of having shamefully acquiesced to Hulagu Khan, the Mongol leader who was seen by most Muslims as an invader of the Muslim world. Tusi accepted Hulagu's favors (including an observatory and excellent research conditions) and thought that continuing his work was more important than resisting the new regime. Ibn Khaldun, who asserted that scholars should by their very nature steer away from politics, thought Tusi was the most brilliant of all the Persians he read.

The moral promise of democracy is that it allows for more equality. Each individual citizen is invested in the laws, and they, hence, must play a role in deciding what the law is. This argument can only be accepted squeamishly by well-trained Muslim legal scholars. They can concede that the diffusion of knowledge needed for lawmaking allows specialists to weigh in on all matters of the law, but they can hardly move from that to supporting a layperson's law based on collective preference. As we noted, social standards are a basic consideration in Islamic legal reasoning, and the extent to which these are accepted varies between different jurists and different environments. But making the leap to lawmaking individuals who create their own moral commitments is a different matter.

On the other hand, a jurist-legislator makes law in the limited sense of describing the general rules, accompanied by legal scenarios and cases, that allow the judge to decide what may be called "easy" or standard cases. Modern (democratic) legislative bodies also leave areas of unclear law or undecided matters to the courts. They are similar to jurist-legislation in this sense. But legislative bodies are much more comprehensive in their scope, and much faster in their ability to respond to change in society, than medieval jurists. Even when the US Congress is accused of being slow and ineffective, it handles many more issues than did the average medieval jurist, who wrote perhaps one or two legal commentaries in his entire lifetime. These points need to be taken into account when a premodern critique of democracy is studied today.

3 Moving parts

Today, events are moving fast. Let us take a final look at the national and post-national views of our triangle (society, law, and government). We will take Pakistan's privatized national law, and Egypt's über-constitutional debates.

3.1 Public and private criminal shari'a

Pakistan was accused of privatizing criminal law when it introduced the *hudud* ordinances in 1979. Islamic criminal law does allow the family a say in criminal cases, where their forgiveness of the killer removes the punishment (the death penalty) and could also remove any financial liability to pay blood money. As I stated earlier, in some premodern applications of this rule, the family may even apply the punishment itself, as attested in the writing of Muhammad ibn al-Hasan al-Shaybani.

Abdul Ghafoor v. State (2000) was one example of this so-called privatization of criminal law, where the family's forgiveness led to removing both the death penalty and the blood-money compensation. The defendant in the case, however, was sentenced to ten years in prison, given the fact that the victim was a police officer, and his murder was hence a matter of public law aside from the family's jurisdiction (Tahir Wasti, *The Application of Islamic Criminal Law in Pakistan* (Leiden: Brill, 2009), p. 21).

What this example illustrates is the hybridity of legal practice in this country, a case for which many analogies can be found across the Muslim world. Each Muslim nation hosts within it communities of various moral commitments that could relate to different aspects of old shari'a and modern morality to different degrees. One of the moving parts in visions of law, society, and government in the broader Muslim world is how these hybrids will continue to evolve.

3.2 Über-constitutional shari'a

An uprising in Egypt began on January 25, 2011. Several weeks later, on February 11, the resignation of the president was announced, and an entity called the SCAF (Supreme Council of the Armed Forces) took over. In March 2012 a constitution amendment regulated what were meant to be fair parliamentary elections (held between November 2011 and January 2012) and presidential elections (held in June 2012). Muhammad Morsi, a member of the Muslim Brotherhood, won the presidential elections and took the oath of office.

Most of this new parliament and president's actions were challenged in courts, and the government was increasingly seen as ineffective. In November 2012, Morsi issued a declaration that made some of his decisions immune to judicial review. He was also perceived to bow to orders and expectations from the Muslim Brothers' chief officers. Whether for this or other reasons, the army performed a coup in July 2013, almost exactly a year after the president had taken office. The leader of the coup, General A. Sisi, installed the Chief Justice of the Constitutional Supreme Court as interim president, then he himself stood for and won presidential elections a year later.

If you can believe it, this is a case of Islamic, rather than international, justice in the eyes of Muslim jurists. Two rulings were issued here. The first, by Qaradawi (b. 1928), states that the coup was a usurpation of legitimate power. The rationale was that Morsi was elected as the people's choice, which is the modern equivalent of election by people's representatives (*ahl al-hall*) in medieval Islamic jurisprudence. In contrast to this view, Ali Jum'a (b. 1952) ruled that General Sisi was the legitimate ruler because Morsi was a usurper of power and his party a group of bandits (*khawarij*) outside of the consensus of the Muslim community, which medieval Muslim jurists agreed must be fought. But, now, we must back up to unpack the case.

3.2.1 A CLASH OF FATWAS

After the Egyptian military seized power in the country in July 2013, arresting the previous president and eventually administering new elections, two Egyptian Muslim jurists clashed over the legitimacy of the action from the viewpoint of Islamic law. Both Yusuf al-Qaradawi (b. 1928) and 'Ali Jum'a (b. 1952) have established personal legitimacy and a large following. The more senior, Qaradawi, has been more prolific and more acknowledged than Jum'a, who is a generation younger. Their disagreement about the legitimacy of Egypt's 2013 *coup d'état*, using traditional jurisprudential language, highlights the relevance of shari'a to public discourse in the Muslim world.

Old legal discussions

In a Muslim community where multiple factions claim to have their own legitimate government, traditional Islamic jurisprudence, as we noted, asks "who is the government and who is the rebel (*baghi*)?" A rebel group, according to the Sunni view of the matter, arises when a settled government has been acknowledged and obeyed by the population. The rebels then make an argument that the government is not legitimate, and form their own authority. The rebels have to have an argument against the existing government, a prima facie grievance; otherwise they are deemed vagabonds.

In principle, a rebellious group (*bughah*) is a protected group that can only be opposed but not pre-emptively attacked. The standing government is not liable, however, for reasonable resistance of rebellion. At the same time, the rules of the government within the state or region in which the rebellion rises, are considered valid, as long as the rebellion lasts. Rebels are held responsible for excessive destruction of property, for example, by all Sunni schools of law. If a rebellion ends in failure, the government retains its comprehensive power and jurisdiction. If the rebellion succeeds in building a new, stable order, opposing this new government becomes a new rebellion.

The oldest model of a rebel group in Islamic history is the *khawarij* (lit. seceders), who allied themselves with the then Caliph Ali B. Abi Talib (d. 40/660) then rebelled against him. They went on to reach an excessive view that all those who did not follow them were not Muslims. The *khawarij*, a group of pious but politically misguided individuals, are the juristic model for a rebellious group in Islamic law. This was Ibn 'Abidin (d. 1836), a Syrian scholar who characterized Wahhabi revolts against Ottoman authorities in the early 1800s as a replication of *khawarij* action.

Back to the present

In the 2013 conflict in Egypt, the two aforementioned scholars disagreed as to who was legitimate and who was a rebel. Qaradawi thought the coup was led by a rebel (General Sisi), while Jum'a thought the Muslim Brotherhood's government, even though it had won the elections, were the rebels, because they attempted to overreach in their government activities and seek a high degree of control over the people's lives (June 2012– June 2013) and later resisted the new order that was legitimized by the people's June 2013 uprising.

Jum'a further argued that Egypt's President Morsi lost his legitimacy as a leader of his Muslim community by losing his freedom. This is a traditional view, which many medieval Muslim jurists would accept (while modern Muslims would clearly disagree as to whether it applies in this case). You may remember that Mawardi's theory of legitimate government allowed for the seizing of power added to the element of time to create legitimate government that may not be resisted. Qaradawi argued that Morsi's legitimacy could not simply be taken away by brute force. He then argued that rebellion against the usurper of legitimate power, General Sisi, had become a religious duty for Egyptians. On this reasoning, General Sisi himself would be vulnerable to being punished as a usurper of legitimate power. This is also a traditional view held by many scholars who discuss the laws of rebellion in Islam. This clash of *fatwas* shows a heightened sense for both scholars that the new conditions of Egyptian Muslims may still be governed by traditional shari'a views, even as these scholars disagreed.

3.3 If God Were Alive Today

This irreverent title of Kurt Vonnegut's unfinished, final novel expresses the foundation for much of the speculation and experimenting about new Muslim societies today. Just as it is too early to write an obituary for all nationalism, it is hard to imagine these experiments about new Muslim governments coming to naught. Some new experiment will end up catching fire and becoming a new standard for some Muslim societies in the next century or two. Current Muslim societies are a mix of what is offered by both modernity and a long Islamic tradition. Each local setting will experiment differently, and the surviving models will also be different in different settings.

The post-Arab Spring debates on legitimate government, which we discussed in this final Unit, teach a threefold lesson. First, an Islamic government is nothing but a government led by Muslims. The reason Muslim governments or Islamic governments differ from one time and place to another is that they are led by different individuals, people of different education, character, and aspirations. Second, a Muslim society can only be a society of Muslims if being Muslim means something, rather than being a matter of inheritance. There can never be a way to speak of Islamic life or Muslim life while excluding the agential side of how individuals and families choose to live their lives. Third and finally, the jurists whose disagreement is blamed for problems that take place in the Muslim world are children of the same context that created their contemporaries, leaders, and populace, and can only reflect the context in which they live.

> IT IS SUFFICIENT FOR A GROUP TO BE COSIDERED KHAWARIJ (SECEDERS) IF THEY BELIEVE THAT THOSE MUSLIMS THEY REBEL AGAINST ARE UNBELIEVERS, SUCH AS WHAT WAHHABIS IN OUR TIME HAVE DONE. KHAWARIJ, ACCORDING TO THE MAJORITY OF JURISTS AND TRADITION SCHOLARS, FALL UNDER THE CATEGORY OF REBELS (BUGHAH).
>
> B. 'Abidin (d. 1252/1836) in *Radd al-Muhtar*, his Commentary, Vol. 3, pp. 309–10, Dar Ihya' al-Turath al-Arabi, Beirut, 1987. *Ahkam a-Bughah*.

Idealists continue to function on different wavelengths. The question of what would happen if God were alive in Muslim societies today, *as desired by those who lament the absence or short supply of Muslim values*, is a question of what would happen if Muslims were believers in God *in the manner in which those who ask the question wanted them to be*. You remember that Hanafi and Shafi'i jurists disagreed as to whether a judge's law is God's law or something the loser in the case must tolerate without any faith in it. They both still thought the buck of human authority ends with this judge, but God knows best. Shi'i jurists, who go even further than Shafi'is and discredit most political actions over the long Islamic history, also believed in complex ways to live a virtuous life until the time comes when a final vindication of the correctness of their way arrives. Until then, Islamic law is what Muslims make it to be, and it will be this for us and generations to come.

4 Conclusion

A religious legal system such as Islamic law with its personal, social, national, and transnational sides requires, in addition to a following of individuals who seek their personal betterment in it, supporting powers, ones within national mechanisms and ones that transcend the nation. In building mechanisms for power, revolution has been employed at times, coupled with a re-articulation and re-interpretation of how modern political and social power can support Islamic law:

1. Most nationalist Muslims accept that creating strong, modern Muslim nations is both faithful to the tradition and sufficient for the purposes of Muslims today and tomorrow.
2. An alternative view, however, is attached to old forms of government in Islamic history or attempts to take advantage of a weakening international order to innovate and create new forms of government within Muslim societies.

Review VIII

- There is no right to revolution, but there may be an obligation to revolution, if and when injustice is so dominant that the existing regime is seen as no regime at all.
- A good Muslim regime is neither populist nor dictatorial. It is based on principles of justice.
- Legitimacy in the time of revolution is contested, because the juristic tradition, which was mostly disorder-averse, still allowed for new regimes to change existing injustice after their success.

Problem

- If uncertainty persists for a long time as to who commands obedience in a Muslim society, what is the way out, from the principles you learned?

Meditative essay

- What do you really think of critiques of democracy? Is it actually the best of all possible worlds of systems of governance?

Final Review

Section 1

This section aims to prompt you to review the relevant sections in the book.

Premodern

1. If you had to say that Islamic law was Qur'anic law, Muhammad's law, or a *jurists'* law—what would your answer be?

    I would say a jurists' law, but I would also say that medieval governments and societies played a role in shaping it.

    Can you go on?

2. Who were these *jurists*?

    Private scholars who lived in the eighth and ninth centuries, who formed schools of law or *madhhabs*, and who over the centuries commanded a large following of law scholars. Their followers and critics augmented the early forms of the law to such an extent that ultimately no one could make a full claim to it.

3. What were these schools of law or *madhhabs*?

    Four Sunni *madhhabs* known as the Hanafi, Maliki, Shafi'i, and Hanbali *madhhabs* commanded the largest presence, followed by a minor school called the Zahiri school; in the Shi'i world, two schools, the Ja'fari and the Zaydi, are known; there was also a slighter presence of Ibadi schools or *madhhabs*. *Madhhabs* that did not survive the test of time (in terms of retaining a large popular following) are also found in medieval sources.

4. What is medieval Islamic law based on?

    Assumptions about human nature and justice, generalizations from the language of texts, and customary local practices.

    Can you give examples?

Modern

1. What sources compete for space with the shari'a in modern national laws?

   New local social standards, old and established legal principles and practices from colonial times and agreements with foreign powers, as well as new principles of natural law as interpreted by modern Muslim scholars.

   Can you give this concise statement some texture?

2. Do new medical developments change everything in Islamic legal reasoning?

   No. Many of the old legal principles still function, and modifications are made mostly where presumptions about gender are questioned. Islamic law can be more relaxed about genetic and medical intervention than many other traditional religious systems.

3. Does the transnational shari'a diverge with modern national laws in Muslim countries?

   Quite a bit, just as national laws in different Muslim lands do not always align with each other. Many post-national views of the world threaten Muslim nations that were created in the twentieth century. And the jury is still out on what jurisdiction will be conceded to these areas of thought and practice.

Section 2

The purpose of the following section is to allow you to write a short essay on the main qualities of Islamic legal reasoning.

1. Is there genuinely a symbiotic relationship between Sunni and Shi'i law?
2. What does nature, as it was understood in the premodern age, tell us about the shari'a?
3. How many basic principles do you remember operating in this area? How different are contracts of sale, rent, and marriage?
4. Individuals are free to do as they wish in private, but what could they *not* do in public?
5. Does Islamic law have wealth redistribution mechanisms? If yes, how strong are these?
6. What principles and cases did you note that governed Muslim/non-Muslim relations? List these then review the relevant sections for details.

Section 3

Review these summaries to refresh your memory about key information.

Unit 1: Three cases

Extramarital sexual relationships incur severe penalties, including corporeal punishment and loss of custody of any children. While Saudi applications of probate and family laws have their unique points, the standards they follow are conceded in Muslim societies in principle. The "family" is understood to consist of a man and a woman and sometimes children. When you look at the full picture of social laws, you notice that a very traditional sense of natural roles that need not be disturbed is at work.

Reconciling a duty (understood to fall on men) to support one's family and perform prescribed religious rituals on time is a basic goal in Islamic legal reasoning. License to defer and combine rituals may be given when hardship reaches a degree that makes normal life difficult to manage.

Inheritance schemes in Islamic law are complex, although they are based on fairly simple principles. *Children, spouses* and *parents* are favored over siblings, and siblings are prioritized over other relatives. Though there is a good amount of disagreement among Sunni and Shi'i jurists (and additional disagreement has also been identified among modern, hybridized inheritance laws), the older structure provides a departure point to fall back on.

Unit 2: *Madhhabs*

Islamic law started as a private initiative among scholars at the eastern end of Arabia (Kufa, Iraq) and its western end (Medina, where the Prophet Muhammad is buried) in the first/seventh and second/eighth centuries. Each of the resulting schools of law, or *madhhabs*, spread in different areas in the Muslim world. Hanafi law dominated the Sunni world but came to follow Shafi'i and Hanbali law's turn to "reports" of the Prophet's life as a foundation for legal provisions. The reports, however, are bones that need "flesh" and the flesh remains legal reasoning of a kind more similar to *madhhab* reasoning—all the way to this fifteenth/twenty-first century of ours.

Unit 3: Theorizing the shari'a

For Muslim jurists to build a system of reasoning, they must think of a target or *fruit* for their research (target: categorizing human actions, between obligatory and prohibited) and a set of sources to employ to arrive at these categories for the actions (sources: revelation, Prophet's practice, and reason). One must also look beyond actual cases that require answers to imagine legal scenarios, ask about how to distinguish cases, and develop a theory of the elements that decide where to go one way or another in deciding ostensibly similar cases differently, and ostensibly different cases similarly.

Jurists disagree, but the agreement of a large group of them is instructive. Consensus, in theory and in practice, is a way to define the borders of a community. When arguments seem *equal* in power but lead to *opposite* conclusions, there must be tools to decide that either their *equality* or *contradiction* is illusory.

Unit 4: The social shari'a

The Muslim society is one loose unit that operates on a degree of solidarity, below a socialist system and above a capitalist system. Roles and functions that are regarded as having been given by nature are questioned only when strong evidence suggests they need to be modified. Individual property is respected, and consent is an essential element in deciding ownership.

Unit 5: The personal shari'a

A Muslim decides his or her personal commitments to Islam in a manner that often, but not always, accepts social restrictions. This includes questions about diet and fasting, religious rituals and vows. The personal shari'a also addresses life and death questions, including abortion, surrogacy, and cloning.

Unit 6: The national shari'as

Many Muslim national legal documents include provisions that allow their lawyers and judges to draw on traditional standards of Islamic legal reasoning. In large numbers of Muslim countries, modern laws that were introduced in the fourteenth/twentieth century, some of which already have old shari'a elements, are reviewed and streamlined with new laws that show stronger shari'a impact. In other countries, lawmakers claim that the whole system is designed based on principles of Islamic law in family, civil, and criminal matters.

Unit 7: The transnational shari'a

Islamic financial jurisprudence is opposed to creating economic value based on stretched "derivatives." Credit must be short-term and reviewable. While seemingly believing in an invisible, fair, hand of God, it actively protects the weak in contractual dealings, revoking contracts that include elements of ambiguity, duress, or undue pressure. Modern Islamic financial institutions, however, are a hybrid of capitalist and Islamic legal principles.

Cyber Islamic law covers any area the student learned about in this text. Its most creative areas are where national laws are either silent or weak. Cyber Islamic jurisprudence is also blamed for mobilizing non-state actors against modern states, which are seen as having lost their legitimacy because of the past behavior of their leaders.

Unit 8: The triangle of society, law, and government

Muslim government can take different forms. The caliphate is an important historical institution, but it is also one that lost its coherence close to a millennium ago. Historical and current forms of Muslim government still presume a multi-ethnic, multi-faith community that respects the Islamic character of the society.

The very, very short list of essential Arabic terms

Fatwa: Extra-judicial case-law.

Fiqh: The art of legal reasoning.

Ijtihad: Legal research, reasoning, leading to an answer to a question.

Madhhab: School of law, such as the Hanafi or Ja'fari school.

Qiyas: Lexically measuring; legally either reasoning from analogy or the apparent broad principle.

The long, short list

Ashab al-Ra'y (Un. 7, Sec. 1, Intro): Jurists with a lower focus on Prophetic practice, most prominently Hanafi jurists

Dhimma (Un. 3, Sec. 1.2): An imaginary depository of rights and responsibilities associated with each human being

Dhimmi (Un. 4, Sec. 1.1): A non-Muslim living under Muslim government

Gharar (Un. 4, Sec. 2.1): An ambiguity in an economic activity that may affect either or both parties

Hadith (Un. 1, Sec. 1.2.1): (Also Sunna): Reports of the Prophet Muhammad's sayings, actions, and tacit approvals (for reporters who don't work with law, they add 'bodily descriptions of the Prophet himself')

Harbi (Un. 4, Sec. 1.1): Broad sense: A non-Muslim who is also a non-Dhimmi; narrow sense: A non-Muslim without license to be present in Muslim lands

Imam (Un. 8, Sec. 2, intro): Leader of Muslim government; in Shi'i law: True authority in the law (E.g., Un. 3, Sec. 3.3)

Istihsan (Un. 2, Sec. 2.1; Un. 3, Sec. 2.2--2.5; Un. 7, Sec. 2.4): Justifying the exception, rather than the rule; (Un. 5, Sec. 2.1): Rules of moderation

Kaffarat (Primary Source II): Expiatory acts (such as a two-month fasting after engaging in an inadvertent manslaughter)

Khalwa (Un. 1, Sec. 1.2): A female presence-alone with one or multiple unrelated males

Khul' (Un. 6, Sec. 2.5): Divorce at the wife's initiative

Mudaraba (Un. 7, Sec. 2.3): A partnership with money/assets provided by one side and effort/expertise by the other (where both money and expertise are exposed to the same degree of risk)

Mufti (Un. 1, Sec. 2.4): A religious adviser (check the very, very short list of terms for a related term.)

Musta'man (Un. 4, Sec. 1.1): A non-Muslim living temporarily under a Muslim government

Qiyas al-shabah (Un. 3, Sec. 2.3): Reasoning from analogy without a reliance on a cause that brings two acts to the same ruling

Riba (Un. 4, Sec. 2.1): An agreement that guarantees an increase for only one party in a contract or an economic activity

Salah (Un. 5, Sec. 3.1): Daily prayers

Sharikat al-Abdan (Un. 7, Sec. 1, Intro): Partnership among individuals with few or no true assets

Shuf'a (Un. 6, Sec. 2.5): Pre-emption of sale based on ownership of proximate property

Shi'i Law: Ja'fari, Zaydi (esp. Un. 2, Intro, Sec. 1.1, 1.2): Shi'i schools whose founders lived in the 1st/7th and 2nd/8th centuries

Sunni Law: Hanafi, Maliki, Shafi'i, Hanbali (esp. Un. 2, Intro, Sec. 1.1, 1.2): Sunni schools whose founders died in the 2nd/8th and 3rd/9th centuries

Tarjih (Un. 3, Sec. 3.3): Preferring one argument over another or one source of law over another

Wilaya (Primary Source IV): Authority; also see 'guardianship' (Un. 1, Sec. 1.4)

Wilayat al-Faqih (Un. 6, Sec. 2.1): Leadership of the jurist

Zahiri (esp. Un. 2, Sec. 1.2.4, 2.1): A school of law notorious for rejecting reasoning based on the analogy of cases

Appendix I: A debate between Shafi'i (d. 204/820) and Ahmad Ibn Hanbal (d. 241/856)

(On a Muslim who does not deny the prayers are obligatory but does not perform them.)

This debate appears in different versions in different, mostly Shafi'i sources. One version is found in Subki's (d. 771/1369) Biography of Shafi'i Jurists (*Tabaqat al-Shafi'iyya*), relating from the authority of Abu Ali al-Hasan ibn 'Ammar, a student of Fakhr al-Din al-Shashi (d. 507/1113). Modern Hanbali jurists vehemently dispute that this debate ever took place, but its line is consistent with the principles of the two debaters.

Shafi'i: You hold someone who does not perform the daily prayers to be a non-Muslim, an unbeliever, even if she or he does not deny the prayers are an obligation?

Ahmad: The Prophet states that "the line between Muslim and non-Muslim is the daily prayers; whoever fails to do these is a non-Muslim."

Shafi'i: How would this non-Muslim then become a Muslim?

Ahmad: S/he ought to recite the *shahada* (I testify there is only one God and Muhammad is his messenger).

Shafi'i: S/he does that. [This is a believing Muslim who does not pray.]

Ahmad: S/he ought to pray, then.

Shafi'i: The prayer is a ritual, and a ritual could not be accepted from a non-Muslim.

Ahmad: . . .

(silence indicates concession and failure to counter the argument)

Appendix II

Map of Muslim populations around the world

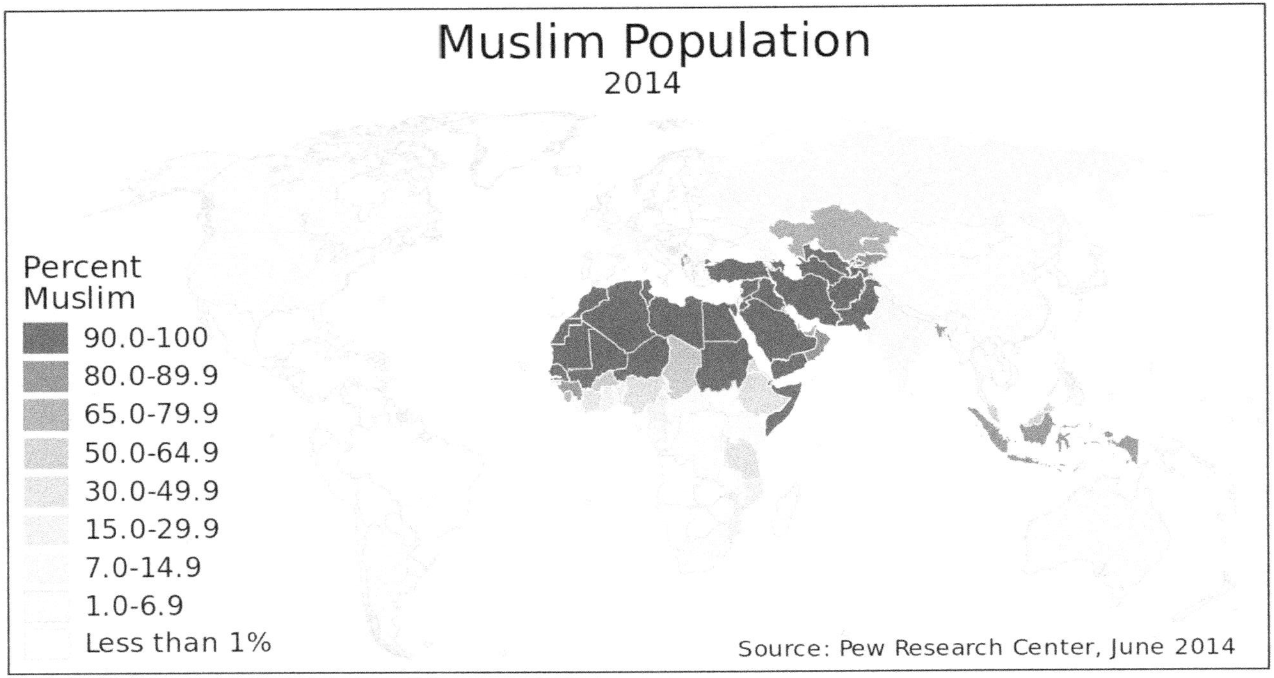

Muslim Population 2014

Percent Muslim:
- 90.0–100
- 80.0–89.9
- 65.0–79.9
- 50.0–64.9
- 30.0–49.9
- 15.0–29.9
- 7.0–14.9
- 1.0–6.9
- Less than 1%

Source: Pew Research Center, June 2014

Appendix III   Preamble to Pakistan's Constitution (4/12/73)

Whereas sovereignty over the entire universe belongs to Allah Almighty alone and the authority which He has delegated to the State of Pakistan, through its people for being exercised within the limits prescribed by Him is a sacred trust;

This Constituent Assembly representing the people of Pakistan resolves to frame a Constitution for the sovereign independent State of Pakistan;

Wherein the State shall exercise its powers and authority through the chosen representatives of the people;

Wherein the principles of democracy, freedom, equality, tolerance and social justice as enunciated by Islam shall be fully observed;

Wherein the Muslims shall be enabled to order their lives in the individual and collective spheres in accordance with the teachings and requirements of Islam as set out in the Holy Quran and the Sunnah;

Wherein adequate provision shall be made for the minorities to freely profess and practice their religions and develop their cultures;

Wherein the territories now included in or in accession with Pakistan and such other territories as may hereafter be included in or accede to Pakistan shall form a Federation wherein the units will be autonomous with such boundaries and limitations on their powers and authority as may be prescribed;

Wherein shall be guaranteed fundamental rights including equality of status, of opportunity and before law, social, economic and political justice, and freedom of thought, expression, belief, faith, worship and association, subject to law and public morality;

Wherein adequate provisions shall be made to safeguard the legitimate interests of minorities and backward and depressed classes;

Wherein the independence of the Judiciary shall be fully secured;

Wherein the integrity of the territories of the Federation, its independence and all its rights including its sovereign rights on land, sea and air shall be safeguarded;

So that the people of Pakistan may prosper and attain their rightful and honored place amongst the nations of the World and make their full contribution towards international peace and progress and happiness of humanity.

Appendix IV Inheritance tables

http://www.saaid.net/book/11/3993.pdf

Appendix V   Islamic mortgage resources

1. https://www.alrayanbank.co.uk/home-finance/home-purchase-plan/
2. http://www.stewart.com/en/stg/massachusetts/memo-islamic-financing.html
3. http://www.bankislam.com.my/home/personal-banking/financing-products/home-financing-i/
4. https://www.rhbgroup.com/products-and-services/personal/islamic/financing/equity-property-financing-i
5. https://uk.practicallaw.thomsonreuters.com/3-500-6260?transitionType=Default&contextData=(sc.Default)&firstPage=true
6. http://icho.ca/

Further reading

Primary Arabic sources in English translation will take some getting used to, but they are the best option if you become interested in Islamic legal reasoning and want to read more widely. Item 1 on the list below is an example of *comparative madhhab* law, which focuses on the reasons why different jurists come down one way or the other in their opinions. Item 2 situates government in a clear relationship to laws but is not comprehensive in its treatment of the substantive laws. Four years of Arabic will certainly allow you to do some guided reading of Arabic sources in this list. With these, quality must be emphasized over quantity.

Academic articles on the subject and court decisions (such as the *Lim Kok Hoe* case published in *Cambridge Law Journal*, #5 below) are an opportunity for a thorough and measured reading, while full-length books may be skimmed or consulted in part. If your interest in modern national laws that have an Islamic element is stimulated, move to Robert W. Hefner's edited collection (#9 below). As you read Hefner's and identify points of divergence between the collection's eight authors and this one, instead of losing your interest and confidence, ask yourself about the sources of this divergence.

Older titles allow you to see how the subject was introduced before certain academic fashions took hold over academic practices in the field. Don't dismiss a piece because it is "dated."

English

Primary in translation

1. **Ibn Rushd (d. 595/1198) (trans. I. Niyazi)**, *The Distinguished Jurist's Primer* (Reading, UK: Garnet, 2000).

2. **Mawardi (d. 450/1058) (trans. W. Wahba)**, *Ordinances of Government* (Reading, UK: Garnet, 2000).

Secondary

3. **Amin, S. Husayn**, *Remedies for Breach of Contract in Islamic and Iranian Law* (Glasgow, UK: Royston, 1984).

4. **Ball, John**, *Indonesian Law: Commentary and Teaching Materials* (Sydney: University of Sydney Law School, 1981).

5. **Bell, John** (ed.), Bimb vs Lim Kok Hoe & Other Appeals, *Cambridge Law Journal* 2009, 6 (Cambridge: Cambridge University Press, 2009), pp. 22–40. The same case appears in the *Malayan Law Journal* [MLJ] December 17, 2016, pp. 839–55.

6 **Bernard-Maugiron, Natalie**, *Egypt and Its Laws* (Leiden, the Netherlands: Brill, Springer, Arab and Islamic Laws Series, 22, 2002).

7 **Bowen, John R.**, *On British Islam: Religion, Law, and Everyday Practice in Sharia Councils* (Princeton: Princeton University Press, 2016).

8 **Ebrahimi, S. N.**, "Child Custody '(Hizanat)' under Iranian Law: An Analytical Discussion." *Family Law Quarterly*, Vol. 39, No. 2, Symposium on Comparative Custody Law (Summer 2005), pp. 459–547.

9 **Hefner, Robert W.**, *Sharia Politics: Islamic Law and Society in the Modern World* (Bloomington: Indiana University Press, 2011).

10 **Hussin, Iza R.**, *The Politics of Islamic Law: Local Elites, Colonial Authority, and the Making of the Muslim State* (Chicago: The University of Chicago Press, 2016).

11 **Lev, Daniel S.**, "The Supreme Court and Adat Inheritance Law in Indonesia." *The American Journal of Comparative Law*, Vol. 11, No. 2 (Spring 1962), pp. 205–24.

12 **Milhaupt, Christopher (& Katharina Pistor)**, *Law and Capitalism: What Corporate Crises Reveal about Legal Systems and Economic Development around the World* (Chicago: Chicago University Press, 2008).

13 **Munir, Muhammad**, *Precedent in Pakistani Law* (Oxford: Oxford University Press, 2014).

14 **Wasti, Tahir**, *The Application of Islamic Criminal Law in Pakistan* (Leiden: Brill, 2009).

Arabic

15 **Hasan b. Yusuf, al-'Allama, al-Hilli (d. 726/1325)**, *Mukhtalif al-Shi'a* (Qumm: Islamic Publications Co., 1991).

16 **Miqdad b. Abdullah al-Hilli (d. 826/1423)** (ed. A. Kuhkamri), *Nadd al-Qawa'id al-Fiqhiyya 'ala Madhhab al-Imamiyya* (Qumm: al-Khayyam Press, 1992).

17 **Abdulla b. Ahmad = Ibn Qudama (d. 620/1223)** (ed. Turki and Hilw), *al-Mughni* (Cairo: Dar Hajar, 1992).

18 **Muhammad b. al-Hasan al-Shaybani (d. 189/805)** (ed. Turki and Hilw), *al-Hujja 'ala Ahl al-Madina* (Cairo: Dar Hajar, 1992).

19 **Nawawi (d. 676/1277)** (ed. M. N. Muti'i), *al-Majmu'* (Cairo: Maktabat al-Irshad, 1992).

20 **Ibn Qutlubugha (d. 879/1474)** (ed. A. & A. Darwish), *Majmuat Rasa'il Ibn Qutlubugha* (Damascus: Dar al-Nawadir, 2013).

21 **Al-Zarqa, Ahmad (d. 1938)**, *Sharh al-Qawa id al-Fiqhiyya* (Damascus: Dar al-Qalam, 1993)

Chibli Mallat's *Introduction to Middle Eastern Law* (Cambridge: Cambridge University Press, 2007) remains an unparalleled text. It is probably where you want to go next, if you have developed a strong interest in Islamic and Middle Eastern law, but it is a print companion that will take a while to finish and comprehend.

Index

'Abdullah ibn al-Hasan (d. 143/762), 111
Ibn Abi Layla (Abu Isa, 'Abd al-Rahman ibn Yasar, d. 83/702), 37
Ibn 'Abidin (d. 1252/1836), 58, 59, 85, 86, 88, 91, 100, 119, 180, 181
Algeria, 5
'Ali ibn Abi Talib (d. 40/660), 28, 54, 101, 113, 171, 180
'Ali 'Abd al-Raziq (d. 1966), 166
'Ali Jum'a (b. 1952), 179, 180
Amidi (Sayf al-Din, d. 631/1233), 67, 114 (n)
'Amili (Jamal al-Din Makki, d. 786/1385), 68
'Amili (Zayn al-Din ibn 'Ali, d 966/1558), 63, 64, 68
Asamm (Abu Bakr 'Abd al-Rahman, d. 279/892), 111, 155
Abu Bakr al-Siddiq (d. 13/634), 30, 36, 60, 61, 62, 66, 68, 120, 170, 171

Baqillani (Abu Bakr, d. 402/1013), 66, 67
Bishr al-Marisi (d. 218/833), 111
Bali (Indonesia), 128
Bukhari (Muhammad ibn Isma'il, d. 256/870), 45

Cairo, 28, 30, 83, 109, 175,

Damascus, 30
Dawud al-Zahiri (d. 270/884), 37

Egypt, 121–4, 128–33, 136, 137, 166, 168, 175, 178–81

Frederick II (Hohenstaufen, d. 1250), 175
Abu Bakr ibn Furak (d. 406/1015), 61

'Abd al-Ghani 'Abd al-Khaliq (d. 1983), 63

Ibn Hajar al-Asqalani (d. 852/1448), 44–6, 83 (in 83, only for distinction with the following item)
Ibn Hajar al-Haytami (d. 974/1556), 83, 116

M. al-Hajawi al-Tha'alibi (d. 1376/1965), 33
Ibn al-Hajib ('Utham ibn 'Umar, d. 646/1248), 67
Ahmad ibn Hanbal (d. 241/855), 30, 32, 75, 102, 152, 189
Abu Hanifa (d. 150/767), 30, 32, 34, 35, 36, 48, 57, 59, 75, 143, 144, 156
Hilli (Ibn al-Mutahhar, al- 'Allama, d. 726/1325), 44, 45, 48, 55, 64, 117

Indonesia, 1, 120, 122, 124, 126–8, 137, 138, 176
Iran, ixv, 1, 4, 5, 7, 28, 29, 31, 36, 37, 43, 45, 117, 123, 124–6, 138, 159, 165, 167, 173, 174, 176
   Supreme Leader of, 88, 162
Iraq, 19, 28, 29, 31, 32, 37, 43, 45, 163, 169
   Al-'Allama al-Hilli of, 117

Ja'far ibn Muhammad al-Sadiq (d. 148/765), 30, 36, 64
Jamil b. Khamis al-Sa'di (fl. around 1256/1840), 43, 69, 111–14
Joseph Story (d. 1845), 25
Jubba'i (Abu 'Ali, d. 303/916), 66
Jubba'i (Abu Hashim, d. 321/933), 66
Juwayni (Abu al- Ma'ali, Imam al-Haramayn, d. 478/1085), 56, 60, 170, 174, 175

Khalil ibn Ishaq (author of al-Mukhtasar, d. 768/1365), 134

Lebanon, 29, 37, 43, 45, 97, 117

Mahmud (Ghazan, Mongol emperor, d. 1304), 98
Malik ibn Anas (d. 179/795), 27, 30, 32, 33, 35–6, 41, 59, 115
Mawardi (Abu al-Hasan, d. 450/1058), 169–72, 174, 176, 181
Mawsili (Ishaq ibn Ibrahim — the musician — d. 850), 152

Miqdad al-Suyuri al-Hill (d. 826/1423), 54, 64, 68
Murteza Ansari (1781–1864), 68, 136

Nawawi (Muhyi al-Din, d. 676/1277), 32, 33, 45, 46, 48, 76, 77, 116, 117

Oliver Wendell Holmes (d. 1935), 100

Pakistan, 117, 124, 133–5, 179, 193

Qaradawi (Yusuf Abdullah, b. 1928), 109, 179–81
Ibn Qudama (d. 620/1223), 45, 75, 78, 86, 117, 146, 162

Razi (Fakhr al-Din, d. 606/1209), 61, 67, 70
Riaydh (Saudi Capital), 14
   Police Facility of, 9
   Supreme Court in, 12
Ibn Rushd (d. 595/1198), 41, 43, 122, 137, 169, 170, 176, 177

Salahuddin (Yusuf ibn Ayyub, d. 1193), 171
Sanhuri (Abd al-Razzaq, d. 1971), 53, 97, 118, 121, 124, 130, 155
Sarakhsi (d. circa 500/1106), 84
Saudi Arabia, 25, 73, 87, 93, 123, 168, 176
   Islamic law in, 9–13, 25, 26, 74, 124, 131–3, 137, 138, 184
Shafi'i (Muhammad ibn Idris, d. 204/820), 17, 30–4, 38, 41, 48, 54, 57, 73, 74, 75, 93, 94, 102, 111, 122, 172

Shashi (al-Qaffal al-Kabir, d. 365/976), 78
Shashi (Fakhr al-Din, d. 507/1113), 189
Shaybani (Muhammad ibn al-Hasan, d. 189/805), 30, 32–6, 47, 57, 98, 99, 101, 116, 120, 143, 179
Sufi Abu Talib (d. 2008), 129
Sufyan al-Thawri, 29, 37, 43
Suyuti (Jalal al-Din, d. 911/1505), 59
Syria, 5, 79, 97, 108, 169, 171, 175

Tabari (Muhammad ibn Jarir, d. 310/923), 29, 37, 102, 169
Ibn Taymiyya (d. 728/1328), 31, 62
Tusi (Abu Ja'far, d. 460/1067), 37
Tusi (Nasir al-Din, d. 672/1274), 45, 170, 178

'Umar ibn al-Khattab (d. 24/644), 28, 34, 35, 90, 113, 171
'Uthman ibn 'Affan (d. 35/656), 171

Al-Walid ibn Abd al-Malik (d. 96/715), 171

Yemen, 5, 16, 29, 36, 43

Zarqa (Ahmad Muhammad, d. 1938), 51, 72, 80, 108, 138–41
Zayd ibn 'Ali (Zayn al-'Abidin, d. 122/741), 30, 36, 42, 48, 109
Zayd ibn Haritha (d. 8/629), 109
Ziryab (d. 857), 152